GUILTY OR NOT GUILTY?

GUILTY OR NOT GUILTY?

An Account of the Trials of
THE LEO FRANK CASE
THE D. C. STEPHENSON CASE
THE SAMUEL INSULL CASE
THE ALGER HISS CASE

By FRANCIS XAVIER BUSCH

Biography Index Reprint Series

BOOKS FOR LIBRARIES PRESS
FREEPORT, NEW YORK

INTERNATIONAL STANDARD BOOK NUMBER:

0-8369-8039-5

LIBRARY OF CONGRESS CATALOG CARD NUMBER:

77-136644

PRINTED IN THE UNITED STATES OF AMERICA

DEDICATED TO

THE IDEAL IN THE ADMINISTRATION OF CRIMINAL JUSTICE:

A VERDICT COURAGEOUSLY REACHED BY A JURY

AFTER A CONSCIENTIOUS CONSIDERATION

OF THE LAW AND THE EVIDENCE

FOREWORD

THE out-of-the-ordinary criminal case enlists universal interest because it is usually a threefold drama: the crime; the identification, apprehension and accusation of the suspect; and the trial and its consequence.

But the public interest in the trial of a defendant for a shocking crime has something in it far more significant than the high drama usually involved. Courts are established and their procedures regulated by basic constitutions or by the executive or legislative branch—whichever happens to be dominant—of the government. The administration of criminal law necessarily mirrors the government of which it is a part.

Crime itself through the ages has changed little or not at all, but the attitudes of particular societies toward persons accused of crime and the methods of dealing with such persons have changed, even in our own time, and are constantly changing. It has, therefore, been said with truth that the degree to which the ordinary citizens of a commonwealth are sensitive to wrongdoing and the degree to which, by their institutions and practices, justice is arrived at is a just measure of the civilization of that commonwealth.

Trial by jury of persons defending against accusations of crime is essentially an Anglo-Saxon institution. The thirteen American colonies adopted it as their own common law. One of the complaints in the long list of grievances against the English crown contained in the Declaration of Independence was the deprivation of what the colonists had come to regard as the sacred right of trial by jury. Today, after eight centuries of testing and despite occasional miscarriages of justice, it remains the most perfect instrument yet devised for the protection of the inalienable individual rights of life, liberty and property. Americans and Englishmen alike generally subscribe to the oft-quoted eulogium of Blackstone:

The founders of the English laws have with excellent forecast, contrived that no man should be called to answer to the King for any capital crime, unless upon the preparatory accusation of twelve or more of his fellow subjects, the grand jury: and that the truth of every accusation, whether preferred in the shape of indictment, information, or appeal should afterwards be confirmed by the unanimous suffrage of twelve of his equals and neighbors, indifferently chosen, and superior to all suspicion.

The four American criminal jury trials presented in the succeeding pages have been selected not only because their dramatic quality attracted nationwide attention, or because they were major forensic battles in which great advocates displayed their skills and wits. In each of these trials the scene is laid against a background peculiar to American life, and each trial possesses a special social significance. Taken together, the trials described in this book can be said to typify the administration of criminal justice in the United States of America.

The plan followed in the work has been influenced to an extent by that most excellent series of seventy-five volumes of *Notable British Trials* (William Hodge & Company, Ltd., London, Edinburgh and Glasgow) . Each volume of that series is devoted to a single case. An "introduction," which briefly describes the crime and the suspected criminal, is followed by a verbatim transcript or full abstract of the trial proceedings—the opening statements, the evidence, the summations, the Court's charge and the verdict. Because of their resulting technical character, the appeal of *Notable British Trials* is largely to the legal profession. In the cases treated in this work, an introduction on the English pattern is followed by a nontechnical condensation of the court proceedings and their consequences. The result is a fairly brief but accurate account of four notable American trials, specially designed for the general reading public.

The accounts of the four trials which follow are based either on the stenographic trial record or the printed appeal record in the particular case.

My acknowledgments are due to the clerks of the courts and other officials and librarians in public and private libraries and newspaper offices in Chicago, Atlanta, Washington, New York and Indianapolis for courtesies extended in making records available; to Mrs. Marian A. Hodgkinson and Mrs. Virginia Weissman and my daughter, Mrs. Frances Busch Zink, for library research, copying, comparing and proofreading manuscript; and to my wife for her valuable suggestions, encouragement and inexhaustible patience.

FRANCIS X. BUSCH.

CONTENTS

I

The Trial of

    LEO FRANK

for the Murder of

    MARY PHAGAN

    (1913)

The Leo Frank Case

THE SIGNIFICANCE *of the Leo Frank case lies not in the nature of the crime, but in the publicity which was given to it and the extraordinary consequences of that publicity. The trial would probably have attracted no attention outside of Fulton County, Georgia, had it not been for the illadvised activities of a coterie of Frank's friends and coreligionists who raised the issue of religious prejudice. During the trial and the course of the case in the upper courts, this group made repeated public appeals, through newspaper advertisements and mailing circulars, for funds to aid Frank in his defense. The basis of the appeals was that Frank, an innocent man, was being persecuted because he was a Jew. These solicitations went to every part of the country, but were directed particularly to the North. The already high feeling against Frank in Atlanta was aggravated by these appeals. It was charged in the Southern press that $250,000 had thus been raised "to make certain that the guilty Jew Frank escaped the gallows."*

After Frank had been convicted and sentenced to death, the Northern press, almost without exception, denounced the verdict as a travesty of justice. Some leading Northern papers went so far as to send detectives and well-known lawyers to Atlanta to "investigate" and "review" the case. They all reported that Frank was innocent and that his trial had been a farce.

Then the case came before the Supreme Court of the United States; and the dissenting opinion of Justice

*Holmes and Chief Justice Hughes that—assuming the truth
of facts alleged in a petition for a writ of habeas corpus—
"lynch law [was] as little valid when practiced by a regularly drawn jury as when administered by one elected by
a mob intent on death" gave the Northern press sensational
material to work with. The majority opinion, which denied the writ on the ground that all of the points raised had
been passed on by the Supreme Court of Georgia, was
ignored.*

*Editorial comment in the Northern press grew increas-
ingly bitter. Georgia was denounced as a community of
bigots; its courts were branded as incompetent and coward-
ly. An aroused Southern press met this attack with re-
sponses equally vitriolic. The North, it retorted, had its
own unenviable record of crime and incompetency and corruption in its courts; let it put its own disordered house
in order; its characteristic intermeddling in the purely
domestic affairs of the South was officious, gratuitous and
unwarranted.*

*The commutation of Frank's sentence to life imprison-
ment was regarded throughout the South, and particularly
in Georgia, as the consequence of Northern propaganda.
In some quarters the direct charge was made that it had
been brought about by bribery. When Frank was forcibly
taken from the state penitentiary by a mob and hanged, the
battle between the Northern and Southern press was in-
tensified. The North saw in the lynching a complete vindication of its previous strictures. Although a few of the
Southern papers condemned the lawlessness of the mob,
many condoned it, finding in it only a justifiable execution
by outraged citizens of the righteous judgment of its courts.
After Frank's death the excitement gradually subsided;
but, as Mark Sullivan says in his Our Times, the Frank
case "fanned into a new flame for the moment the old ani-
mosities of the North and South of fifty years before."*

SPRING ARRIVES early in Georgia. Flowers, wild and cultivated, always in profusion during the long spring season, are at their height in April. It was probably for this reason that Georgia, when it was freed of the domination of Northern "reconstruction," designated April 26 as a memorial day on which to honor its Confederate dead.

In 1913 the day perhaps had a greater significance in Atlanta than elsewhere in the state. Many were still living who remembered the "March to the Sea" and its attendant death and destruction. Memorial Day in Atlanta was as much a reminder of that "unforgivable infamy" as it was a tribute to the fallen wearers of the gray.

On Memorial Day stores and factories closed. Gentle hands placed bouquets and wreaths on cross-and-flag-marked cemetery mounds. There was the parade of soldiers, old and young, with the dwindling line of veterans of the War between the States in the place of honor and, at the climax, the oration of the day—flaming apostrophes which recalled immortal sacrifices for the "lost cause."

In 1913 Memorial Day fell on a Saturday. Thirteen-year-old Mary Phagan was only one of a thousand little girls who wanted to see the parade. She had been employed at the National Pencil Company factory. Her job had been to fasten metal caps on the ends of lead pencils; but at the close of the workday on the previous Monday the supply of metal had run out, and she had been "laid off." For her work she was paid ten cents an hour, and there was one dollar and twenty cents due her for her twelve hours' work on Monday. Because of the holiday, most of the help had been paid off on Friday, but Saturday was the usual payday. Mary had been told by one of her fellow workers that there would be someone at the factory on Saturday from whom she could get her "envelope." She told her mother she would call at the factory, get her money and then go downtown and watch the parade.

She dressed for the occasion—her best dress, her blue hat with the ribbons and flowers and her "Sunday shoes." She carried the only accessories she possessed: a little variegated parasol and a mesh bag. She was a pretty child—well developed for her age, blond, blue-eyed and rosy-cheeked. Though her clothes were of the cheapest she wore them proudly and made a pleasing picture.

Mary lived with her mother and stepfather in Bellwood —then a suburb of Atlanta—and reached the factory by streetcar. At 11:45 A.M. on April 26 she boarded the car near her home and arrived at the street intersection nearest the factory a few minutes after noon. It was only a three-minute walk from there to the factory. The conductor and the motorman saw her leave and start to walk toward the factory. The evidence as to what happened afterward is uncertain and conflicting. It is known that she entered the factory and while in there was brutally violated and murdered.

In the early morning of Sunday April 27, about three-thirty, central police headquarters received a telephone call. An excited voice reported that the dead body of a "colored woman" had been found in the basement of the pencil factory. Two police officers were immediately dispatched to the scene. There they were met by one Newt Lee, Negro night watchman, who was the only person at the factory. It was Lee who had found the body and notified the police. He told the officers he had gone to the basement to use the toilet and had then discovered the body. He led them to the basement.

The only light was from a single gas jet, turned down so low that it afforded little illumination. One of the policemen turned the jet on full. On the floor in front of the furnace was the cold, rigid corpse of a white girl who was later identified as Mary Phagan. She was lying face downward. Her golden hair was matted with blood, and her face was swollen and black from dust and dirt. There was a deep cut on the back of her head and a cord, pulled tightly around her neck, had cut into the flesh. A strip of white cloth, torn from the girl's underskirt, was also wrapped loosely around her neck. A shoe was missing from one foot. It was later found some 100 or more feet away. The girl's hat and bloodstained handkerchief lay on a trash pile a short distance from the body. The little parasol, undamaged, was found[1] at the bottom of the near-by elevator shaft. Near the girl's head the police discovered two small sheets of paper, one white and one yellow, on which were scrawled in uncertain writing[2] two separate pencil notes:

mam that negro hire doun here did this i went to make water and he puch he doun that hole a long tall negro black that hoo it wase long sleam tall negro . . . wright while . . .

he said he would . . . play like nigt witch did it but that long tall black negro did it buy hisself.

The papers on which the notes were written had apparently come from an order pad, a number of which lay on a trash pile near the body.

The body was removed to a mortuary. Later medical examination established that death had been due to strangulation. According to an autopsy and microscopic analysis, there was no indication of spermatozoa on the clothing or body; yet the epithelium of the walls of the vagina had been torn and bruised.[3] The girl's drawers had been cut or ripped up the seam and were stained with blood and urine.

As the morning wore on, more police arrived at the building and a thorough search was begun. Nothing further of significant importance was discovered. The layout of the building, which assumed an importance later in the

---

1 The mesh bag was never found.
2 Dots indicate where the words were illegible.
3 This was a matter of dispute during the trial.

trial, was noted. The building occupied by the National Pencil Company was a four-story brick-and-frame structure with a basement. The factory had a frontage of seventy-five feet on South Forsyth Street and a depth of one hundred and fifty feet to a public alley. The main entrance was from Forsyth Street through a hallway on the first floor. Within this hallway, and some twenty-five or thirty feet from the entrance door, was a stairway which led to the upper floors of the building.

The second floor was shut off from the stairway by a partition, and access to it was obtained by a door. This floor contained the company's offices. The superintendent's inner office was separated from the outer office by a partition. Also on the second floor was the machine or metal room, also partitioned off. In this room there were numerous machines and inner, partitioned dressing and toilet rooms for female employees. Mary Phagan and a number of other young girls worked in the metal room.

There was an enclosed elevator shaft in the outer hall which extended from the basement to the fourth floor. The elevator was operated electrically. In addition to the iron stairs leading from the first floor to the basement there was, immediately behind the elevator shaft on the first floor, an opening or hatchway from which a ladder extended to the basement. When the factory was in full operation more than 100 persons, mostly women and girls, were employed on the first, second, third and fourth floors of the building.

Lee, the night watchman, told Police Captain Starnes, who was in charge of the investigation, that after he found the body he tried several times, but without success, to get in touch with Leo Frank, the superintendent of the factory, by telephone. The captain also put in repeated calls, but it was not until 7:00 A.M. that Frank answered the phone. Starnes asked him to come immediately to the factory. Frank replied that he had not had his breakfast, and asked where the night watchman was. Starnes told him that it

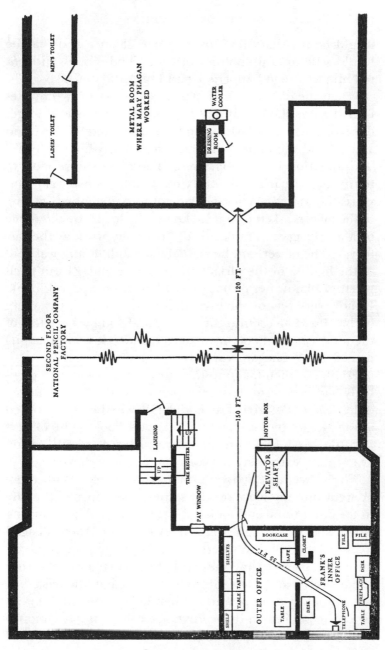

MEN'S TOILET

LADIES' TOILET

**METAL ROOM
WHERE MARY PHAGAN
WORKED**

WATER COOLER

DRESSING ROOM

**SECOND FLOOR
NATIONAL PENCIL COMPANY
FACTORY**

120 FT.

150 FT.

UP

UP

LANDING

TIME REGISTER

PAY WINDOW

MOTOR BOX

ELEVATOR SHAFT

BOOKCASE

35 FT.

SHELVES

SHELF

TABLE

TABLE

OUTER OFFICE

SAFE

CLOSET

FRANK'S INNER OFFICE

FILE

FILE

TABLE

DESK

DESK

FIREPLACE

TABLE

TELEPHONE

SECOND FLOOR OF THE NATIONAL PENCIL COMPANY FACTORY—PARTIAL FLOOR PLAN.

21

would be necessary for him to come at once and that he would send an automobile for him. The captain did not tell him what had happened, and Frank did not ask.

When the officers called at Frank's house a few minutes later, Frank asked what had happened. He was told to get dressed, go to the factory and see for himself. He then asked, "Did the night watchman report anything to you?" This question was also ignored. The officers were later to testify that during this interview Frank seemed very nervous and excited. When he had got into the police car, one of the officers asked him if he knew a little girl by the name of Mary Phagan. Frank asked, "Does she work at the factory?" The officer said he thought she did. Frank was told of the finding of the girl's body; then he said, "I can't tell whether I know her or not until I look on my payroll book. I know very few of the girls that work there. I pay them off but I seldom go into the factory and I know very few of them. I can look on my payroll and tell you if a girl named Mary Phagan works there."

Frank was then taken to the mortuary to which the girl's body had been removed. He glanced at the body, said he didn't know the girl, but could tell whether she worked at the factory by looking at his payroll book. The officers later declared that during this attempt at identification Frank was "extremely nervous" and "badly shaken."

The police next drove Frank to the factory. With them he went into the office on the second floor, opened the safe in the outer room and took out a time book. After running down the list of employees, he said, "Yes, Mary Phagan worked here. She was here yesterday to get her pay. I'll tell you the exact time she left here. My stenographer left about twelve, and a few minutes after she left, the office boy left, and Mary came in and got her money and left." Frank asked the policemen if the envelope containing her money had been found. According to the officers, he still seemed to be in a highly nervous and excited state. Frank asked to see where the body had been found. He accompanied the officers to the basement, and the place was pointed out to him. Witnesses were later to testify that during this time also Frank showed intense agitation.

Captain Starnes at this stage saw nothing suspicious in Frank's story or his actions. He ascribed Frank's agitation —at the mortuary and on being shown where the body was found—to the natural reaction of a man confronted with news of the murder of one of his employees and concern for the effect the publicity might have on the pencil company's business.

Lee, meanwhile, had been arrested. A shirt with blood spots on the front of it had been found in a trash barrel near his home. He denied it was his, and no evidence was developed to prove the contrary. Despite police abuse (he was manacled to a chair, which made either rest or movement difficult) and almost continuous questioning, he stuck to his original story. Such additional details as he gave were consistent with it and were verified by investigation.

Soon after Lee had been placed in custody the police officers asked Frank to talk with Lee privately to see if he could obtain additional information from him. Frank, after conversing alone with Lee for some time, reported that he had talked freely, but had told him nothing he had not already told the police.[4]

On Sunday Frank suggested to the police that they might do well to question Jim Conley, a Negro roustabout worker at the factory, and J. M. Gantt, a white man and former employee, who had recently been discharged because of a shortage in his accounts. Frank told the police that Gantt "had been on intimate terms with Mary Phagan."

Gantt, who had known Mary Phagan and her family for several years, was arrested. He was held in custody and

---

4 Lee gave a different version of this conversation at the trial. Reference to this will be made later.

questioned for several days, but had comparatively little difficulty in convincing the police that he knew nothing of her murder. Conley was arrested the Thursday following the murder. He had a police record of convictions for a number of petty offenses and a generally bad reputation among both blacks and whites. In spite of his repeated protestations that he had been drunk all of Memorial Day and nowhere near the factory, the police were apparently convinced from the start that he knew something of the crime. They kept him in close custody and, in the language of one of the later witnesses, "continued to work on him."

It was determined almost immediately that the penciled notes found near Mary Phagan's body had not been written by her. Mary Phagan had had only two or three years' schooling, but specimens of her writing produced by her mother and friends were entirely unlike the writing in the notes and showed, moreover, that she capitalized properly and spelled and punctuated fairly well. The police quite logically concluded that the notes had been prepared and planted by someone who hoped thereby to divert suspicion from himself.

The elimination of Gantt as a suspect, the failure of the police to turn up any evidence directly incriminating Lee or Conley, and the piecing together of what the police deemed peculiar circumstances shifted suspicion to Frank. On April 29, three days after the crime, he was arrested, lodged in jail and booked on a charge of suspected murder.

Leo Frank was a native of Texas but had spent his boyhood and early manhood in Brooklyn. He attended the public schools there, took some preparatory work at Pratt Institute and matriculated at Cornell University. He graduated from this institution in 1906 with a degree of Bachelor of Engineering. His uncle had organized and established the National Pencil Company in Atlanta; so, after working for a short time in Boston, Frank went to Atlanta to learn, and to grow up with, the business. Starting as a draftsman, he became by successive promotions superintendent and vice-president. He was married but had no children. At the time of the Phagan murder he was twenty-nine years old. The newspapers described and pictured him as a slight, thin-faced, rather frail-looking individual, with heavy black hair, a prominent nose and "stary" eyes. This last feature was accentuated by the thick-lensed glasses he habitually wore. He was of medium height and weighed about 130 pounds.

The morning after the murder Frank called in one of the regular attorneys for the company, a Herbert Haas, "to protect the pencil company's interests." Ostensibly for the same reason, he asked the Pinkerton Detective Agency to make an "independent investigation" of the crime. The manager of the Atlanta Pinkerton office—a man named Scott—accepted the employment. An ordinance of the City of Atlanta licensed private detectives and required, as one of the conditions for the license, that when engaged in work on criminal cases they should promptly report their findings to the municipal police and co-operate with them in the apprehension and prosecution of criminals. Scott's relations with the Atlanta police were extremely friendly; and, in accepting the pencil company's employment, he made it clear to Frank that he intended to "work with the police" to discover the murderer "regardless of who it might turn out to be." Frank told Scott that Detective Black seemed to suspect him; but he professed his complete satisfaction with Scott's declared intention to "get to the bottom of the matter."

The police ordered the factory closed on Monday so they might make a more leisurely and thorough inspection of it. Scott participated with the officers in the inspection. Some stains which looked like human blood were found on the floor of the metal room near the dressing room. An attempt had apparently been made to obliterate or obscure the stains by rubbing some white substance over them. On the handle of a bench lathe near Mary's machine were some strands of what looked like human hair. Employees who operated near-by machines were questioned. All were certain that neither the stains nor the hair had been there when they had left the factory the Friday before. The parts of the cement floor containing the stains were chipped out and, together with the supposed human hair, were preserved for possible future use as evidence.

Scott took a complete statement from Frank. It was substantially the same statement he made a few days later at the coroner's inquest and, except for slight modifications, was consistent with his longer and sworn statement made on his trial. Scott, however, found a number of items in the statement which, he later decided, convinced him that Frank was not telling the full or exact truth. Scott indignantly repudiated a suggestion that his reports should be submitted to Frank's attorney before they were shown to the police. This, it would appear, increased Scott's suspicion that Frank was in some way involved. Frank or Haas terminated the employment of the Pinkerton agency on Wednesday—the day before Frank's arrest—but Scott continued to work on the case with the Atlanta police. When official suspicion was definitely directed toward Frank, Scott made no effort to allay it; on the contrary, as new evidence against Frank came to light, he was one of the first to merge suspicion into accusation.

In their re-examination and appraisal of Frank's conduct the police recalled a number of circumstances which they now deemed suspicious: In the early morning of the twenty-seventh, following the discovery of the girl's body, Frank had not answered the repeated telephone calls made by Lee and Captain Starnes. He had balked when Starnes had said he should come to the factory immediately. When asked by the officers if he knew Mary Phagan he had answered that he could not tell; that he knew very few of the factory girls by name. These circumstances were compared with his statement, made immediately afterward at the office, in which he said: A girl named Mary Phagan worked there, and she had got her pay on Saturday. He could tell the exact time she came and left. His stenographer had left at twelve o'clock, and his office boy had left a few minutes later. Mary came in after that.

To the conclusion which they drew from this comparison the police added another observation: Right on the heels of Frank's declaration that he did not know Mary Phagan he had directed suspicion to Gantt by saying that Gantt had been "intimate" with her. The police recalled Frank's extreme nervousness and agitation on Sunday morning when the officers had called at his home and had taken him to the mortuary to see the dead body of the girl and to the basement of the factory where the body had been found. Both Lee and Gantt had since told them of Frank's apparent fright when he had encountered Gantt at the door of the factory at six o'clock Saturday.

The police now regarded it as significant that before and after Frank reached the factory on Sunday morning he had asked if they had found the girl's pay envelope. Lee had denied Frank's statement that Frank frequently called him at the factory after hours to inquire if everything was all right. He said that his call at seven o'clock on the twenty-sixth was the first such call he had made. Lee had also told the police that when Frank had talked to him privately in his cell Frank had said, "If you keep up like this, both of us will go to hell."

In later searches of the factory premises the police had discovered several pieces of cord identical with the cord which had been used to strangle the girl; some of it had been found in the metal room.

The police arrested one Mineola McKnight, the Negro cook in the Frank home. She was detained for some time and questioned. Among other things, she told the officers that when Frank came home Saturday night he was drunk and that he talked wildly and threatened to kill himself.[5] By persistent questioning, the police also obtained statements from a number of girls who worked at the factory. They said Frank had embarrassed and annoyed them with his attentions.

On Monday April 28 the county coroner summoned and swore a jury to inquire into and determine the manner and agency by which Mary Phagan had come to her death. After viewing the body and the factory premises, the jury continued the taking of testimony to May 6. On that day Frank, Gantt, a number of factory workers, policemen, and relatives and friends of Frank appeared and testified. Frank, represented by Luther Z. Rosser of the firm of Arnold & Rosser—one of the best-known criminal-trial lawyers in the South—took the stand and submitted patiently to three and one-half hours of examination.

This was Frank's story: On Saturday April 26 he arrived at the pencil company's office at about 8:30 A.M. He intended to work all day, because he had to get out his end-of-the-month financial statements. When he reached the factory the day watchman and an office boy were already there. Two carpenters were also there, changing some partitions on the fourth floor. Several other employees came in, between 8:30 and 9:30. Between 9:30 and 9:45 he left the factory in the company of a man named Darley, general superintendent of the pencil company, and a man named Lyons, superintendent of a near-by factory.

Continuing his testimony, Frank stated: He stopped at the near-by office of Montag Brothers, an affiliate of the pencil company in the same block, to see if he could get that company's stenographer Mattie Hall to come over to the pencil company and do some work for him. He spoke briefly with some of his friends at Montag Brothers and

---

5 She later repudiated all of these statements. She said that the police had abused and threatened her and that she had answered "yes" to everything they had asked in order to escape their brutality and get out of jail.

then returned to his office at 11:05 A.M. Miss Hall was already there. A Mrs. White, wife of one of the carpenters, was also there. She asked and received his permission to go up to the fourth floor to see her husband. Between 11:05 and 11:45 four other people came into the office and left.

Frank further stated in his testimony the following: He told the day watchman he could leave as soon as he got certain work done, and the man left about 11:45 A.M. It was ten or fifteen minutes later that the little girl, whom he afterward learned was Mary Phagan, came into his office and asked for her pay envelope. He asked her what her number was. She told him. He went to the cash box, identified her envelope by number, took it out and handed it to her. As she started to leave she turned around and asked if the metal had come yet. He told her, "No."[6] He heard her footsteps as she went away. He did not see her again until he was shown her dead body in the mortuary on Sunday morning. About five minutes after the girl left, one Lemmie Quinn, a foreman at the pencil factory, came in, and they talked for a minute or two.[7]

Frank, in his testimony in the inquest, was positive in the timing of his actions, At 12:45 P.M. he telephoned the cook at his house to inquire when lunch would be ready. Then he went to the fourth floor to tell the carpenters that he was locking up. The men said they would work through until he got back. Mrs. White followed him down the stairs and left the building at 12:50. He returned to his office, put away his papers, went downstairs, locked the outside factory door and left about 1:10. He reached home about 1:20, had lunch, lay down and rested for a while. Then he got up and telephoned his brother-in-law and told him that because of work at the office he could not go with him to the

---

6 In an earlier statement to the police and to Scott Frank said that his answer to her was that he didn't know; much was later to be made of this variation at the trial.

7 In his earlier statements to the police and to Scott Frank made no mention of Quinn.

ball game as previously planned. He took a streetcar back to the factory and arrived there shortly before 3:00.

The carpenters had just finished their work, Frank said, and they left the building at 3:10 P.M. At 4:00 Newt Lee, the night watchman, came in. He had told Lee the day before to report at that hour, because he (Frank) had expected to go to the ball game. However, there was no work for Lee to do; so he told Lee to go off and amuse himself and come back at 6:00. After Lee left he continued to work until 6:00, at which time Lee returned. He closed his office, went to the front door of the factory and there found Gantt talking to Lee. Gantt wanted to go up to the fourth floor to get a pair of shoes he said he had left there, and he (Frank) told Lee it would be all right to let Gantt into the factory for that purpose.

Frank said he then left the factory, performed some errands and arrived home about 6:25 P.M. He called Lee on the telephone around 7:00 to ask if Gantt had got his shoes and if everything was all right at the factory. Then he had supper and read the newspapers. Some friends came in and played cards with his parents-in-law, and he retired about 10:30. The telephone in the house, Frank explained, was in the dining room on the first floor, and the sleeping rooms were on the second floor; this accounted for the fact that he had not heard the early calls from Lee and Starnes. He said he awoke at 7:00 just in time to answer the last of Starnes's calls. Frank denied positively that he had ever spoken to Mary Phagan before the twenty-sixth when she came in to get her pay or that he had known her by name before the tragedy.

The coroner's inquest was concluded on May 8. The jury returned a verdict of murder at the hands of a person or persons unknown. While it does not appear in the verdict, the questions and comments of the coroner and jurors indicated their theory: that the murder had taken place on one of the upper floors of the factory and that the body had been carried to the basement and placed in front of the furnace, with the intent of later burning it. There were suggestions, too, that the factory had been regularly used as a love rendezvous and that Frank had been guilty of improper relations there with some of the female employees.

Meanwhile on May 3 a public announcement was made stating that Solicitor General Hugh A. Dorsey had assumed personal direction of the investigation to discover the murderer of Mary Phagan. On May 6 a grand jury was impaneled by Judge Ellis in the Fulton County Superior Court. He referred to the "unsolved Phagan case" and directed, because of the revolting nature of the crime and the public agitation over it, that it be given top priority in the jury's considerations.

Following the coroner's verdict a new and, as the event proved, most important witness appeared. One of the factory girls—one Monteen Stover—made an affidavit in which she said that she called at Frank's office at five minutes after twelve on Saturday the twenty-sixth to get her pay and that Frank was not in his office. She said she waited for him for about five minutes and then left. This was a direct contradiction of Frank's statement that he was continuously in his office from 11:05 to 12:45.

Another girl—one Helen Ferguson—told the police that on Friday the twenty-fifth, when she got her pay, she told Frank that Mary Phagan had asked her to get her envelope. Frank refused to give it to her. He said that Mary would have to call for her pay herself. This was balanced against the admitted fact that pay envelopes of employees were frequently delivered to their fellow workers or relatives.

Apparently the solicitor general was in serious doubt as to whether he should ask for a true bill against Frank or Newt Lee. He had a form of indictment prepared and in hand to fit either of them, and kept both names before the jury until the last witness had been heard. On May 24, however, he determined the question by asking for a true bill against Frank. The jury accordingly returned a no bill against Lee and an indictment against Frank charging him with first-degree murder.

By a strange coincidence, the Atlanta newspapers on the same day released a "confession" which the police had secured from Jim Conley. In it he charged Frank with the murder and confessed that at Frank's direction and with his assistance he had removed the body from the metal room on the second floor to the basement and left it in front of the furnace. Conley also declared that at Frank's dictation he wrote the notes which were found near the girl's body.

The death notes were compared with admitted specimens of Conley's handwriting. A similarity was apparent. No expert testimony on this point was offered on the trial, but Albert S. Osborn of New York, the most famous questioned-document expert in the United States, later declared that in his opinion there was no doubt that the notes had been written by Conley.

The case of the State of Georgia against Leo N. Frank came for trial at Atlanta in the Fulton County Superior Court on July 28, 1913. Presiding was the Honorable L. S. Roan, a veteran jurist of wide experience—able, conscientious, impartial and kindly. Appearing for the State were Solicitor General Hugh A. Dorsey, Special Assistant Solicitor Harry Hooper and Assistant Solicitor E. A. Stephens. Frank was represented by Reuben R. Arnold, Luther Z. Rosser, Stiles Hopkins and Herbert Haas. Solicitor General Dorsey carried the burden for the prosecution. He was a large, strikingly handsome man and a determined and forceful advocate. He was fully convinced of Frank's guilt, as were most of the citizens[8] of Atlanta, and conducted the trial throughout with an intensity of emotion

---

8 One of the Atlanta newspapers estimated on the basis of informal polls that four out of five of the townspeople held this view.

that electrified the crowds which daily jammed the courtroom. Arnold and Rosser shared the work of Frank's defense. They were old hands at the game and, realizing the
evidence and prejudice they had to overcome, sought by
all legitimate means to impeach the State's witnesses and
to build up an affirmative case for Frank of such preponder-
ating weight that it would compel a verdict of acquittal.

One hundred and forty-four veniremen were summoned.
Despite the publicity given the crime—the police investigation, the inquest, the grand-jury proceedings and the activities of the police department and the solicitor general's
office in the preparation of the case for trial—it took less
than four hours to select and agree on a jury of twelve men
who swore they had no preconceived opinions of Frank's
guilt or innocence, and could give him a fair and impartial
trial. Of the twelve chosen, eleven were married and five
of them fathers. They were of widely diverse occupations:
two salesmen, two machinists, a bank teller, a bookkeeper,
a real-estate agent, a manufacturer, a contractor, a mail
clerk, an optician and a railroad claim agent.

Special Assistant Solicitor Hooper in short and dramatic
sentences outlined the State's case against Frank: The evidence would show that thirteen-year-old Mary Phagan
came to her death as the consequence of a premeditated
rape of her person by the defendant. Frank had previously
seduced and taken indecent liberties with a number of
other young factory girls, and had made unsuccessful advances to Mary Phagan. Frank knew she was coming to the
factory on Saturday because one of her fellow employees
had asked him the day before for her pay envelope, and
Frank had said that she would have to come herself and
get it. To aid him in his lecherous activities Frank had
trained the Negro Conley to act as a lookout and to see
that he was not interrupted during his immoral and per-
verted acts. Conley had been told to report to the office
on Saturday April 26 for another of these occasions.

It would be the contention of the State, supported by evidence, said Hooper, that Mary Phagan came to Frank's office at 12:10 P.M. Hooper sketched in the details of what then occurred: Frank was alone in his office. After he had given the girl her pay envelope she had asked him if the metal for her work had come. He had answered he didn't know and, ostensibly to find out, had followed her into the metal room. While in there he had made advances to her which she had repulsed. He had then knocked her down, rendered her unconscious and raped her. In a panic of terror lest she recover consciousness and accuse him of rape, he had strangled her to death. He had left the body in the metal room while he went up to the fourth floor; he wanted to get the people out of the building in order that he might dispose of the body. After he had got rid of Mrs. White he called Conley and told him that the little girl had refused him and that he "guessed he had struck her too hard." The two of them then dragged the body to the elevator and took it to the basement. They made plans to burn the corpse later. Frank gave Conley $2.50 and, later, $200. But almost immediately he asked for and got the $200 back, after promising Conley he would pay him when the job was finished.

Hooper outlined briefly the remainder of the State's evidence, emphasizing particularly the expected testimony of Monteen Stover that Frank was not, as he had told the police and the coroner, in his office continuously from 11:05 A.M. to 12:45 P.M., but was out of his office when she came there looking for him at 12:05; that she had waited for him for five minutes; and that when, in leaving, she had tried the door to the metal room, she had found it locked.

The first witness called by the State was Mary Phagan's mother. Mary, she said, would have been fourteen years old had she lived until the first of June. She was a pretty girl and well developed for her age. On Saturday April 26 at 11:30 A.M. Mary had eaten a hearty dinner of bread and cabbage. About 11:45 she had left the house. She said she was going to the pencil factory to get her pay, and from there she was going to see the Memorial Day parade. She wore a lavender dress trimmed with lace, a blue hat with flowers in the center, and carried a little parasol and a German silver-mesh bag. Mary's mother identified the dress, underclothing, hat and parasol shown her as the things Mary had worn and carried when she last saw her alive.

One George Epps, a fourteen-year-old boy who lived "right around the corner" from Mary, testified he got on the same streetcar with her about 11:50 A.M. and rode with her until she got off the car at Forsyth and Marietta streets. It was then about 12:07.

The next witness was Newt Lee, the night watchman. He testified in substance as follows: His regular working hours were from 6:00 P.M. to 6:00 A.M., except on Saturdays, when he reported for work at 5:00 P.M. He got to the factory a few minutes before 4:00 on Saturday and found the outside door and the double inside doors to the upstairs locked. In the previous three weeks of his employment at the factory he had never found either of these doors locked when he came on duty in the afternoon. He had keys to the doors and opened them. As he unlocked the double doors Frank came "bustling out of his office," a thing he had never seen him do before. Frank said, "Come here a minute, Newt. I am sorry I had you come so soon. You could have been at home sleeping. I tell you what you do. You go downtown and have a good time." Frank had never let him off like that before. He then told Frank he would lie down in the factory's shop room. At that Frank said, "Oh, no. You need to have a good time. You go downtown and have a good time. Stay an hour and a half and come back at your usual time at six o'clock." He (Lee) then left.

Lee continued his testimony: He returned to the factory

a few minutes before 6:00 P.M. He was standing at the front door when J. M. Gantt came from across the street. Gantt told him he wanted to go up to the fourth floor and get a pair of shoes he had left there. He told Gantt that he was not allowed to let anyone into the factory after six o'clock. He was still talking to Gantt when Frank opened the front door and came out. When Frank saw Gantt he jumped back as if he was "frightened." Gantt told Frank he wanted to go upstairs to get his shoes. Frank said, "Well, I don't know." Then Frank "sort of dropped his head." He looked up and said to him (Lee), "You go upstairs with him and stay until he finds his shoes." He followed Frank's instructions. He went upstairs with Gantt, found the shoes, came downstairs and saw Gantt leave the building. At some time after seven o'clock Frank called him on the telephone and inquired, "Is everything all right?" He replied that everything was all right so far as he knew. It was the first time that Frank had ever called him on the phone.

Lee then repeated the story he had told the police. His account included his discovery of the body, his calling the police station, his unsuccessful attempts to reach Frank by telephone, and of the arrival of the officers and his directing them to the body. He testified he didn't see Frank after that until sometime between seven and eight o'clock, and then he did not speak to him.

The next conversation Lee had with Frank was two days afterward, on Tuesday evening, at the police station. He was at that time under arrest, and the officers had brought Frank into his cell. This is Lee's story of their meeting: He was handcuffed to a chair. Frank sat down in another chair and "hung his head." When they were alone he said to Frank, "Mr. Frank, it is mighty hard for me to be handcuffed here for something I don't know nothing about." Frank answered, "What's the difference? They have got me locked up and a man guarding me." He then asked Frank,

"Mr. Frank, do you believe that I committed that crime?" Frank said, "No, Newt, I know you didn't, but I believe you know something about it." In answer to Frank's statement he said, "Mr. Frank, I don't know a thing about it any more than finding the body." Frank then said, "We'll not talk about that now. We will let that go. If you keep that up we will both go to hell." At that time the officers came in and took Frank out.

Lee's testimony was not weakened by Rosser's careful and exhaustive cross-examination. Some beneficial qualifications were developed: The locked double doors inside the entrance to the building would not have prevented anyone from going to the basement. The front door and the double doors were unlocked when Lee returned to the factory at six o'clock. Frank had previously told Lee that Gantt had been discharged and that if he saw him hanging about the factory to watch him. Lee also said that Gantt was "a big fellow about seven feet tall." Gantt may have startled Frank. Lee in making his rounds after six o'clock had gone through the machine room and the ladies' dressing room every half hour and noticed nothing unusual. When he first saw the body he thought it was that of a Negro because her face was so black and dirty. When he was in the basement with the policemen, one of them showed him the notes they had found near the body. He swore he had never seen them before.

Various members of the police department gave their testimony[9] as to their notification of the murder, their going to the factory, their conversation with Lee, the finding of the body, the position and condition of the body and its removal to the mortuary. The notes found near the body, the girl's clothing and the parasol were identified and received in evidence. Other officers told of the telephone calls to Frank and their conversations with him at his

---

[9] In the narrative of this case the exact order in which the witnesses were called has been disregarded.

home, at the undertaker's and in the factory. All agreed that during the entire morning Frank was in a highly nervous state—"his hands shook," "he appeared excited," "was jumpy," "talked rapidly," at times "hung his head," and asked the same questions over and over again.

Harry Scott, superintendent of the local branch of the Pinkerton Detective Agency, testified in substance as follows: He was employed by Frank to represent the National Pencil Company and to "endeavor to determine who is responsible for this matter." He questioned Frank closely as to his movements on Friday and Saturday. Frank answered all of his questions readily and told him substantially the same story that he later told at the coroner's inquest. Frank, in his statement to him, declared positively that he was continuously at his desk in the inside office from the time he got back from Montag Brothers at 11:05 A.M. until 12:50 P.M., at which time he went upstairs to the fourth floor to tell the carpenters that he was leaving the factory to go home to lunch. Frank was equally positive that Gantt had paid a good deal of attention to Mary Phagan and had been "intimate" with her.

Scott, continuing his testimony, stated that after Frank was arrested on April 29 and confined in the same police barracks as Lee, Detective Black suggested to Frank, in his (Scott's) presence, that he did not believe Lee had told all he knew; that Frank was his employer and ought to be able to get more out of him than anyone else. Then Black asked if Frank would talk to Lee. Frank readily consented, was taken to Lee's cell and left alone with Lee for about ten minutes. He (Scott) didn't hear all that was said, but he did hear Lee say, "It's awful hard for me to be handcuffed here to this chair." Later he heard Frank say, "Well, they have got me, too." After Frank left Lee's cell Black asked if Lee had told him anything and Frank replied Lee had not. Lee had stuck to his original story. Frank, when he came out of Lee's cell, appeared "extremely nervous," "hung his head," "shifted his position," "sighed heavily," "took deep swallows" and "hesitated."

Scott and Black both testified to finding a bloodstained shirt in a trash barrel at Lee's house the Tuesday morning following the murder. The city chemist, who examined the shirt, refused to swear positively that the stains were human blood. He said the shirt showed no signs of having been worn since it had last been laundered.

Two of the factory machinists, who reported as usual for work Monday morning, testified to finding some splotches which looked like blood on the floor near the ladies' dressing room in the metal department. Some "white stuff" which they thought might be potash or "haskoline" had been smeared over the spots. They found also some strands of what looked like hair on the handle of a bench lathe near the machine where Mary worked. Neither the spots nor the hair,[10] they said, had been there the previous Friday.

A number of police officers and other witnesses testified the spots were pointed out to them and looked like blood. Witnesses identified pieces of cement chipped from the floor, which showed the stains. The city chemist had also examined and tested these. He testified he was unable to declare positively that the stains were human blood.

Several witnesses testified there were pieces of cord in the machine room of the same kind as that which had been used to strangle the girl. They said that similar cord was used throughout the factory and could be found on any of the floors.

Much of this testimony was uncontroverted and, with the exception of Lee and Scott, the cross-examinations were relatively brief. One of the witnesses—Darley, general manager of the pencil-company factory—was friendly to-

10 It had been determined before the trial that the supposed human hair found near Mary Phagan's machine was not of the same color or texture as her hair.

ward Frank, and both on direct and cross-examination, did everything he could to aid him. There was nothing significant, he said, about Frank's nervousness on Sunday after he had been told of the crime. Frank was naturally high-strung and became nervous and excited at any unusual occurrence. Darley admitted having seen the supposed blood spots on the metal-room floor but said he frequently saw blood and "white stuff" on the floor in and around the ladies' dressing room. The factory was a very dirty place, he added.

The undertaker who embalmed the body, and two physicians gave testimony as to its condition. The undertaker testified: When he saw the body—about 9:00 A.M. Sunday morning—it looked as though the girl had been dead for ten to fifteen hours. There was a scalp wound two and one-half inches long on the back of the head, but the skull was not fractured. The girl's hair was clotted with blood and around her neck there was a cord drawn so tightly that it cut into the flesh. He said he examined the girl's clothing. The right leg of her drawers had been slit with a knife or torn up the seam. There were stains of urine, some discharge and dried blood on them.

The undertaker's testimony was corroborated in part by that of the county physician. He testified in substance as follows: The head wound had been made before death. The cuts on her face and the bruises and scratches on her right elbow and left knee had been made after death. The cord around the girl's neck was imbedded in the skin, and her tongue protruded an inch and a half through her teeth. There was no question that she had died of strangulation. Although he found blood on her private parts he found no evidence of violence to the girl's female organs. The hymen was not intact, but she had normal genital organs which were somewhat larger than usual for a girl of her age. This condition could have been produced by penetration immediately preceding death.

On cross-examination the county physician testified that the blood he found might have been menstrual flow. He said that he discovered no "outward signs" of rape.

The testimony of Dr. H. F. Harris, who made a postmortem examination of the body, was considerably at variance with that of the county physician. Dr. Harris testified: The vagina definitely showed evidence of some kind of violence before death—an injury made by a finger or by other means. The epithelium was pulled loose from the inner walls and completely detached in some places. The violence which had produced this condition had occurred before death. He found evidence of internal bleeding. It would have taken considerable violence to tear the epithelium to such an extent that bleeding would ensue. He had also examined the stomach contents. The digestive process had ceased with her death. In his opinion the girl had lived for from one half to three quarters of an hour after she had eaten her meal of bread and cabbage.

Helen Ferguson, who worked in the metal room with Mary Phagan, testified she saw Frank at seven o'clock Friday night when she got her pay. She asked him to give her Mary's envelope so that she might take it to Mary and save her a trip to the factory, but Frank said she could not have it. On previous occasions she had got Mary's pay envelope for her but not from Frank.

J. M. Gantt gave testimony which was highly damaging to Frank. He testified in substance as follows: He had known Mary Phagan ever since she was a little girl. Frank knew her too. One day she came into his (Gantt's) office to get her time corrected, and after she left Frank said, "You seem to know Mary pretty well." He had not previously told Frank that the girl's name was Mary. He went to the factory Saturday afternoon to get his shoes. When Frank came out of the door and saw him he "jumped," "looked pale" and "hung his head."

Gantt admitted on cross-examination that Frank had discharged him on the previous April 7 for an alleged shortage in the payroll and that when he testified at the coroner's inquest he had said nothing about Frank's having known Mary Phagan.

Mrs. J. A. White testified: She went to the factory Saturday morning about eleven-thirty to see her husband. Frank permitted her to go up to the fourth floor, where her husband was working, and she stayed there until 11:50. She then left the factory. She returned at 12:30 and again went up to the fourth floor. When she talked to Frank at 11:30 he was in the outside office. When she went upstairs at 12:30 he was standing in the outside office at the safe. Frank came up to the fourth floor at one o'clock and said that unless she wanted to stay until three o'clock she had better leave because he was going to lunch and was locking up the factory. She left shortly afterward, and as she passed Frank's office she saw him at his desk writing.

She concluded her testimony with a statement of which much was to be made in later argument. She said as she was going out of the building she saw a Negro sitting on a box on the first floor, just inside the door. On cross-examination she said she paid no particular attention to the man and could not identify him.

Fourteen-year-old Monteen Stover gave damaging testimony against Frank. She repeated the story she had told the police. She was positive she reached the factory at 12:05 P.M. on Saturday. She waited in Frank's office for five minutes. Since he was not there she concluded that he had gone for the day. She was sure of the time, she said, because she had looked at the clock. She testified further that she had intended to go to the ladies' dressing room, inside the metal room, but when she tried the door she found it locked.

Albert McKnight—the husband of Mineola McKnight, who was the Negro cook in the house where Frank lived with his wife's parents—gave testimony which was directly contradictory to the statement Frank had made to the police and the testimony he had given at the inquest. McKnight swore he was in the kitchen with his wife when Frank came home about 1:30 P.M. and that Frank did not eat any lunch. Frank, said McKnight, left the house after five or ten minutes.

The State's star witness, who was one of the last called, was James Conley, the Negro. Conley told a long and startling story: He worked days at the factory as a general handy man, a roustabout. He had worked at the pencil factory for a little over two years. On Friday afternoon, about three o'clock, Frank came up to the fourth floor, where he was working. Frank said he wanted him to come to the factory Saturday morning at 8:30 because there was some work for him to do on the second floor. He followed Frank's instructions and came to the factory about 8:30 on the twenty-sixth and found Frank there. Frank said, "You are a little early for what I want you to do for me, but I want you to watch for me like you have been doing on the rest of the Saturdays."

Conley explained Frank's order by stating that on several previous Saturdays and on Thanksgiving Day 1912 he had stayed on the first floor by the door and watched while Frank and "some young lady" were on the second floor "chatting." He and Frank had a code of signals by which when the right lady came along Frank would "stomp" on the floor and Conley would lock the door. When Frank "got through with the lady" he would whistle, and this meant that Conley should unlock the door so the lady could get out. Conley said that when Frank told him he didn't need him for a while he left. He returned to the factory at some time between 10:00 and 10.30 A.M. He was standing at the corner of the building when Frank came out of the factory door, passed him and said he was going to Montag Brothers but would be right back. Frank told him that he should wait right where he was.

When Frank came back (Conley did not state the time) both he and Frank walked to the front door of the factory and stepped inside. Frank then showed him how to turn the catch on the knob, on the inside of the door, so that no one could get in from the outside. Then Frank pointed to a little box near a trash barrel just inside the door and gave him his instructions: He (Conley) should sit on the box, keep out of sight as much as he could and keep his eyes open. Later on, said Frank, there would be a young lady come along, and she and Frank were "going to chat a little." Frank said that when she came he would "stomp" as he had done before; then Conley should shut and lock the door. Later he would whistle; then Conley would know he was through and should unlock the door and come upstairs to the office. This would give the young lady time to get out.

Conley said he promised Frank to do as he was directed. Frank then went upstairs. Conley told of seeing various people come into and leave the factory. After these people had come and gone he said he saw a girl, whom he afterward found out was Mary Phagan, come to the door, enter the building and go upstairs. Later he heard footsteps going toward Frank's office. After that he heard the footsteps of two people. It sounded as if they were walking out of the office toward the metal room. Shortly afterward he heard a lady scream, and then he didn't hear any more sounds. The next person he saw, according to his testimony, was Monteen Stover. He described what she wore. He said she stayed in the factory for a short while; then she came down the steps and left. After that he heard someone run out of the metal room—running as if on tiptoes—and then he heard somebody tiptoe back toward the metal room. Following this, he said, he must have "kinda dozed off to sleep." The next thing he knew Frank was over his head "stomping." He got up and locked the door. Then he sat on the box for a little while until he heard Frank whistle.

Conley did not attempt to fix the time of these sequences. He said that when he heard the whistling he unlocked the door and went upstairs. There he saw Frank standing at the door of his office "shivering and trembling and rubbing his hands." His "face was red" and "he looked funny out of his eyes." In one of his hands, said Conley, Frank held a piece of white cord. Conley said it was "just like this here cord"—the one in evidence.

Conley continued: After he got to the top of the stairs Frank asked him, "Did you see that little girl who passed here just a while ago?" Conley replied he had seen one girl come in and go out; and then another girl came in, but she didn't come down. Then Frank said, "Well, that one that you say didn't come back down, she came into my office awhile ago and wanted to know something about her work, and I went back there to see if the little girl's work had come, and I wanted to be with the little girl and she refused me, and I struck her and I guess I struck her too hard, and she fell and hit her head against something, and I don't know how bad she got hurt." To this Frank added, "Of course, you know I ain't built like other men."

Conley testified that Frank asked him to go back to the metal room and bring her out so that they could put her somewhere, and to hurry; there would be money in it for him. Conley said that he then went back to the metal room and saw the girl lying on the floor with a rope around her neck. Another piece of cloth was around her head to catch the blood. He noticed the clock at that time; it was four minutes to one. He saw that the girl was dead and immediately ran back to Frank and told him so. Frank said, "Shh," and told him he should go back to the cotton box, get a piece of cloth, wrap it around her and bring her out.

Conley said that he did as he was directed, but when he tried to lift the body he found that it was too heavy for him to carry. He returned to Frank and told him that he could not move the body alone; Frank would have to help him. Together they carried the girl's body to the elevator, and after Frank had got the key and opened the elevator door they put the body in the cab and ran the elevator to the basement. There they rolled the body out onto the floor and left it. Then they went back upstairs to Frank's office.

Conley said they had hardly reached the office when Frank jumped up and said, "My God! Here is Emma Clark Freeman and Corinthia Hall. Come over here, Jim; I have got to put you in this here wardrobe." Frank put him into the wardrobe, and he stayed there until the women left—it seemed a long time to him. After the women left the office Frank opened the wardrobe and said, "You are in a tight place; you done very well."

Conley continued his testimony: They sat down and Frank handed him one cigarette and then the broken package which contained several more. Frank said "Can you write?" He answered, "A little bit." Frank gave him a lead pencil and dictated a number of notes. The first notes evidently did not satisfy Frank, but after four or five attempts he (Conley) wrote a note which Frank "laid on his desk" and "looked at smiling." Frank "pulled out a nice little roll of greenbacks" and said, "Here is $200." Frank looked at him and added, "Now, you go down in the basement and take a lot of trash and burn that 'package' that is in front of the furnace." He told Frank that he was afraid to go down there by himself. Frank asked him for the roll of bills, and he gave them back to Frank.

After that, according to Conley, there was the following conversation: Frank said, "Why should I hang? I have wealthy people in Brooklyn." Conley said, "What about me?" Frank replied, "Don't you worry about anything; you just come back to work on Monday morning like you don't know anything and keep your mouth shut. If you get caught I will get you out on bond and send you away. You can come back this evening and do it." Conley asked if he was going to get any money. Frank said he was going home but would be back in about forty minutes and fix everything. Conley told Frank, "All right," he would be back in about forty minutes.

After that, Conley said, he went across the street to the nearest saloon. When he went to take a cigarette out of the package Frank had given him he found it contained also two one-dollar bills and two silver quarters. He had a drink, went home, fell asleep and did not wake up until six-thirty the next morning. The next time he saw Frank was the following Tuesday morning on the fourth floor of the factory. Frank passed him and said, "Keep your mouth shut. If you had come back here Saturday and done what I told you there wouldn't have been any trouble."

Conley, when asked what Frank had meant by his statement that he was "not built like other men," testified the reason Frank had said that was "because he had seen him (Frank) in a position I haven't seen any other man that has got children." On two or three occasions before Thanksgiving he had seen Frank in the office "with a lady in his office, and she was sitting in a chair and she had her clothes up to here—" indicating above his waist—"and he was down on his knees, and she had her hands on Mr. Frank." At another time he had seen Frank in the back room with a young woman lying on a table.

Conley testified that sometimes when Frank had a woman with him and he (Conley) was "watching" for him a man by the name of Dalton was also there with a woman; that Frank, Dalton and the two women frequently had soft drinks and beer in Frank's private office. Dalton, he said, occasionally handed him a half dollar or a quarter after the parties were over. At one such time Frank gave him fifty cents and told him to keep his mouth shut.

Conley was subjected to a long and grueling cross-examination. Under pressure he said Daisy Hopkins was the name of one of the women who had been with Frank and

Dalton. He told of an occasion when Frank and Dalton had gone into the basement with another woman whom he did not know. Conley said Frank once talked to him about watching within the hearing of another Negro employee who responded to the nickname "Snowball." He repeated his direct examination as to the persons he had seen come into and leave the factory Saturday morning, but he said he had no recollection of having seen either Mrs. White or the office boy, Alonzo Mann. He denied having told a Mrs. Carson and a Miss Fuss that "Frank was as innocent as the angels in Heaven" or of having ever admitted to anyone that he (Conley) had killed a girl.

Conley admitted that he had lied to Scott in a statement made shortly after his arrest and that he had lied to the police in at least four statements prior to his alleged confession. For nearly a month after the murder he had maintained, in spite of almost continuous questioning, that he knew nothing whatever about the murder. He said he had done this to protect Frank, because Frank was a white man and his boss and had been good to him—had not docked him for some of the times he had been drunk and had failed to punch the clock. It was brought out that Conley had been arrested and convicted a half-dozen times for drunkenness and disorderly conduct and had served several jail sentences. He admitted that the police had questioned him night and day and would not let him sleep, but he denied that they had abused or threatened him to force his confession.

On redirect examination Conley testified that he had seen Mary's mesh bag in Frank's office and had seen Frank put it in his safe. He described the bag as "a wire-looking, whitish pocketbook."

The impression created by a witness on the jury which hears and sees him cannot be read on the printed page; but by judging from what he reads in cold type the disinterested investigator can only conclude that Conley and his loose and disconnected story were wholly discredited by Rosser's devastating cross-examination.

Conley's story was corroborated to a degree, however, by the testimony of Dalton, the man he had named as Frank's companion in some of his unmoral relationships. Dalton testified he knew Frank and Conley. He said that he and Frank had frequently had relations with women at the factory and that on such occasions Conley had acted as their "lookout." He had given Conley a half dollar or a quarter probably a half-dozen times. He also said there were a stretcher and an old cot in the basement. The cross-examination of Dalton was scathing. He was badly confused, repeatedly contradicted himself and was made to admit that he had been convicted and had served time for larceny in the state penitentiary.

Mrs. White was recalled and asked if she could identify Conley as the Negro she saw sitting on the box at the foot of the stairs on Saturday. She was unable to do so.

The statement Frank first made to the police and his testimony at the coroner's inquest, authenticated by the testimony of the stenographic reporters who took them, were offered and received in evidence.

Two witnesses called by the State proved more helpful to the defense than to the prosecution. Darley, the general superintendent of the pencil company, testified there never had been a bed, cot or sofa in the factory. Halloway, the Negro day watchman, corroborated Frank's statement: He saw Frank arrive at the factory Saturday morning at eight-thirty and go to his office. Frank left about 10:00 A.M. to go to Montag Brothers. He returned a few minutes before 11:00 and went immediately to his office on the second floor. Miss Hall, the stenographer, was already there. At Frank's suggestion he left the factory for the day about 11:45. A short distance from the factory he met Mrs. Freeman and Corinthia Hall. One of them asked him if Frank was in his office, and he answered that Frank was. Hallo-

way further testified he had frequently seen bloodstains in
and near the entrance to the ladies' dressing room in the
metal department and that potash and haskoline—both
white substances—were often accidentally spilled and
smeared on the floor.

Both Halloway and Darley declared there was no lock on
the metal-room door. Both also testified they saw nothing
of Conley on Saturday. They said they saw him Monday
morning; his furtive actions made them more suspicious
of him than of anyone else. They had never seen Frank
"jolly" Conley or act familiarly toward him. Halloway did
admit, reluctantly, that Conley did not always "punch the
clock" as the rest of them did; he did about as he pleased
and got his pay just the same.

The foregoing summarizes the State's case in chief.

Frank's attorneys properly concluded that the successful
defense of their client required (1) corroboration of the
previous statements he had made to the police and at the
coroner's inquest, and the statement he would later make
to the jury; (2) testimony which would so completely discredit Conley and Dalton that the jury would be compelled to reject their evidence; (3) testimony which would
negative the inferences to be drawn from the testimony of
the State's witnesses, particularly that of Lee, Gantt, Helen
Ferguson, Monteen Stover and the police officers; and (4)
testimony which would establish Frank's general reputation as a law-abiding citizen and his particular reputation
for morality and uncriticizable conduct toward the female
factory employees.

The record reveals a thoroughness in investigation and
pretrial preparation which resulted in the production of a
mass of evidence—nearly 200 witnesses—to satisfy these re-
quirements. Neither Frank nor his attorney ever contended
that there had been any abridgment of his constitutional
rights to summon witnesses in his own behalf and make a
full and complete defense.

These were Frank's contentions: He had got to the factory on Saturday the twenty-sixth at 8:30 A.M. He was in his office until 9:30 or 9:40 when he left to go to Montag Brothers. He returned to the factory and went to his office at 10:55. He stayed there continuously until 12:45 or 12:50. He left the factory shortly after 1:00 and returned just before 3:00. He remained there until about 6:00 when he left for home. He arrived at his home about 6:25, had dinner shortly afterward and retired at 10:30. He knew nothing of the crime until he heard about it the next morning.

More than twenty witnesses were called to corroborate these place-and-time sequences. Mattie Hall, the stenographer borrowed from Montag Brothers, Robert Schiff, the assistant superintendent of the pencil factory, Corinthia Hall, Emma Clark Freeman and the office boy Alonzo Mann swore that Frank was in his office on the second floor from eleven o'clock until noon and that during that hour he talked to several people. Lemmie Quinn, one of the factory foremen, testified he saw Frank in his office about 12:20 P.M. White and Denham, the carpenters, testified Frank came up to the fourth floor about one o'clock and told them he was locking up to go to lunch. One Helen Kerns, an employee of Montag Brothers, testified she saw Frank at Alabama and Whitehall streets, a short distance from the pencil factory, at 1:10. A Mrs. Levy, who lived across the street from Frank's home, testified she saw him get off a streetcar between one and two o'clock and cross the street to his home. Frank's father-in-law and mother-in-law testified Frank came in at 1:20, ate his lunch and left about 2:00.

Three witnesses corroborated Frank's statement that he called his brother-in-law, Ursenbach, on the telephone at 1:30 or 1:40 P.M. to say that he could not go to the ball game. Six witnesses swore they saw Frank at two o'clock. Two of them testified they saw him get on a streetcar which was traveling in the general direction of the pencil factory.

A forelady at the factory and her mother testified they saw
Frank looking at the parade in downtown Atlanta between
2:30 and 2:35. Denham and White testified they saw him
at 2:50 when he returned to the factory.

Frank's father-in-law and mother-in-law testified Frank
came home for dinner about 6:30 P.M. Dinner was served
at seven o'clock. About eight o'clock some friends of theirs
came in to play cards. Frank did not play but read the
newspapers and retired at 10:30. The four persons identified by Frank's parents-in-law as the persons who came in
to play cards testified they arrived at the Frank home about
eight o'clock and saw Frank there. According to their
recollections, however, Frank excused himself about nine
o'clock and went upstairs.

Twelve of the fifteen witnesses who saw Frank after one
o'clock testified they were close to him and noticed no
bruises or scratches on his face or hands, and he appeared
and acted as usual.

With the exception of Quinn the testimony of none of
these witnesses was weakened by the solicitor general's
cross-examination. As bearing on the interest of the several witnesses, it was developed that all who were not employees of Montag Brothers or the pencil company were
relatives by marriage or close friends of Frank. Quinn,
under a slashing cross-examination, failed to stand up to
his declaration made on direct examination that he had
seen Frank in his office at 12:20 P.M. Quinn was bitterly
denounced in the State's closing arguments as a perjurer.

Mineola McKnight, the Negro cook in the Frank house-
hold, contradicted the testimony of her husband, who had
been a State's witness. She swore that her husband was not
at the Frank residence at any time on Saturday. Frank, she
said, came home to lunch about 1:20 P.M. and left about
2:00. She next saw him when he ate dinner with the family
at night. She said the police tried to get her to say that
Frank would not allow his wife to sleep the night of the

twenty-sixth and wanted to get a gun and shoot himself; that that was not true; that the police took her to the station house in a patrol wagon and locked her up, and she then told the police anything they wanted her to say so they would let her out of jail; that any statement she might have made to them was untrue. She denied that Mrs. Selig, Frank's mother-in-law, had raised her wages or given her any extra money since Frank's arrest. Mrs. Selig corroborated this statement.

Emil Selig, Frank's father-in-law, testified in refutation of Newt Lee's testimony that he had frequently heard Frank call up the night watchman at the factory from his home at night.

To account for Frank's presence at the factory on Saturday afternoon three witnesses testified to the volume of end-of-the-month work Frank had to do. They said that it would have taken a diligent and skilled bookkeeper from three and one-fourth to three and one-half hours to complete it. The stenographer Miss Hall, in addition to her testimony corroborative of Frank's story, testified that Frank asked her to stay and help him with his work Saturday afternoon. She told him she could not do so on account of a previous engagement.

Magnolia Kennedy, one of the factory workers, testified that when the girls lined up for their pay on Friday she was right behind Helen Ferguson. Helen Ferguson did not ask for Mary's pay envelope; moreover, although Frank sometimes "paid off" he had not paid the employees on Friday the twenty-fifth. Schiff, the assistant superintendent, testified that he, not Frank, paid the employees on Friday April 25. He said that Helen Ferguson did not ask for Mary's pay and that one employee could not get the pay envelope of another without a written order.

W. M. Matthews and W. T. Hollis, motorman and conductor of the English Avenue streetcar, testified that Mary Phagan was a passenger on their car on April 26 and that

she got off at Hunter and Broad streets, about a block from
the pencil factory. They said their scheduled arrival time
was 12:07½ P.M.[11] and that the car was on time on April
26. A superintendent of the streetcar company corroborated
their testimony as to the schedule and running time between various points. The testimony of the conductor and
motorman, so far as it was designed to establish the exact
time Mary Phagan got off the car, was considerably weakened by the cross-examination of the superintendent, who
testified that the English Avenue schedule was a difficult
one to maintain and that the company frequently had occasion to suspend trainmen for "running ahead of schedule."

Two civil engineers were called to testify they made accurate measurements of the distances between the front
door of the factory and certain street intersections and of
the length of time it would take, walking at a fair pace, to
cover those distances. The distance from the pencil factory
to Marietta and Forsyth streets was 1,016 feet, and it took
them four and one-half minutes to walk that distance. The
distance from the factory to Whitehall and Alabama streets
was 831 feet, and it took them three and one-half minutes
to cover that distance. The distance from Broad and
Hunter streets was 333 feet, and to cover that distance it
took them one and three-quarters minutes.

More than a dozen of the witnesses called gave testimony
either to impeach Conley or discredit his story. Nine witnesses swore that his general reputation for truth and veracity was bad and that they would not believe him under
oath. Eight defense witnesses testified they were at the factory at various times Saturday morning and at no time did

---

11 Much was made of the exact time Mary Phagan left the streetcar at
Broad and Hunter, or Broad and Marietta, streets. If the time of the arrival
of the car was 12:07½ P.M. and it took three or four minutes to reach the
factory, Monteen Stover, according to her own positive testimony, would
have left the factory before Mary Phagan arrived, and Frank's absence from
his office between 12:05 and 12:10 would lose its significance.

they see Conley. A Mrs. Carson and her daughter testified they saw Conley at the factory on Monday morning. He told them he had been so drunk all day Saturday he could not remember where he was or what he did. Conley told them that "Frank was as innocent as a child." Another factory worker, a Miss Fuss, testified she talked to Conley on the Wednesday following the murder, and he said that "Frank was as innocent as the angels in Heaven." These and other witnesses who saw Conley on Monday, Tuesday and Wednesday following the murder testified that he was nervous, avoided answering questions and acted suspiciously.

Several witnesses swore that Conley could read and write. One of the girls testified that on Monday he borrowed some money from her to buy newspapers and that he was so excited he bought two copies of the same edition.

A reporter for one of the Atlanta papers testified he talked with Conley on May 31—after Conley had made his confession—and Conley told him he finished his work and left the factory at 1:30 P.M. on April 26 and that he had never seen any mesh bag.

Some of the factory help testified they were regularly or frequently at the plant on Saturday afternoons and at no time saw Conley there. Witnesses did testify that Conley was at the factory on Thanksgiving Day 1912, sweeping up and doing his regular work, but they said Frank left the building shortly after twelve o'clock on that day and did not return. They also testified that Frank usually worked Saturday afternoons, but there were never any women in his office, nor was there any drinking there. None of them had ever seen Dalton in the factory on Saturday afternoons. They all testified that to their knowledge none of the outside or inner doors of the factory were ever locked on Saturdays, that Frank's office was always open and that the blinds and shades in his office were never drawn.

Daisy Hopkins, named by Conley as one of the girls Dalton brought to the factory for the Saturday-afternoon assignations, swore that she had never been at the factory with Dalton or anyone else, that she did not know where the basement was and that she had never spoken to Frank. She admitted on cross-examination that she had been arrested and charged with fornication but had never been tried. Two other women who had been suggested in the State's case as companions of Dalton at the factory took the stand; one denied that she had known either Dalton or Frank, the other denied that she had ever been at the factory with Dalton. Eight witnesses were called who declared that Dalton's reputation for truth and veracity was bad and that they would not believe him under oath.

Gordon Bailey, the Negro worker at the factory known as "Snowball," denied that he had ever seen Frank and Conley talking together or heard Frank say anything to Conley about "watching" for him.

Four factory employees testified that when the elevator ran it made a very loud noise and jarred the floor when it stopped. Denman and White, the carpenters who were working on the fourth floor of the factory all day Saturday up to three o'clock, corroborated this testimony and also testified that from where they were they could have seen the wheels in the upper part of the elevator shaft turn and that those wheels did not turn at any time Saturday while they were there.

A Dr. Owens testified he conducted a series of experiments to determine how long it would have taken Conley and Frank to do what Conley said they did after twelve o'clock Saturday noon. He said the actions described could not have been performed in less than thirty-six and one-half minutes and that was not allowing any time for the dictation and writing of the notes as testified to by Conley. He said from twelve to sixteen minutes would have to be added for that action.

A number of factory employees testified they frequently

saw splotches of blood on the second floor in the metal
room and in and around the ladies' dressing room. The
operators often got their fingers cut or crushed in the machines and bled. The floors were never kept clean and
white substances—potash and "haskoline"—which were
used in the factory were frequently spread on the floor to
cover the blood spots. One witness, a machinist, testified to
two specific instances when employees working around the
machinery had been quite badly injured and suffered a
serious loss of blood. Lemmie Quinn, the metal-depart-
ment foreman, testified the girls "fixed their hair" in the
metal room, and many times their combings were scattered around the room.

The defense called three physicians—one of them was a
professor of physiology and physiological chemistry at the
Atlanta College of Physicians and Surgeons—who testified
it might take as long as four and one-half hours for cabbage
to digest and pass from the stomach into the intestines. It
all depended, they said, on mastication, and from an examination of the stomach contents one could not tell within
two and one-half hours how long the digestive process had
been going on before death.

Three other physicians testified they had examined
Frank and that he was a sexually normal person. They also
testified there was nothing significant in the post-mortem
finding that the epithelium had apparently been torn loose
from the walls of the dead girl's vagina. Such a condition,
they said, could have been due to the embalming of the
body and did not indicate violence to the vagina before
death.

Fifty-six witnesses—associates of Frank at Cornell University and in Brooklyn and Atlanta—testified that his general reputation as an upright, law-abiding citizen was good.
Forty-nine of the women employees at the pencil factory
testified that not only was his general reputation good but
also that his reputation for moral rectitude was good. Spe-

cifically they said that they had never heard of his being otherwise than a gentleman where women were concerned or of his ever "having done anything wrong." The testimony of one of these witnesses did not stand up too well on cross-examination. She testified that on two or three occasions she had heard "remarks" about Frank's coming into the women's dressing room and staring at the girls and that she herself was in the dressing room on one such occasion when he came in.

The defense was concluded with Frank's statement.[12] While it was very lengthy—eighty pages of typewritten record—it added very little beyond details to the statements he had previously made. The only significant variation was his attempt to avoid a direct clash with Monteen Stover, who, it will be remembered, testified in the State's case that when she went to Frank's office at 12:05 P.M. he was not there and that she waited until 12:10 and when he did not appear concluded he was not in the factory and left. In Frank's statement to the jury he said that to the best of his recollection from the time the twelve-o'clock whistle blew[13] until 12:45 when he went upstairs to talk to the carpenters he did not leave his inner office. "But it is possible," said Frank, "that to answer a call of nature or to urinate I may have gone to the toilet. Those are things a man does unconsciously and cannot tell how many times nor when."

The defense had made a strong case. It was destined, however, to be badly riddled by rebuttal. Under the law the State could not attack the general or specific reputation of the defendant until the defendant first put his reputation in issue. Frank had done that. He had produced more than 100 character witnesses. The State had a score of witnesses

---

12 Under Georgia practice a defendant in a criminal case is not a competent witness in his own behalf. He may, however, if he desires, make a sworn or unsworn statement, but he is not subject to cross-examination.

13 This was a slip on Frank's part, and he was to hear from it in the solicitor general's summation. April 26 was a holiday. The factory was closed, and the whistle did not blow that day.

in readiness to meet this mass of negative testimony with positive testimony of the most damaging character.

The State called more than seventy witnesses in rebuttal.

Gantt testified he knew exactly how long the work Frank had to do for the end-of-the-month records would take; that he had seen Frank do the entire job in an hour and a half.

One R. L. Craven, a friend of Mineola McKnight's husband, swore he went to the police station with McKnight to see if they could have her released from police custody. He was present, he said, when she made and signed a statement to the police. In that statement she said that when Frank came home on Saturday evening he showed signs that he had been drinking; that after he went to bed he did not rest well, made his wife get out of bed and wanted her to get a pistol so he could shoot himself. Craven's testimony was corroborated by George Gordon, a lawyer, who said he went to the police station with a writ of habeas corpus to get Mineola McKnight out of jail, and she told him she had made a complete and true statement to the police of everything she knew. Another witness who worked for the same company as Albert McKnight testified he went to the station with McKnight to see Mrs. McKnight, who told him that Mrs. Frank and Mrs. Selig had given her a lot of extra money and cautioned her not to talk.

Two men, Tillander and Graham, who had gone to the factory Saturday morning to get their sons' money, testified they arrived there about 11:40 A.M. Frank, they said, was in his inner office. The stenographer was in the outside office. They had a few minutes' conversation with Frank, got their boys' pay envelopes and left. Both said that as they entered the factory from the street they saw a Negro in the dark passageway. They asked him where Frank's office was. Neither would identify Conley as the man they saw, but both said he was about the same size as Conley.

Another witness testified he saw Conley at the corner of

Forsyth and Hunter streets between one and two o'clock
on Saturday April 26, and so far as he could observe Conley was not drunk.

One of the male factory workers testified he frequently
saw Conley at the office when he came there on Saturday
afternoons around two o'clock.

Eight witnesses testified that Daisy Hopkins' reputation
for truth and veracity was bad. One of them said he had
seen her at the factory talking to Frank. Another testified
to having had an assignation with her at 8:30 P.M. on a
Saturday, and she told him she had been at the pencil factory during the afternoon.

Fourteen witnesses testified that Dalton's reputation for
truth and veracity was good. Another witness swore he had
seen Dalton come into the factory with a woman in July
1912 on a Saturday afternoon between one and two o'clock.

Six employees of the Atlanta Streetcar Company testified. The consensus of their testimony was that the English
Avenue car was scheduled to arrive at Broad and Marietta
streets at 12:07, not 12:07½ P.M., and that it frequently arrived ahead of schedule as much as four or five minutes
because the trainmen wanted that additional time for dinner and a layover. One witness testified he was at the corner of Forsyth and Marietta streets on Saturday April 26
when the English Avenue car operated by Matthews and
Hollis arrived at 12:03. Another witness, one McCoy, testified he saw Mary Phagan in front of Number 12 Forsyth
Street. She was walking toward the pencil factory, and it
was not later than "three or four minutes after twelve."

L. T. Kendrick, a factory employee, testified there was
no unusual noise in the operation of the elevator, and he
did not believe one could have heard the elevator running
if one were hammering on one of the floors some distance
away from the shaft.

One of the witnesses referred to in the defense testimony
as having been hurt by one of the machines in the metal

room testified that the blood from his wound dripped on the floor alongside the machine where he was working. None of it was anywhere near the ladies' dressing room, he said.

Three witnesses, employees or former employees of the pencil company, testified they had frequently seen Frank talk to Mary Phagan and that he called her by her first name. One of them said that during her employment in March 1913 these conversations occurred two or three times a day, and that she had seen Frank "standing pretty close" to Mary, "leaning over her face" and "have his hand on her shoulder." Another witness told of an occasion in the middle of March 1913. Mary, this witness said, was going to work and Frank stopped her. Mary told him she had her work to do, but Frank said he was the superintendent of the factory and wanted to talk to her. Mary "kind of backed off," but Frank kept following her, still talking to her.

Twenty girls, former employees of the pencil company, testified that Frank's reputation for lascivious conduct was bad. None of these was cross-examined, a significant circumstance of which much was made later in the State's arguments. One of these witnesses testified to an occasion when she was in the dressing room with another one of the women employees. While they were undressing "Frank stuck his head inside the door and stood there and laughed." Another testified that on one occasion Frank went into the dressing room with one of the factory girls and stayed for some time.

Three physicians who had not previously appeared in the case were called. Two of them were recognized stomach specialists. They refuted the testimony of the defense witnesses, declaring it was possible from an examination of the stomach's contents after death to tell at what stage digestion had been arrested and that the process of the digestion of the cabbage in Mary Phagan's stomach had ceased an hour after she had eaten it. The third physician, who had also participated in the post-mortem examination, testified that in his opinion the epithelium had been torn loose from the walls of the vagina before death.

There was very little surrebuttal. Frank made a supplemental statement denying the testimony that he had forced his conversation upon Mary Phagan and that she had backed away from him. It was possible, he said, that on some occasion he might have passed through the metal room and talked to the girl about her work, but he never called her by her first name because he did not know it. He positively denied the testimony of the two factory girls by saying that he had never looked or gone into the ladies' dressing room.

Four witnesses were called by the defense to testify that George Kendley, a streetcar-company employee and one of the rebuttal witnesses, had publicly expressed himself as violently antagonistic to Frank—that "he was nothing but a damned Jew and should be taken out and hung," that he was as "guilty as a snake" and that "ninety per cent of the best people in the state think he is guilty and ought to hang." It was on this note—a most unfortunate one—that the evidence closed.

Special Assistant Solicitor Hooper commenced the summations for the State. He spoke for over two hours. He carefully reviewed the prosecution's testimony. That testimony, he said, was consistent and plausible. The murder had occurred in the metal room sometime between 12:05 and 12:20 P.M. Frank had made indecent proposals to Mary Phagan or had attacked her, and when she repulsed him he had struck her and knocked her down. In falling she had hit her head against something which had rendered her unconscious. Then Frank, in a panic of fear lest she recover consciousness and accuse him of having attempted to rape her, strangled her to death with a piece of cord which he picked up in the metal room. Frank, fearing discovery and not knowing what to do with the body, left the metal room, locked the door and returned to his office. At 12:30 he might possibly have been seen by Mrs. White or Lemmie Quinn. After Quinn had left, Frank tried to get everybody out of the building and that was the reason for his trip to the fourth floor at 12:45. It was after this he called Conley, and between 12:50 and 1:20 they removed the body to the basement.

Hooper argued that Conley had told the truth; Conley had no motive for doing otherwise. Hooper laid great stress on the fact that defense counsel had not cross-examined any of the twenty young women, called by the State, who had sworn that Frank's reputation for lewd, lascivious conduct was bad. The prosecutor supplied the reason:

The conduct of counsel in this case . . . in refusing to cross-examine these twenty young ladies refutes effectively and absolutely [the testimony] that Frank had a good character. . . . If this man had a good character no power on earth would have kept him and his counsel from asking these girls where they got their information and why it was they said the defendant was a man of bad character. . . . I have already shown you that under the law they had a right to go into that character, but you saw that on cross-examination they dared not do it. And their failure [to cross-examine] . . . is a circumstance against them. . . . You know, as twelve honest men seeking to get at the truth, that the reason these able gentlemen did not ask "those harebrained fanatics," as Mr. Arnold called them before they ever went on the witness stand—those girls whose appearance is as good as any they brought, those girls that you know by their manner are telling the truth, those girls who were unimpeached and unimpeachable—you know the reason they did not cross-examine them. They did not dare to do so!

Hooper closed with the declaration that the guilt of Frank was as clear as the noonday sun and demanded a verdict of death as the only penalty that would "fit this horrible crime."

Both Arnold and Rosser argued at length for the defendant. Their combined arguments lasted better than a day. In blistering terms Rosser scored Conley, Dalton, Scott and the police officers. They were perjurers and sub-orners of perjury bent only on the destruction of Frank. Arnold followed much the same line. His attack on Conley was savage. "My brother Hooper," declared Arnold, "says that Conley had nothing to hold him on the stand but the truth. My God! He had the desire to save his own neck. What stronger motive could a man have on the stand? The whole case against Frank is based on Jim Conley's testi-mony. If the prosecution can't hobble to a conviction on that broken crutch, then they know they will fail. Before I get through I am going to show you there was never such a frame-up against a man since God made the world as that which has been concocted against this defendant."

Arnold faced the question of religious prejudice square-ly. "Leo Frank," he said, "comes from a race of people who have made money and that has made some people envious. I tell everybody, all within the hearing of my voice, that if Frank had not been a Jew he never would have been in-dicted. That nigger Conley has been brought into court to tell his long tale; not corroborated but prompted. I am asking my kind of people to give this man fair play. . . . This is a case that has been brought about by the story of a monstrous perjurer by the name of Conley, and they ask you to believe this nigger against Frank." Arnold then dwelt at length on the 100 or more witnesses who had come to testify to Frank's good character; no man with such testi-monials could be guilty of the fiendish crime which had been charged against him, said Arnold.

Dorsey concluded the summations. The solicitor gen-eral attempted no detailed defense of Conley, nor did he reply to Arnold's repeated characterizations of him as "a lousy nigger," "a dirty, black nigger" and "a lying nigger scoundrel." Instead he countered with an argument well calculated to appeal to the white Georgians on the jury: The job of the police and the prosecution would have been infinitely easier had they been able to unearth evidence to fasten the crime on Conley. Conley was a "nigger"— shiftless, penniless, friendless—with a chain-gang record. Frank was a white man with powerful and influential relatives and friends who were prepared to spend and had spent thousands of dollars in his defense.

Dorsey repudiated the suggestion that Frank's religion had had anything to do with his indictment or prosecution. He outdid Arnold in his tributes to the Jewish people and in citing their contributions through the ages to the advance of civilization. He argued, with great eloquence and persuasiveness, the testimony of Lee, Gantt, Monteen Stover, the police and the witnesses who testified to Frank's relations with women and declared that that evidence, even without the testimony of Conley, established Frank's guilt.

Frank's defense, declared Dorsey, was negative—over 100 witnesses testified that he bore a good reputation and that they had never heard anything against him. In the face of positive evidence of criminal conduct such testimony, said Dorsey, was utterly worthless. He recalled the cases of Oscar Wilde, "an Irish knight, a scholar, a literary man, brilliant, the author of works that will live through the ages," of Abe Ruef, "a Jew, the boss of San Francisco, respected and honored," of McCue of Charlottesville, "a man of such reputation that his fellow citizens had elevated him to the head of their municipality, and yet he tired of his wife and shot her to death in a bath tub," of Richeson, "the Boston preacher who had seduced a poor servant girl," of Beatty of Richmond, "a man of good reputation from one of the oldest and finest families" who had murdered his wife, of Crippen, "an eminent physician of England," who had murdered his wife that he might elope with his secretary. All of these, said Dorsey, had good reputations, yet all were proved to have committed despicable crimes, and their good reputations did not avail to save them from the consequences.

Dorsey closed with a stirring plea to the jurors to base

their verdict on the evidence of what had happened in the pencil factory on Saturday April 26, 1913. That evidence, he said, pointed unmistakably to Frank as the defiler and murderer of Mary Phagan.

At the conclusion of the summations and before Judge Roan began his charge, Defense Counsel Arnold asked that the jury be excused. The jury was withdrawn and the defense formally moved the Court to declare a mistrial. In that motion it was charged that the conduct of the spectators throughout the trial had been "disgraceful." They had frequently applauded statements of the solicitor general and rulings of the Court which were adverse to Frank. Repeated pleas of the defense to clear the courtroom had been denied. Large crowds, unable to get into the courtroom, had gathered daily in front of the courthouse and, in the hearing of the jury, had loudly cheered Solicitor General Dorsey whenever he entered and left the building. These demonstrations were designed and tended to intimidate the jury and influence its verdict. The Court overruled the motion, declaring that the crowds and the noise were inseparable from any trial in which the public interest and curiosity had been aroused. Judge Roan did, however, clear the courtroom on the last day of the trial.

The summations were concluded about noon on August 25. Although the courtroom had been cleared hundreds of persons stood in the streets outside the courthouse awaiting the outcome of the case. There was no disturbance; rather, an ominous quiet. Before Judge Roan commenced his charge to the jury he summoned counsel into private conference and suggested the possibility of danger to the prisoner and his counsel if the jury should disagree or return a verdict of not guilty. He asked, in the interest of avoiding possible trouble, that counsel agree that the prisoner need not be present when the verdict was received and the jury polled. In the absence of, and without the knowledge of, the defendant both sides consented.

The judge then proceeded with his charge to the jury. It was a simply worded, dispassionate statement of the law of the case; its impartiality was attested by the fact that very few of the numerous assignments of error on appeal attacked the charge and such of them as were argued were clearly shown to have been without merit.

The jury was out for a little more than two hours. Neither Frank nor his counsel was present in the courtroom when the verdict was received. When the verdict—guilty of murder in the first degree—was pronounced, and before more than one juror could be polled, there was such a roar of applause from the crowd outside that the polling could not go on. A semblance of order was restored, but even then the continuing noise was such that it was difficult for the Court to hear the answers of the jurors although he was only ten feet away from them.

Thus ended the longest and most celebrated trial in the history of Georgia.

Defendant's counsel urged over 100 different grounds for a new trial. Judge Roan held the motion under advisement for more than two months. When he handed down his ruling on October 31 he declared the case had troubled him more than any case he had ever tried. He said that while personally he was not thoroughly convinced of Frank's guilt the jury had undoubtedly been so convinced; that, after all, the jury, under the law, was the judge of the facts, and he felt it to be his duty to overrule the motion. Frank was sentenced to death by hanging.

AFTERMATH

And now commenced Frank's long fight through the upper courts. Exhaustive and able briefs were filed in the Supreme Court of Georgia. That Court, on February 17, 1914, handed down its decision affirming the judgment of the lower Court. Two of the six justices dissented.[14] The

---

[14] 141 Ga. 243.

date for the execution of the sentence, which had been postponed on appeal, was fixed for April 17.

On April 16 an extraordinary motion in the nature of a petition for a new trial was presented to the Supreme Court of Georgia. It was taken under advisement, and the date of execution again postponed. On November 14 the Court denied the motion. Another motion in the nature of a writ of error, which, if allowed, would have nullified the judgment of the lower Court, was immediately filed. This, too, was overruled.

All of the approaches to the state courts having been closed, resort was now had to the Federal courts. Applications for writs of error were successively presented to Supreme Court Justices Lamar and Holmes and lastly to the full bench of the Supreme Court of the United States. All were denied. One last hope remained—a petition for a writ of habeas corpus based on the ground that errors in the conduct of the trial in the state court amounted to a deprivation of the defendant's liberty without the "due process of law" guaranteed by the Fourteenth Amendment to the Constitution of the United States. Such a petition was filed in the United States District Court of Georgia. It was heard by District Judge W. T. Newman and denied December 21, 1914. On application made, Supreme Court Justice Lamar granted a certificate of importance so that the matter could be reviewed by the Supreme Court of the United States.

On April 19, 1915, the Supreme Court of the United States handed down its decision affirming the judgment of the lower Federal Court denying the writ.[15] Two of the justices dissented. The opinion of the majority held that Frank had been formally accused of a crime cognizable solely by the courts of the State of Georgia. He had been afforded a fair trial by a court of competent jurisdiction

---

[15] 237 U. S. 309.

in that state. He had been found guilty and sentence had been pronounced pursuant to the laws of that state. By three different proceedings his case had been reviewed or considered by the Supreme Court of Georgia, and every ground urged in his present petition for habeas corpus had been urged and adversely passed on by Georgia's court of last resort. It was their final conclusion that Frank was "not shown to have been deprived of any right guaranteed to him by the Fourteenth Amendment or any other provision of the Constitution or law of the United States. . . . "

The dissenting opinion was written by Justice Oliver Wendell Holmes and concurred in by Chief Justice Hughes. Basing their view on the theory that the allegations of the petition were untested, the dissenters felt that the defendant should be permitted to make proof of his contentions that the atmosphere of prejudice and hostility which surrounded him had infected the jury and made a fair trial impossible. If the allegations were found to be true, it was clear, said the dissenting justices, that Frank had been deprived of his liberty and was about to be deprived of his life without due process of law and in violation of the Fourteenth Amendment. Justice Holmes, as was his wont, used vigorous language in expressing this view, which was quite generally misinterpreted by the press and the lay public as a statement by him of the undisputed facts of the case. The contrary is clearly shown by the opinion itself. Justice Holmes said:

The single question in our minds is whether a petition alleging that the trial took place in the midst of a mob savagely and manifestly intent on a single result, is shown on its face. . . . This is not a matter for polite presumptions; we must look facts in the face. Any judge who has sat with juries knows that in spite of forms they are extremely likely to be impregnated by the environing atmosphere. And when we find the judgment of the expert on the spot, of the judge whose business it was to preserve not only form but substance, to have held that if one juryman yielded to the reasonable doubt that he himself later expressed in court as the result of most anxious deliberation, neither prisoner nor counsel would be safe from the rage of the crowd, we think the presumption overwhelming that the jury responded to the passions of the mob. Of course, we are speaking only of the case made by the petition, and whether it ought to be heard.

Upon allegations of this gravity in our opinion it ought to be heard, whatever the decision of the state court may have been. . . . It may be that on a hearing a different complexion would be given to the judge's alleged request and expression of fear. But supposing the alleged facts to be true, we are of opinion that if they were before the Supreme Court [of Georgia] it sanctioned a situation upon which the Courts of the United States should act, and if for any reason they were not before the Supreme Court, it is our duty to act upon them now and to declare lynch law as little valid when practiced by a regularly drawn jury as when administered by one elected by a mob intent on death.[16]

Even before the decision of the Supreme Court of the United States was handed down another desperate attempt was made to secure a new trial through a motion to that end in the Circuit Court of Fulton County. It was heard on April 22 by Judge B. H. Hill, who had succeeded Judge Roan, and denied. Frank was resentenced—execution to take place on April 25.

The possibilities of judicial review being now exhausted, an appeal was made to the governor and to the state's Prison Commission for a pardon or commutation of sentence.

Execution of sentence was again postponed, pending investigation and report of the state's Prison Commission. On June 9 that body, by a vote of two to one, denied

16 The above is quoted at length because of the impression created at the time by the publicity given to the great jurist's dissent (which was out of all proportion to that accorded the majority opinion) that Frank had from the outset been the marked victim of mob terrorism.

Frank's plea for clemency. The dissenter argued: Frank
and Conley had equal motive and opportunity to commit
the crime. There was possibly more of a motive for Conley—robbery, in addition to rape. It was undisputed that
Conley had written the notes. The trial judge who heard
the evidence expressed a doubt as to Frank's guilt. There
were what amounted to the opinions of two judges of the
Supreme Court of the United States that Frank had not had
a fair and impartial trial.

Governor Slaton was not satisfied and announced he
would make a personal investigation. He visited the factory and went over the premises. He read and studied the
record of the testimony, the briefs and arguments of counsel and the Courts' decisions in the various appeals. He
announced he would hold public hearings at which any
person with anything to offer for or against Frank might
appear and be heard. A number of such hearings were
held. More than 100 persons appeared and made statements, among them Solicitor General Dorsey and his assistant prosecutors. The proceedings were stenographically
reported and published in full in the daily press. Judge
Roan from his deathbed had written to the governor, urging clemency for Frank.

On July 21 Governor Slaton commuted Frank's sentence to life imprisonment. His statement, accompanying
the official order, merits quotation. After an accurate and
dispassionate summary of the evidence, the governor said:

In any event, the performance of my duty under the
Constitution is a matter of my conscience. My responsibility rests where the power is reposed. Judge Roan, with
that awful sense of responsibility which probably came
over him as he thought of that Judge before Whom he
would shortly appear, calls to me from another world to
request that I do what he should have done. I can endure
misconstruction, abuse and condemnation, but I cannot
stand the constant companionship of an accusing con-
cience which would remind me that I, as governor of

Georgia, failed to do what I thought to be right. There is a territory beyond a reasonable doubt and absolute certainty for which the law provides in allowing life imprisonment instead of execution. This case has been marked by doubt. The trial judge doubted. Two judges of the Supreme Court of Georgia doubted. Two judges of the Supreme Court of the United States doubted. One of the three prison commissioners doubted. In my judgment, in granting a commutation in this case I am sustaining the jury, the judge and the appeals tribunals and at the same time I am discharging that duty which is placed upon me by the constitution of the state. Acting, therefore, in accordance with what I believe to be my duty under the circumstances in this case, it is ordered that the sentence in the case of Leo M. Frank is commuted from the death penalty to imprisonment for life.

The governor's action aroused a storm. There were anti-Frank demonstrations throughout the state. A regiment of the state militia was called out to guard the executive mansion. The Southern press generally denounced the action or remained silent. A few of the more responsible and influential papers, following the lead of the Atlanta *Journal,* called the governor's act one of high courage.

Despite the threatening signs no actual trouble eventuated, and Frank was safely removed to the state penitentiary at Milledgeville.

The case was now thought to be closed, but within a month and in circumstances never fully explained Frank was attacked while he slept by a fellow convict who cut a seven-inch gash in Frank's throat with a butcher knife and severed the jugular vein. Had the alarm not been instantly sounded and medical aid rushed to him, Frank would undoubtedly have bled to death. As it was he hovered for days between life and death.

Four weeks went by. Frank was still convalescing from his wound when a mob of probably not more than forty unmasked men forced their way into the prison, held the guards at bay with guns and dragged Frank from his bed. Handcuffed and with a rope tied around his ankles Frank was thrown into the rear of an automobile and, escorted by three other loaded cars, driven to Marietta,[17] the birth and burial place of Mary Phagan. There in the early morning of August 16, 1915, he was hanged from a pine tree not far from her grave.

Governor Harris, who had succeeded Governor Slaton, denounced the lynching and promised a "thorough investigation." Three days later he issued a statement that the mobsters were unknown. They had cut all telephone and telegraph lines in and out of Milledgeville, said the governor, and entered the prison with drawn revolvers in such overwhelming numbers that resistance would have been foolhardy. He concluded the prison authorities were "absolutely blameless."

The Northern press condemned the lynching as the "work of lawless fanatics" and consistent with the lawlessness which had characterized the case from the beginning. Marietta's local newspaper declared it was not the act of lawless fanatics but of "a body of law-abiding citizens who had simply carried out a righteous sentence, the execution of which had been postponed by the unjustified and illegal interference of a misguided retiring governor." The Atlanta *Journal* and other leading dailies in the South denounced the lynching as "mob murder" which had "outraged and endangered a commonwealth" and "assassinated the character of a law-abiding state."

Was Frank guilty? After one has read the record and all of the available literature on the case, the most one can say is: He may have been guilty, and he may have been innocent. One simply cannot, with evidence supporting reason, declare unequivocally that he was guilty or that he was not

---

[17] About 150 miles from Milledgeville.

guilty. There is evidence and reasonable probability to support either conclusion.

It may be significant, as has been argued in support of the jury's verdict, that in the passage of nearly forty years since Frank's brutal execution not a single additional fact pointing to his innocence has come to light. Nevertheless, from the present perspective a conscientious reader of the record puts it down with the uncertain and troubled feeling that Frank's guilt was not proved beyond a reasonable doubt and that he may have been the victim of one of the most flagrant miscarriages of justice recorded in American criminal annals.

II

The Trial of

D. C. STEPHENSON

for the Murder of

MADGE OBERHOLTZER

(1925)

2

The D. C. Stephenson Case

THE SIGNIFICANCE *of this case lies in the fact that the defen-*
dant David C. Stephenson, before he was charged with the
murder of Madge Oberholtzer, typified the growing polit-
ical importance, in the North as well as the South, of a new
legion of racial and religious intolerance and hate which
styled itself, after a more ancient and moribund organiza-
tion, the Ku Klux Klan. Although Stephenson had recent-
ly broken with the national organization, the accusation,
trial and conviction of the erstwhile Grand Dragon and
most influential Klansman in the North of what the press
throughout the country called the "unspeakable crime"—
murder resulting from a brutal attempt at rape accom-
panied by the most revolting perversions—created such a
revulsion of feeling against the Klan, its hypocrisies and its
sinister potentialities that as an influence it withered and
died. This was true not only in Indiana but throughout
the United States. It was surely no mere coincidence that
within three years after Stephenson's conviction the Klan,
which had boasted a membership of ten million, was re-
duced to a few, scattered, impotent thousands.

The case has its special interest to lawyers. The murder
was not of the usual type: the natural *consequence of a de-*
liberate act. The charge on which Stephenson's conviction
was obtained and sustained was that the victim, as the re-
sult of a criminal assault, became mentally deranged and
while in that condition took poison which ended her life;
and that because of the "causal connection" between the

assault and the ensuing suicide, the defendant was guilty
of murder. Such a charge necessarily involved the exten-
sive use as witnesses of expert physicians and toxicologists.
The experts called by the State were men of outstanding
professional attainments; both sides were ably represented;
and the record of the trial—in the archives of the clerk of
the Supreme Court of Indiana—constitutes for the student
of forensic medicine a source of invaluable material.

H AD THE DEFENDANT in this case been plain Jim
Doakes, the case would probably never have been
heard of outside the county where the crime was
committed. Jim would have been speedily tried, convicted,
sentenced and forgotten. But because the defendant was
David C. Stephenson and because David C. Stephenson was
what he was, the case became Indiana's most famous *cause
célèbre* and claimed front-page space in practically every
daily newspaper in the United States for more than six
months.

Who was David C. Stephenson?

David Curtis Stephenson was born in Texas in 1891. He
received a grade-school education—the early part of it in a
Catholic parochial institution. His early employments,
which began when he was sixteen years old, seem to have
been principally in various printing shops and newspaper
offices in Texas, Oklahoma and Iowa. He first worked as
an apprentice and later as proofreader and linotype operator. In Oklahoma he joined the Socialist party and wrote
some articles and made a number of speeches in behalf of
its principles and candidates.

In 1915 he married and, according to later divorce-court
records, deserted his wife in the same year, shortly before
their only child was born.

In July 1917 he joined the Iowa National Guard and
soon after entered an officers' training camp at Fort Snell-
ing, Minnesota. In November he was commissioned a sec-

ond lieutenant and assigned to active duty. Although he and some of his friends later boasted that he had been a fighting major of infantry at Belleau Wood, the record is clear that he never got closer to France than Camp Devens, Massachusetts.

After his honorable discharge from the service in February 1919 he married again. He lived with his second wife less than a year. In 1924 she divorced him.

Stephenson's first appearance in Indiana seems to have been in Evansville in 1920. According to one account he worked there for a brief period as a printer. It is known that he sold securities in a coal-mining company in which, in some way not disclosed, he had obtained an interest. About this time he left the Socialist party and registered as a Democrat.

Just when Stephenson's association with the Ku Klux Klan[1] commenced is uncertain—probably in 1921 or 1922.

---

[1] "The original Ku Klux Klan was organized by the ex-Confederate element to oppose the Reconstruction policies of the radical Republican Congress and to maintain 'white supremacy.' After the Civil War, when local government in the South was weak or nonexistent and there were fears of Negro outrages and even of an insurrection, there was formed in almost all communities informal vigilante organizations or armed patrols. These were linked together in societies. . . . The Ku Klux Klan was the best known of these, and as it spread it absorbed many of the smaller organizations. It was organized at Pulaski, Tenn., in Dec., 1865. . . . A general organization of the local Klans was effected in April, 1867, at Nashville, Tenn. General N. B. Forrest, the famous Confederate cavalry leader, was made Grand Wizard of the Empire. . . . General Forrest, in Jan., 1869, seemingly under some apprehension as to the use of its power, ordered the abandonment of the Klan and resigned as Grand Wizard. Local organizations continued, some of them for many years. . . . The second Ku Klux Klan was founded by William J. Simmons, an ex-minister and promoter of fraternal orders, in 1915; its first meeting was held on Stone Mt., Ga. The new Klan had a wider program than its forerunner, for it added to 'white supremacy' an intense nativism and anti-Catholicism (it was also anti-Semitic) closely related to that of the Know-Nothing movement of the middle 19th cent. Consequently its appeal was not sectional, and, aided after 1920 by the activities of Elizabeth Tyler and Edward Y. Clarke, professional promoters, it spread rapidly throughout the North. . . . Professing itself nonpolitical, the Klan nevertheless controlled politics in many communities and in 1922, 1924, and 1926 elected many state officials and a number of Congressmen. Texas, Oklahoma, Indiana, Oregon, and Maine were particularly under its influence." *The Columbia Encyclopedia*, ed. William Bridgwater and Elizabeth J. Sherwood (2nd ed.; New York: Columbia University Press, 1950). Quoted by permission of the publisher.

His rise in the organization was meteoric. He was well
equipped for the role he elected to play. He had read
widely and had participated extensively in political and
other public discussions. Though not a particularly impressive physical figure he was alert, friendly, ingratiating,
well poised and confident. He was a tireless worker with a
real genius for organization and executive direction. In
addition he possessed a native wit, a gift of phrase and an
oratorical ability which aroused and persuaded audiences.
In 1922 he was appointed by Hiram W. Evans, Imperial
Wizard and dictator of the Klan, King Kleagle[2] of the
Realm of Indiana. His amazing job of proselyting and organizing enrolled, in less than two years, over 300,000
robed and hooded fanatics.

July 4, 1923, at a grand conclave at Kokomo a tremendous crowd[3] gathered at the fairgrounds to witness the in-
stallation of Stephenson as the Grand Dragon[4] of the
Realm of Indiana. Stephenson excelled in showmanship,
and it was here he put on his bravest act. The arrival of
celebrities at public gatherings by automobile had become
commonplace. Stephenson's arrival was not commonplace.
At the appointed hour, by prearrangement with trusties
scattered through the crowd, a great shout went up. Fingers
pointed to a brilliant object in the sky. Sailing majestically
over the heads of the crowd was an airplane of gleaming
gold. It circled the field a dozen times, bearing ever closer
to the ground, before it landed. When the door of the plane
opened a figure clad from head to foot in royal purple
stepped out. It was Stephenson. Enveloped and surrounded by these imperial trappings, the Grand Dragon of
the Realm of Indiana made his acceptance speech. It was
a carefully prepared speech in the best Klan tradition, and

---

2 A title given the head of a realm not yet chartered.
3 Varying accounts place the number of the crowd at anywhere from 20,000
to 200,000.
4 The title given to the supreme head of a chartered realm.

it was magnificently delivered. The vast audience was awed, thrilled and satisfied.

This was honor, but honor alone would not satisfy Stephenson. He saw to it that there were other rewards—material ones. He secured a contract from the Klan by which he became its supreme organizer in nineteen other Northern states. Out of every ten-dollar initiation fee—"donation" in Klan parlance—he retained four dollars. The Klan regalia sold at six dollars a set. Stephenson had these sets manufactured at a cost to him of one dollar and seventy-five cents. The difference went into his pocket. According to the circulated stories, which may have been exaggerated, Stephenson's "take" in eighteen months aggregated over $2,000,000. The outward signs of his prosperity were not wanting. He purchased a palatial home in a spacious setting of oaks and maples in Irvington, a suburb of Indianapolis. For a time he maintained an expensive yacht on which he entertained United States senators, governors, mayors of cities and lesser dignitaries. He had a well-appointed suite of offices in the city's most pretentious skyscraper. A "fleet of Cadillacs" served the Grand Dragon and his host of hangers-on.

The entente between Grand Dragon Stephenson and Imperial Wizard Evans was short-lived. Both were bent on absolute, undivided power, and both were utterly ruthless and unscrupulous in the choice of methods to obtain it. Evans had ousted his predecessor, Simmons, from the leadership of the Klan through deceit and trickery. Stephenson set out, by whatever means might come to hand, to supplant Evans or, failing in that, to split off and rule the Northern and more profitable segment of the organization.

The points of friction between them were immediate and many. There was the Northern voice of the Klan—*The Fiery Cross*—a weekly Klan organ with a circulation of nearly 500,000. Stephenson succeeded for a time in controlling it and making it a sounding board for his campaign

against Evans. Stephenson's contract with the Klan provided that Klan regalia should be purchased from Atlanta
and that the profit between the manufacturer's price and
the retail price would go into the treasury of the parent
body. Stephenson, as we have seen, handled this business
for his own account. Control through auxiliary organizations of the women relatives of Klansmen was another bone
of contention. Evans had such an auxiliary, "The Women
of the Ku Klux Klan." Stephenson had one, "The Queens
of the Golden Mask." Simmons, struggling to regain his
lost power, had another, "The Kamelia." Stephenson conceived the idea of taking over the financially sick Valparaiso University and converting it into a school for the
children of Klansmen. He sought a contribution of Southern funds. Evans refused his aid and opposed the project.
Stephenson wanted more "Northern representation"—
which, translated into reality, meant more of his hench-
men—on the Imperial Kloncillium, or grand council, of
the Klan. Evans, the thought of self-preservation upper-
most in his mind, rejected the suggestion.

The fight increased in bitterness. *The Fiery Cross* pulled
no punches. The Southern Klansmen were characterized
as "ignoramuses," "rebels" and "thieves." Evans personally was accused of the mishandling of Klan funds.
Through the medium of other Klan publications which did
his bidding Evans retaliated in kind. The climax was
reached when Evans succeeded regaining control of *The
Fiery Cross* and defeated Stephenson's cherished plan to
take over Valparaiso University.

In November 1923 Stephenson seceded from the national
organization. Henceforth, he announced, with the assured
help of Providence, he would guide the Indiana faithful
to their appointed destiny. With his ever-present consideration for things material he included a direction to all
Klaverns[5] to hold all funds in their treasuries "until the

---

5 The name given to local Klan organizations.

millions that have been taken from the Hoosiers have been accounted for." Most of the Indiana Klansmen seemed disposed to follow him.

Although the Klan was not avowedly political Stephenson manipulated his dupes to nominate and elect candidates of his choice. Great as his influence, supplemented by liberal campaign contributions, undoubtedly was he exaggerated it into a repeated, loud-voiced claim that he and he alone "delivered the Klan vote." Most of the politically ambitious believed him.

It would appear that Stephenson was not without personal political ambitions. He had unsuccessfully attempted in 1920 to obtain a Democratic nomination for Congress. After his defeat he switched his talents and pinned his hopes to the Republican party. In the 1924 primary campaign he repeatedly declared to his friends that he would seek nomination to the United States Senate at the first opportunity. To some of his intimates he is said to have confided his most cherished ambition—that in the not-too-distant future he might lay aside the easy-to-be-won toga and don the mantle of the chief executive.

In the spring of 1924 hundreds of avowed and prominent Klansmen were nominated on the Republican ticket for the legislature and various county and municipal offices throughout Indiana. Many other successful nominees, not openly professing Klan allegiance, owed their nominations to Klan support. Among these was the Republican candidate for governor, "Ed" Jackson, a close friend of Stephenson. The Grand Dragon boasted he had spent $120,000 to insure Jackson's nomination.

In the fall of 1924 the Republicans swept the state. Jackson was elected governor. A majority of the elected members of the state's House of Representatives were beholden to the Klan for their nomination and election. Stephenson noisily took credit for all of these victories. He epitomized his fancied eminence in the oft-repeated declaration: "I am the law in Indiana." While there was a large element of braggadocio in all this, it is undeniable that Stephenson wielded a tremendous influence with the new administration. He participated in the dispensation of patronage. He sponsored bills, good and bad, which passed; he killed other bills which he considered obnoxious to his plans— of that much the record is clear.

As it turned out, however, this was only a surface indication. The foundations beneath him, never too solid, were being slowly but surely undermined. Evans was a powerful and resourceful enemy. Many of the details of Stephenson's disgraceful private life must have been known to Evans. So long as Stephenson was useful to him and so long as his lecheries and debaucheries did not become too notorious, they could be tolerated.

Hypocrisy among the higher-ups in the Klan was a mask they wore as comfortably as their hoods. When, however, it suited Evans' purposes to strip aside the mask and strike at Stephenson the setup was perfect. The Klan, with its program of discrimination, intolerance and hate, and persecution of Negroes, Catholics and Jews, had an associated program which preached virtue, the curse of alcoholism and the sanctity of womanhood. This begat in the rank and file a delusion of knight-errantry which expressed itself in stern reprisals against notorious offenders. In the dead of night prostitutes were taken from their beds and flogged; whoremongers and notorious habitual drunkards were tarred and feathered. And so when stories, cleverly planted by Evans, began to circulate that Stephenson, the bumptious ex-Dragon of the North, was a secret lecher and drunkard some of the more pious of the brethren took action.

Evidence of Stephenson's immoralities was not hard to obtain. He had been initiated and held membership in the Evansville Klavern. Whether it acted on its own initiative or at the express direction of Evans is obscure, but in January 1924 Stephenson was formally charged by that body with "gross derelictions"—specifically, that he had attempted to seduce a virtuous young woman of Evansville and had committed numerous "immoralities" in Columbus, Ohio, Columbus, Indiana, Atlanta, Georgia, and "on trains and boats." He was secretly tried, found guilty and "banished" from Klan association.

Such was Stephenson and such was his position in Indiana when he met Madge Oberholtzer.

Madge Oberholtzer at this time was twenty-eight years old. She was unmarried and lived with her parents in a modest two-story house in Irvington, some two or three blocks away from the Stephenson mansion. Her parents were honest, respected people in moderate circumstances. The father had been employed for many years as a clerk and inspector in the post office. The mother took in roomers to supplement the family income.

Though Madge Oberholtzer was not the outstanding beauty that some of the more imaginative newspaper reporters made her out to be, she was not bad-looking. She was well-mannered, dressed smartly and possessed a better-than-average education. After leaving public high school she had attended Butler College—which was then located in Irvington—and had taken a secretarial course in an Indianapolis business college. She taught in the public schools for part of a term and then worked as a clerk in the offices of two of the larger commercial firms in Indianapolis. When she met Stephenson she was employed in the Indiana State Department of Public Instruction as manager of one of the state's public-welfare activities.

According to the later evidence, Madge Oberholtzer was introduced to Stephenson in January of 1925 at a banquet and ball given in honor of Governor-elect Jackson. They danced together several times and, in the incidental conversation, Stephenson learned where she worked and where she lived. On two or three later occasions she had dinner with him in the public dining room of one of Indianapolis' prominent hotels. At these times he made previous appointments with her by telephone, called for her in his chauffeured car at her parents' home and returned her to her home at an early hour. On one occasion she accepted his invitation to attend a dinner party at his house. It was a large party. In addition to Miss Oberholtzer, the guests included a number of prominent officials and businessmen and their wives. On all these occasions, according to the girl's later story, Stephenson acted as the perfect gentleman.

The next time she heard from Stephenson was on Sunday March 15. She had spent the afternoon and evening with some young people of her acquaintance and returned home shortly before ten o'clock in the evening. Her mother told her that during her absence Stephenson had called her several times and had left a message for her to call him at Irvington 0492; that he had said it concerned a matter important to her.

Miss Oberholtzer made the call. Stephenson answered the phone and said he wanted her to come to his house immediately; that it was about something important to her; that he was leaving for Chicago and had to see her before he left. He added that he would send an escort for her, and she said she would come. Stephenson had previously interested himself in a bill which would have affected her status as a state employee, and it is altogether probable that Miss Oberholtzer thought Stephenson's call had something to do with her employment. She evidently expected to be gone for only a short time because she left without her purse and wore no hat.

In a few minutes a man she had never seen before—but who was afterward identified as Earl Gentry—called for her and together they left for Stephenson's house. Miss Oberholtzer did not return home that night. Her parents had retired early and were not aware of her continued absence until the following morning. Mrs. Oberholtzer was naturally much disturbed, but about eight o'clock she received a telegram, dated from Hammond, Indiana, signed "Madge," which read: "We are driving through to Chicago. Will be home on night train."

Mrs. Oberholtzer met the night train, but Madge was not on it. With a friend and with a lawyer whom Mrs. Oberholtzer had consulted about the girl's disappearance, Mrs. Oberholtzer went to the Stephenson home to inquire of Stephenson about her daughter. They were told that neither Stephenson nor Miss Oberholtzer was there.

Between eleven and twelve o'clock Tuesday morning an automobile drove up to the Oberholtzer home and a man— afterward identified as Earl Klinck—got out. He opened the door, lifted Miss Oberholtzer out of the car and carried her into the house. She was moaning and seemed to be in great distress. The only person in the Oberholtzer home at the time was a roomer, Mrs. Schultz. The man, who gave his name as "Johnson" and said he was from Kokomo, told her the girl had been in an automobile accident. At Mrs. Schultz's direction he carried Miss Oberholtzer to an upstairs bedroom and laid her on the bed. Mrs. Schultz would have questioned him further, but he said he was in a great hurry and left immediately.

Madge Oberholtzer was conscious and asked that a physician—Dr. Kingsbury—be called. Both he and Miss Oberholtzer's mother arrived shortly afterward. To them, between her sobs and groans, the girl told a terrible story. It was the same story which she recited later in a formal, signed statement. Most of it, as her dying declaration, was to become the core of the State's case against Stephenson.

After the door of Stephenson's house closed behind her on Sunday March 15, Gentry hurried her to the kitchen at the rear of the house. There she saw Stephenson. He was quite drunk. His chauffeur, called "Shorty," was with him. Miss Oberholtzer knew Shorty from having previously ridden in the Stephenson car with him. Almost immediately

another man, who was later to be identified as Earl Klinck
and whom Miss Oberholtzer had not previously known,
came in.

The girl by this time realized that Stephenson's house-
keeper was not there. She became frightened and said she
was going home. Stephenson had in his hand a small glass
containing some kind of liquid, which he held out to her.
He said she should drink it. When she refused he and the
others, according to her story, compelled her to drink it.
They refilled the glass twice and made her drain the contents. She said she became ill almost immediately, vomited
profusely, became confused and could scarcely move. She
told Stephenson she wanted to go home and he replied,
"No, you can't go home; you are going with me to Chicago; I love you more than any woman I have ever known."
She tried to reach the telephone but one of the men prevented her.

Stephenson then went upstairs. The men with him
forced the girl to follow him. Stephenson pulled a drawer
out of one of the dressers. It was full of revolvers. He took
a pearl-handled one for himself and had Shorty load it.
Each of the other men took one. The girl said she was
terrified.

She remembered that Gentry called the Washington
Hotel in Indianapolis and talked about reserving a drawing room. She was half carried out of the rear door into
the back yard and pushed into one of Stephenson's automobiles which was parked there. Stephenson and Gentry
followed her. Shorty drove. Klinck remained behind.

The girl begged her captors to drive past her home that
she might get her hat, believing, as she said, that once inside her own home she would be safe from them. They
ignored her pleas and drove on to the Washington Hotel.
The chauffeur got out, presumably to pick up the railroad
tickets. Stephenson and Gentry remained in the car. Miss
Oberholtzer said she made an effort to get out of the car,

but they held her back. She said she was dazed and was terrified that her life would be taken. She remembered Stephenson saying to Gentry how smart he had been to have got hold of her.

When they reached the railroad station they helped her out of the automobile and walked her through the gates to the train and to the Pullman car in which the reservation had been made. There they pushed her ahead of them, up the steps and through the car to the drawing room. She said that during this time she was so weak she could hardly stand and so dazed that she could barely understand what was happening. She could not tell all that occurred afterward. She did remember that the upper and lower berths were made up, that Gentry climbed up into the upper berth and immediately after that Stephenson attacked her.

In her dying declaration she said: "He took hold of the bottom of my dress and pulled it up over my head. I tried to fight but was weak and unsteady. Stephenson took hold of my two hands and held them. I had not the strength to move. What I had drunk was affecting me. Stephenson took all my clothes off and pushed me into the lower berth. After the train had started Stephenson got in with me and attacked me. He held me so I couldn't breathe. I don't know and don't remember all that happened. He chewed me all over my body, particularly my neck and face, chewed my tongue, chewed my breasts until they bled, my back, my legs, my ankles, and mutilated me all over."

She lost consciousness and had no memory of the rest of the night. She remembered hearing a buzzer early in the morning and the porter telling them to get ready to get off at Hammond. Gentry shook her and said it was time for her to get up. Things, she said, became a little clearer after that. She remembered Stephenson flourishing his revolver. He held it against her side and threatened to shoot her. When she begged him to do it he put the gun back in his grip. Stephenson and Gentry then helped her to dress.

They also helped her get off the train. She was able to walk with them to the Indiana Hotel, about a block away. It was now 6:30 A.M. Stephenson registered under an assumed name, Gentry registered for himself, and two rooms —rooms 416 and 417—were assigned to them. The girl had repeatedly begged Stephenson to send her mother a telegram, and when they reached the rooms she asked the bellboy for a telegraph blank. He gave her one, and Stephenson made her write a message as he dictated it. Gentry took it and said that he would send it right away.

The girl was in intense pain, and Gentry put hot towels soaked with witch hazel on her head and bathed the wounds on her body. Stephenson ordered a substantial breakfast and ate heartily. The girl drank some coffee but ate nothing. About this time Shorty, the chauffeur, appeared on the scene. He had driven up from Indianapolis in one of Stephenson's cars.

Miss Oberholtzer said she told Stephenson she had to have a hat but had no money. At Stephenson's direction Shorty gave her fifteen dollars and left the hotel with her. They drove to a near-by store where, in Shorty's presence, she selected and paid for a hat. She had some change left and asked Shorty to drive her to a drugstore that she might get some rouge. Shorty got out of the car at the drugstore but evidently did not stay close enough to her to see what she bought. While at the counter she purchased a box of bichloride-of-mercury tablets and put them in the pocket of her coat.

Shorty drove her back to the hotel and took her up to room 416. Stephenson and Gentry were there. Both had been drinking. Stephenson was lying on the bed. When he appeared to be asleep she went into room 417, laid out eighteen of the bichloride-of-mercury tablets and at once took six of them. "I only took six," she stated in her declaration, "because they burned so." While Gentry was out sending the telegram, she said, she considered seizing Ste-

phenson's revolver and killing herself in his presence, but
then she decided to try to get poison and take it in order
to save her mother from disgrace.

It was about ten o'clock in the morning when she took
the poison. Almost immediately she became violently ill.
Her pain was intense and, to use her own language, she
"vomited blood all day." Shorty came into her room about
four o'clock in the afternoon. She told him what she had
done and begged him not to tell the others. Shorty, however, lost no time in notifying Stephenson and, in a few
minutes, Stephenson, Gentry and Shorty, all very much excited, entered her room.

Stephenson sent out for a bottle of milk and made her
drink it. He suggested driving her to a hospital and regis-
tering her as his wife so that the poison could be pumped
out of her system. The girl refused. He then suggested
that they drive to Crown Point and be married. Again she
refused. Stephenson then said he would drive her home.
He ordered Shorty to pack the grips. This the chauffeur
did and checked out for the party. Stephenson and Gentry,
meanwhile, got the girl to her feet, out of the hotel and
into the back seat of the automobile. Stephenson and Gentry got in beside her; Shorty did the driving. It was about
five o'clock in the afternoon when the 175-mile return ride
to Indianapolis began. To avoid identification Stephenson
ordered the license plates removed from the car. If they
were questioned, their agreed story was that the plates had
just been stolen.

The girl's statement continued: "All the way back to
Indianapolis I suffered great pain and agony and screamed
for a doctor. I said I wanted a hypodermic to ease the pain
but they refused to stop. I said to Stephenson to leave me
along the road some place, that someone would stop and
take care of me if he wouldn't. I said to him that I felt he
was more cruel to me than he had been the night before.
He said he would stop at the next town but he never did.

Just before reaching a town, he would say to Shorty, 'Drive fast but don't get pinched.' I vomited in the car, all over the back seat and grips. Stephenson didn't try to make me comfortable in any way. He said he thought I was dying at one time and said to Gentry, 'This takes guts to do this, Gentry. She is dying.' I heard him say also that he had been in worse messes than this before and he would get out of it. Stephenson and Gentry drank liquor during the entire trip. I remember Stephenson having said that he had power . . . that he was the law."

They reached Indianapolis about an hour before midnight and drove directly to the Stephenson garage. As they reached it Miss Oberholtzer heard Stephenson say, "There is someone at the front door of the house." He told Shorty to go and see who it was. Shorty jumped out of the car and disappeared in the darkness. He came back almost immediately and said, "It is her mother."

Together the men carried the girl to the loft above the garage. She remembered Stephenson telling her that she was staying right there until she married him and that she should say she had been in an automobile accident. He also told her, "What's done has been done . . . you must forget this . . . I am the law and the power." After that she said she remembered nothing until the next morning (Tuesday), when Klinck awakened her and said she had to go home. He helped her to dress and carried her downstairs and put her in the rear seat of the Cadillac. Then he drove her home, carried her into the house and upstairs to her bedroom.

Such was Madge Oberholtzer's story.

Dr. Kingsbury at once instituted the recognized treatment for the elimination of the poison from her system. In the course of the ensuing ten days all of the numerous wounds and bruises on her body yielded to the usual medication with the exception of an incised wound in one of her breasts, which became infected. Her general condition,

however, did not improve. She began to run a temperature, and other physicians were called into consultation.
They pronounced the case hopeless. The girl was told of
her extremity on March 28, and with the realization that
her end was near she, in the presence of Dr. Kingsbury, two
lawyers and a girl friend, made her dying declaration. She
died on April 14, 1925.

When Stephenson boasted that he had got out of worse
jams before and would get out of this one, he failed to ap-
prehend the determination of two important individuals—
George Oberholtzer, the father of the girl; and William H.
Remy, the honest and fearless prosecuting attorney of Marion County, who owed no allegiance to the Klan and who
was not paralyzed at the thought of encountering the supposed power and influence of the erstwhile Grand Dragon
and his self-styled "law in Indiana."

On April 2 the girl's father filed a sworn criminal complaint against Stephenson, Gentry and Klinck. On the following day the prosecuting attorney laid the case before a
Marion County grand jury sitting at Indianapolis. The in-
quisitors promptly returned an indictment against the
three for assault and battery with intent to commit a criminal attack, malicious mayhem, kidnaping and conspiracy
to kidnap. Stephenson's bail was fixed at $25,000. He was
arrested, furnished the required bail immediately and was
released. The arrest of Gentry and Klinck followed shortly.
Their bonds were fixed at $5,000, and with sureties pro-
vided by Stephenson they, too, were promptly released.

Attorneys acting for the father instituted a civil suit on
behalf of the girl for $150,000 damages. Stephenson
promptly engaged the best legal talent available and loudly
declared he was being made the victim of a "frame-up"
and "shakedown" and would fight to the finish.

Immediately following the girl's death the father filed a
new criminal complaint charging Stephenson, Gentry and
Klinck with murder. The prosecuting attorney promptly

presented the evidence to the grand jury, and on the eighteenth of April that body returned a true bill formally charging the three with murder. All were arrested, lodged in the county jail and held without bail.

And now commenced one of the longest and bitterest contests in the history of criminal prosecutions—a contest that even as this is written is still raging.

The immediate strategy of Stephenson's attorneys was to avail themselves of every technical procedure known to Indiana practice to prevent or delay the trial and, that failing, to limit to the utmost the proof available to the prosecution. Pleas in abatement impugning the validity of the evidence submitted to the grand jury, motions to quash the indictment on the asserted ground that it stated no criminal offense and was "ambiguous, duplicitous, indefinite and vague," and motions to strike portions of the indictments for irrelevancy and surplusage were successively made, argued and overruled. A motion to admit the defendants to bail was denied.

The defendants next moved for a change of venue from Marion County, alleging that the general excitement and prejudice of its citizens precluded the possibility of obtaining a fair and impartial trial in that jurisdiction. It was not difficult to sustain this charge. Seven days after Madge Oberholtzer's death, over 500 aroused citizens of Irvington in a mass meeting passed resolutions demanding the immediate prosecution and punishment of the girl's murderers. A flood of similar resolutions followed—from the women's clubs, churches and church organizations, and fraternities and sororities of Butler College. Marion County Klavern Number Three, a lodge of the Ku Klux Klan, gave wide publicity to its repudiation and denunciation of Stephenson. The newspapers, somewhat chary at first, soon sensed the direction of the wind and joined in the general hue and cry.

The judge of the Marion County Circuit Court, after a

comparatively brief hearing, ordered the case transferred to Hamilton County. Noblesville, the county seat, was some thirty miles removed from Indianapolis. The elected judge of the Hamilton County Circuit Court was the Honorable Fred E. Hines, a fair-minded man of unimpeachable integrity. The defendants, however, promptly challenged his competency by a motion for a change of venue in which it was averred that he was personally prejudiced against the defendants. Following Indiana practice, Judge Hines presented the defense with a list of three alternate judges. From this list the State struck one and the defense one. The name remaining was that of the Honorable Will M. Sparks,[6] the elected circuit judge of Rush County.

The filibustering was over. The case came on for trial at Noblesville, in Hamilton County, on October 12, 1925, Judge Sparks presiding. Appearing for the State were William H. Remy, prosecuting attorney for Marion County, Justin A. Roberts, prosecuting attorney for Hamilton County, Charles E. Cox, Ralph Kane and Thomas Kane. For the defense: "Eph" Inman, Ira W. Holmes, Floyd Christian, Ralph Waltz, Alfred F. Corwin, Ralph E. Johnson and John Kiplinger. Remy, Cox and Ralph Kane presented the case for the State; Inman, Christian and Holmes carried the burden for the defense.

Remy, although a comparatively young man, had had several years experience as chief deputy prosecutor before becoming prosecutor. He was in many respects the ideal type of prosecutor: a man of cultural background and splendid education, holding rigid views of right moral conduct, solemn-visaged and serious-minded. He was meticulous in the preparation of his cases and presented them dispassionately but with convincing sincerity.

---

6 Judge Sparks was later appointed to the United States Circuit Court of Appeals for the Seventh Circuit and served there with great distinction until shortly before his death in 1950.

Judge Cox was a sixty-five-year-old man and a veteran practitioner. For six years before his admission to the bar in 1889 he had served as librarian of the Supreme Court of Indiana. He had been successively chief deputy prosecutor of Marion County, judge of a city court of Indianapolis and a justice of the Supreme Court of Indiana. He was a fine legal scholar, painstaking in his assembling of facts, and a skillful direct and cross-examiner. He was charged with the preparation and presentation of the medical evidence for the prosecution, and he cross-examined the experts called by the defense.

Ralph Kane, although an Indianapolis practitioner at the time of the trial, had been born and raised in Hamilton County and had formerly practiced there. He was the "thirteenth juror" type of trial lawyer—knowledgeable, unpretentious, ingratiating, likable—speaking and arguing as a native of farm and crossroads.

"Eph" Inman, who led for the defense, was one of the best-known criminal-trial lawyers in Indiana. His impressive figure—he was well over six feet tall—matched his assurance of manner engendered by many successes. His wide and varied experience, his shrewd judgment of human nature, his resourcefulness and his flair for exploiting dramatic possibilities made him an opponent to be respected and feared.

Floyd Christian was a highly esteemed citizen of Noblesville and an experienced and successful trial lawyer.

Ira W. Holmes, who presented the evidence in behalf of the defendant Klinck, was an Indianapolis practitioner. His experience in both civil and criminal cases had been wide and varied, and he was accounted a clever and able trial lawyer.

Eleven days were spent in selecting and agreeing on a jury. Counsel were permitted an unusually wide latitude in the interrogation of the 400 veniremen called—searching, intimate inquiry into their personal histories, their

business and social connections, their prejudices and scru-
ples, their knowledge of the case and the parties and their
opinions or impressions formed from newspaper or other
comment.

The twelve men finally chosen, mostly farmers, were representative of the community. Challenges, for cause assigned
or peremptory, had eliminated every one called who had
been suspected of affiliation with or sympathy for the Klan.
While all of them had heard of Stephenson, none of them
knew him personally or held a fixed opinion as to his guilt
or innocence. Each of them declared that he could and
would give the defendants a fair and impartial trial according to the evidence and the law. On the twenty-eighth of
October 1925 the jury was formally sworn to try the case.

Judge Cox, for the prosecution, made an impressive
opening statement of what the State expected to prove. The
defense waived its right to make a statement in reply, and
the first of the State's twenty-eight witnesses took the stand.

The facts as to Stephenson's telephone calls, the girl's
leaving in Gentry's company for Stephenson's house, the
receipt by her mother of the telegram on Monday morning,
the fruitless inquiry at the Stephenson home on Monday
night and the return of the girl in one of Stephenson's cars
at noon Tuesday were readily established by the girl's parents, a roomer at the Oberholtzer home and friends of the
missing girl who accompanied Mrs. Oberholtzer when she
called at the Stephenson home late Monday night.

Mr. and Mrs. Oberholtzer, a nurse who was immediately
brought into attendance and other witnesses corroborated
the testimony of Dr. Kingsbury, the family physician, as to
the condition of the girl and the wounds and bruises on
her person after she was brought home. She was, according to this evidence, in a state of profound shock. Her body
was blue and cold, her temperature subnormal and her
pulse rapid. There were cuts and bruises on her face and
mouth. Her tongue was swollen. There were abrasions

and lacerations on her breasts, one quite deep, a wound such as might have been made by teeth. The lower part of her abdomen was bruised. The inner lips of the vulva were bruised and swollen. Her legs down to her ankles were covered with bruises, and there was a particularly large discoloration on her left buttock.

Dr. Kingsbury testified that from the time she was brought home until her death, twenty-eight days later, the girl repeatedly declared she was going to die. He told the jury the story she told him of what had happened to her between the time she left home Sunday evening and the following Tuesday morning. Her statement to the doctor did not vary in any essential detail from what she said later in her dying declaration.

Asa J. Smith, an able and highly regarded Indianapolis lawyer, had been consulted by the father of the girl on Monday March 16 when it was discovered that the girl had not returned home the previous evening. When it became apparent that Miss Oberholtzer was not going to recover, Smith set about preserving her testimony in a statement which would be admissible evidence in the event of a later prosecution of Stephenson and others for causing her death.

From notes made of his previous conversations with her Smith prepared a typewritten statement, and on the evening of March 28 four solemn-faced persons gathered at the girl's bedside. Dr. Kingsbury, having conferred earlier with other physicians called into consultation, told her that she had no chance to recover. She replied that she knew it and was ready to die. Smith then explained to her the purpose of the proposed declaration. Dr. Kingsbury, Asa Smith, an attorney associated with Smith, and a young lady who was probably the dying girl's closest friend were present.

Smith's testimony, corroborated by the others, was that he read the typewritten statement to the girl clearly and slowly. At the end of each sentence he paused and asked her if that was correct. If she answered in the affirmative, he passed on to the next sentence. If she suggested any corrections, he made them with pen and ink and then re-read to her the sentence as amended. When he had finished reading and had corrected the statement, she declared that it expressed the truth and signed it in the presence of the four witnesses.

The statement was offered in evidence. A vigorous general objection to its admissibility was overruled, but on particular objections certain specific statements were deleted. These, for the most part, were recitals of events which preceded March 15. The girl's story of her abduction and assault and of her taking the poison to end her life and save her mother from disgrace went to the jury.

Witnesses were called to corroborate, wherever possible, the facts recited in Madge Oberholtzer's dying declaration.

The manager of the local telephone company serving Indianapolis testified that the D. C. Stephenson residence telephone number was Irvington 0492.

A night clerk at the Hotel Washington in Indianapolis testified that he received a call the evening of March 15 to reserve a drawing room for Stephenson on the Monon night train for Chicago. Later in the evening, the clerk said, someone picked up the reservation and three railroad tickets.

The Pullman conductor on the Monon train which left Indianapolis for Chicago at 1:00 A.M. on Monday identified Stephenson and Gentry as two men who, accompanied by a girl with no hat on, had given him tickets for and occupied a drawing room in one of the cars on the train.

The Pullman porter on the car made a similar identification. He testified that while he was making up the upper and lower berths Stephenson showed him his revolver, and he heard the girl tell Stephenson to put it up because she was afraid of it. Later, he testified, he heard her vomiting.

The hotel clerk who was on duty at the Indiana Hotel at

Hammond in the early morning of March 16 identified
Stephenson and Gentry as two men who had, in company
with a woman who was "pale, with no make-up on and no
hat," entered the hotel about 6:30 A.M. and asked for
rooms. He testified further that Stephenson registered for
"Mr. and Mrs. W. B. Morgan," that Gentry registered as
Earl Gentry, and that the three were assigned to rooms 416
and 417.

The hotel clerk who was on duty in the afternoon testified to the arrival of Shorty in a "big, closed car" and to
his inquiry for Gentry. He further testified that later three
people came down and got into the car, that one of the men
held the woman's arm to support her and that he thought
she was intoxicated but trying to act as if she were sober.

The hotel maid in charge of rooms 416 and 417 testified
that a man, whom she identified as Stephenson, called for
more towels, saying that they had used up all they had for
hot towels. She said she cleaned up the rooms after the
parties had vacated them. In room 416 she found five or
six "bullets" (pistol cartridges) in one of the dresser drawers. She also found and picked up a partially filled whisky
bottle, an empty milk bottle, some witch hazel and some
oranges. The bed in room 417, she said, was "all tore up
. . . one of the pillow slips was wet and bloodstained" and
"the cuspidor looked like it was full of sour milk."

The porter at the hotel identified Stephenson and Gentry. The woman with them, he testified, "looked awful
bad, walked slow and kind of staggered . . . one man got on
each side of her . . . she didn't seem to be quite herself,"
and "she was pale and had a red place on her cheek."

A superintendent of the Western Union Telegraph
Company at Indianapolis identified a telegram received at
the Indianapolis office on March 18 at 8:00 A.M., which
read: "We are driving through to Chicago. Will take train
back tonight." It was signed "Madge."

A housewife whose home was about 300 feet away from

the Stephenson residence testified that near midnight on Monday March 16 she was awakened by a terrible scream which came from the direction of Stephenson's garage and that Stephenson's three police dogs, which he kept near the garage, barked furiously all the rest of the night.

Another neighbor testified that on the morning of March 17 she observed Shorty washing one of the Stephenson automobiles in front of his garage and that all of the cushions had been washed and laid out to dry. She also testified that between eight and nine o'clock she saw Gentry carrying a tray from the house to the garage.

It is in no sense critical of the defense to record that the cross-examination of these witnesses yielded nothing to discredit their several testimonies or to impeach their authors. The stories told by these witnesses, most of whom were entirely disinterested, were unquestionably true. Even the belligerent, rapid, searching cross-fire of Stephenson's chief counsel, "Eph" Inman, produced only minor discrepancies which failed to weaken the force of the evidence. Efforts to impeach two or three of the witnesses by showing alleged variations between their versions on the stand and previous answers on the "bail hearing" and to show, as to one other, an attempt to extort money from Stephenson to compound his alleged crimes failed utterly. The bases on which to conduct successful cross-examinations simply did not exist.

The remainder of the State's case was medical testimony[7] —testimony as to the nature and effect of the internal administration of bichloride of mercury, its proper treatment, the chances of recovery following such treatment, the na-

---

[7] Stephenson, in his later numerous appeals for a retrial and parole, made much of the claim that the State had not established his guilt beyond a reasonable doubt by its failure to call as its witnesses the millinery saleswoman in Hammond who had sold Miss Oberholtzer the hat and the druggist's clerk from whom she had purchased the poison tablets. If the testimony of these witnesses would have impeached the girl's dying declaration, Stephenson could have summoned them as his witnesses. It is difficult to follow Stephenson's argument that failure to corroborate these details in the girl's statement reacted to his prejudice.

ture and consequences of the physical injuries inflicted upon Madge Oberholtzer by Stephenson and the cause or causes of her death.

The trained nurse in attendance from the time the girl returned home until her death testified from her hour-to-hour bedside record to the girl's temperature, pulse, respiration, complaints of pain, the stomach washings, administrations of narcotics and sedatives, foods taken and stool and urine elimination.

The State's chief medical expert was a professor of pathology at the Indiana University School of Medicine and was a highly qualified physician, surgeon and toxicologist. He had previously performed over 900 autopsies. At the request of the Marion County coroner and in the presence of Dr. Kingsbury and three other physicians (all of whom were witnesses for the State), he conducted a post-mortem examination of the body of Madge Oberholtzer.

He testified that he found an acute nephritis, a marked irritation of the intestinal tract and some degeneration of the liver and heart tissues—all, in his opinion, due to bichloride-of-mercury poisoning. He also testified to finding evidences of numerous healed lacerations and that one of these in one of the girl's breasts showed evidence of having suppurated before it healed over. He added that there was an abscess in the lung below it. This abscess, he said, was in the outer portion of the lung adjacent to the pleura and contained pus and staphylococci germs. The kidneys, he found, were infected with the same bacteria.

A biochemist, also a professor in the Indiana University School of Medicine, testified that a microscopic examination of portions of the girl's vital organs which were turned over to him by the post-mortem surgeon revealed the presence of bichloride of mercury in the liver and kidney tissues.

There was complete agreement among the State's medical experts as to the effect of bichloride of mercury taken into the human system internally and the proper treatment of a patient suffering from such poisoning. Two or three grains may constitute a fatal dose, but ensuing death would depend on whether the poison was eliminated or absorbed. The poison in powder form is absorbed more readily than that which is in tablet form. The rapidity of the absorption depends on the promptness with which suitable measures are instituted to cause vomiting and purging.

With prompt and appropriate treatment, recoveries have been known in cases where as much as 40 to 100 grains have been taken. If a lethal dose is taken and there is an absence of treatment, or if the patient does not respond to the usual medical procedures, death generally ensues in from a few hours to twelve days. In rare cases death may be longer postponed. The most extreme case known to the State's experts was one where the poisoned patient lived twenty-five days.

If death occurs within the first four days, it is because of the corrosive action of the poison on the stomach and bowels; if after five but within twelve days, it is the result of the action of the poison on the kidneys causing an acute nephritis. After the twelfth day nature begins a process of absorption of the dead kidney tissue and replacement of it with new tissue. Thereafter, in the absence of new complications, the prospects of recovery improve with each passing day.

The autopsy revealed that the initial injury to the kidneys from the poison had almost entirely healed and that the replacement of the destroyed tissue by new tissue was almost complete.

One of the State's experts, an experienced pathologist, gave testimony based on blood and urine examinations which he made on various days between March 21 and April 10. A secondary infection, he said, in the girl's kidneys, ureter tubes or bladder, superimposed on the nephritis, caused her death.

All of the State's medical witnesses gave it as their definite opinion that the twenty-four-hour delay in instituting proper treatment to eliminate the poison from the girl's system tended to lessen her chances of recovery and to shorten her life.

Judge Cox, the learned special prosecutor, concluded the direct examination of three of the State's experts with a long hypothetical question. It accurately summarized the facts recounted in the girl's dying declaration, epitomized the testimony of the various witnesses as to the girl's condition when she was brought home and to the wounds and bruises on her body, the findings of the attending and consulting physicians, the findings on the post-mortem examination and asked the opinion of the witnesses as to the cause of death. All three of the State's medical experts answered that in their opinion death resulted from the complication of a secondary blood-stream infection, with pus-forming bacteria, superimposed on the nephritis which was the direct result of bichloride-of-mercury poisoning. Such an infection, they said, might have been and very probably had been introduced into the blood stream by a human bite causing the laceration in the breast which later became infected with the pus-forming bacteria; and, in view of the fact that the girl lived twenty-nine days after taking the poison and that the restorative processes in the kidneys were far advanced, she in all probability would have recovered except for this secondary infection.

The probative force of this latter testimony is obvious: The secondary staphylococci infection which manifested itself in the lung abscess and the kidneys was advanced as the *direct* result of a bite which Stephenson in the course of his assault had inflicted on the girl's breast. On this evidence the jury could find Stephenson guilty of murder even if it found that the assault had not put the girl in a state of irresponsible mental distraction in which she took the poison.

Defense Counsel Inman cross-examined all of the State's medical witnesses. He had made a thorough study of the properties of bichloride of mercury, the effects of the poison on the human body and the recognized medical treatment for its elimination. His cross-examinations took two directions: (1) to discredit the witnesses by showing their lack of knowledge of the subject matter, and (2) to elicit additional facts which would corroborate and support the contentions and theories to be advanced later by his own medical experts. The State's witnesses, however, were all men of outstanding professional attainments—undoubtedly the best to be found in Indiana. They knew their subject, and they were not to be confused. The cross-examinations—skillful and persistent as they were—failed utterly to discredit or weaken the direct examinations.

The cross-examiner's efforts to develop new matter in aid of his expected defense were more successful. By adroitly worded direct questions, which compelled categorical answers, he brought out that bichloride of mercury is one of the quickest-acting and most deadly of poisons. When taken by mouth it burns and inflames the tongue and sets up a severe irritation of the mucous membranes of the lips, mouth, larynx, esophagus and alimentary canal. Its particular effect on the stomach would vary depending on the presence or absence of recently eaten food. If taken on an empty stomach, or by a patient whose only food over a long previous period had been a cup of coffee, the absorption of the poison would be more rapid than if taken on a full stomach and the effect on the stomach tissues, the entry of the poison into the blood stream and the attack on the other organs of the body more devastating.

Inman's cross-examinations compelled further admissions: If vomiting occurred immediately after taking the poison, the subsequent effects would depend on how much of the poison remained in the system. Milk was a proper agent to induce vomiting. When bichloride of mercury is taken into the stomach, part of it is immediately absorbed and can be found in the blood stream. If a lethal dose so taken is not entirely eliminated through vomiting within six hours, the unexpelled poison would be absorbed into the blood stream. When the poison gets into the blood stream it exercises an affinity for certain tissues, particularly those of the kidneys and lower bowel, and blood will be found in the intestines and in the stool.

Bichloride of mercury, the State's experts conceded, could be taken into the system through the skin as well as by mouth and cause death. A bichloride douche, sufficiently concentrated, would inflame the mucous membranes of the vagina; and if brought in contact with the skin, would burn it. It was also developed that an abscess of the lung may follow pneumonia and that an attack of influenza, if severe enough to cause death, would cause some degeneration of the kidneys, heart and lungs; that various bacteria, and particularly staphylococci, are commonly found in all of the human organs.

The suggestion that the poison might have been injected into the system other than by mouth was greatly weakened by an answer of the State's chief medical expert, given on cross-examination, that if it had been so taken, it would not have produced immediate and repeated vomiting of blood. The cross-examination was further weakened by a sharply conducted redirect examination which brought out clearly that the wounds and bruises on the girl's body were such that they could not have been produced by the external application of a bichloride-of-mercury solution, and that the post-mortem examination disclosed no pneumococci bacteria in either of the lungs.

Its medical testimony concluded, the State rested its case, and the submission of evidence on behalf of Stephenson and his codefendants commenced.

The lead-off witness for the defense was a resident physician of Indianapolis who professed to have had an extensive experience in cases of mercurial poisoning. His direct examination was extended and established a pattern which was largely followed in the examinations of the six other physicians who were called to testify in behalf of Stephenson and his codefendants. He agreed that bichloride of mercury was a deadly poison and that three or more grains taken internally could be a fatal dose. He supported the contentions suggested in the cross-examinations of the State's experts.

He testified further that if after taking bichloride of mercury the patient vomited and the expelled vomit struck the breast, abdomen and other parts of the human body and remained there for some time, it would have a very marked tendency to inflame and corrode those surfaces. Mercurial poisoning, he testified, is readily absorbed from any of the bodily surfaces, and it is quite common to find that women have been poisoned by using concentrated solutions of bichloride of mercury as a vaginal douche; that a seven-and-one-half-grain tablet, dissolved in a small quantity of water, would produce a solution which, if applied to a mucous surface, would have a very pronounced burning effect and by sloughing would create a general condition as bad as if the poison had been taken by mouth. He said he had known of cases where the frequent use of such concentrations of bichloride of mercury in vaginal douches had resulted in death.

The girl's father had testified that a few months before her death she had had a slight attack of flu from which she had apparently fully recovered. Seizing upon this, the doctor, under Inman's examination, testified that all sorts of complications could follow an attack of flu—affections of the bronchial tubes, tuberculosis, pyemia with pus in the lungs, nephritis and heart disease. He added that the staphylococci bacteria are the most common of the germs; they are everywhere—in the mouth, the throat and the alimentary canal, and they might get into the system as the result of a blood transfusion or a catheterization; that if

a person had an abscess on the lung infected with staphylococci, there was no way of determining where the infection came from. It could have resulted, he said, from a previous flu or from any one of a number of other causes.

Two long hypothetical questions were put to the witness.
The first omitted all reference to the assault. It assumed
the previous attack of flu but made no reference to the evidence that it was slight and that there had been a complete
recovery. It assumed and stressed that bichloride-of-mercury tablets had been dissolved in water and taken on an
empty stomach and that the girl told no one of her action
for six hours; also, that she had then been given milk to
drink and had vomited. The question in further assumptions fairly stated the evidence as to the 175-mile ride in the
automobile from Hammond to Indianapolis, the confine-
ment in the garage until Tuesday morning and the return
of the girl to her home, the attending doctor's discovery of
the symptoms of bichloride-of-mercury poisoning and subsequent treatment. The evidence as to the condition of the
girl when she was brought home and the nature and extent
of the wounds and bruises on her body was minimized by
the assumption that she had "some discoloration and small
abrasions on various parts of her body" and that "one such
abrasion on the chest had suppurated but healed." The
question further assumed and emphasized that while the
autopsy revealed an abscess in one of the lungs there was
none in the kidneys and that bichloride of mercury had
been found in the liver and kidneys. The recitals concluded with an inquiry for the doctor's opinion as to the
cause of death. He answered, "Bichloride of mercury."

The second hypothetical question added to the first an
assumption of the examiner's toned-down version of the
assault. The witness was asked if the facts additionally assumed would change his previously expressed opinion. He
answered they would not. The witness also gave it as his
opinion that, after a six-hour delay in instituting treat-

ment to eliminate the poison, no subsequent medical treatment could have saved the girl's life.

Judge Cox's handling of the cross-examinations of the defense's medical experts was, from the standpoint of advocacy, the most brilliant feature of the trial. He brought out first that the witness knew Stephenson and had "prescribed" for him on three or four occasions. This was followed by inquiries into the doctor's experience in bichloride-of-mercury poisoning. Of his twenty patients who took the poison orally, all but two or three had died. The witness had never seen or treated Madge Oberholtzer and had not seen the autopsy findings. All he knew of the case was what was stated in the hypothetical questions, and his opinions were based solely on the assumptions contained in those questions. He was then tested as to his knowledge of the authoritative literature on toxicology. He professed to have read Blair, Solomon, Woods, Clark, Landers and Milt. He was examined particularly regarding his knowledge of Blair. He admitted that his readings in the field of toxicology had begun about six weeks before the trial.

After the defense had called three other medical experts, whose testimony followed closely the above line, Judge Cox asked that the defense's first expert be recalled for further cross-examination. The witness restated the authorities on toxicology with which he was acquainted and on which he relied, again mentioning particularly Blair's book. Upon further specific questioning he was forced to admit that the book with which he professed such intimate acquaintance was by Blythe and not Blair and that he didn't own a copy but had borrowed one from a doctor friend of his within the preceding week or ten days. On his further cross-examination it developed that Milt's work on toxicology about which he had previously testified was a work on veterinary practice. This was followed by short, rapid-fire questions which elicited the facts that the witness had taught toxicology in a veterinary college and had associated himself with a veterinarian in a patent-medicine company which advertised and sold veterinary remedies. The cross-examination was concluded with additional questions concerning the doctor's relations with Stephenson. After repeated hedgings the witness was compelled to admit that he had treated Stephenson for alcoholism, with the unmistakable suggestion that the condition had bordered upon delirium tremens.

The other defense witnesses, called as medical experts, underwent vigorous and searching cross-examinations. None was of the caliber of the State's expert witnesses and, under Judge Cox's skillful questioning, all were made to admit many of the contentions of the State. The results of these cross-examinations, coupled with the blow which had completely shattered the testimony of the first witness, left the State's medical case practically intact.

One obvious purpose of the defense was to convince the jurors—or at least raise in their minds a reasonable doubt—that the previous relationship between Stephenson and the dead girl had been much more intimate than was to be inferred from her dying declaration, that her trip with him to Hammond had been voluntary, and that there had been no occasion to assault or rape her. It was to this end that there had been brought into the medical testimony the suggestion that bichloride of mercury could be introduced into the system otherwise than by drinking it. In an effort to show that Miss Oberholtzer was not the innocent victim of Stephenson's lust, the defense called an even dozen witnesses. Some of these testified that they had frequently seen Stephenson and Madge Oberholtzer together in Stephenson's office and elsewhere. Others swore they had seen Stephenson and the girl drinking gin together; still others that they had heard her address Stephenson familiarly as "Stevie" and "dear." These witnesses were all intimate friends of Stephenson. A number of them had been associated with him in the activities of the Ku Klux Klan.

Railway employees at the Monon depot testified to the location of entrances and exits, waiting rooms, passageways, gates through which passengers passed to the tracks and waiting trains and the procedure for identifying and collecting tickets. A plat showing the station layout with relevant measurements was identified and received in evidence. The inferences to be drawn from this testimony was that the girl, had she been under the restraint she claimed, could have called for help and been freed from her alleged captors.

Two newspaper reporters testified they had seen the naked body of Madge Oberholtzer during the post-mortem examination and there were no marks on it other than a "faint bruise . . . about the size of a penny" under the left collarbone.

This was all the testimony offered in Stephenson's behalf.

An attempt was made to establish an alibi for Klinck. Four deputy sheriffs, associates of Klinck,[8] testified to having seen him during practically all of March 16 and the morning of the seventeenth. One of them testified to having been with him on the sixteenth when he made an arrest and on the seventeenth when the persons arrested were brought before a justice of the peace. Two of the others testified that on the morning of the seventeenth Klinck delivered a batch of prisoners to the Indiana State Penitentiary Farm by automobile, and papers showing the receipt of certain named persons were offered as corroboration.

Neither Stephenson, Klinck, Gentry nor Stephenson's chauffeur, Shorty, took the stand. Shorty, whose real name was DeFriese, had fled the jurisdiction shortly after the indictment.

In rebuttal the State called two officials of the state penitentiary and four of the prisoners named in the receipts.

---

[8] Both Klinck and Gentry were on the Marion County payroll as deputy sheriffs.

All testified that the prisoners were received at the state penitentiary farm on Tuesday morning March 17 but that Klinck was not in the automobile which delivered them there.

The secretary of the committee on arrangements for the governor's ball on January 12, 1925, testified that he was well acquainted with Miss Oberholtzer and on that evening introduced her to Stephenson. This testimony, if it was believed, completely destroyed the testimony of the witnesses for the defense who had sworn they had seen Madge Oberholtzer and Stephenson together before January 1925.

The State called two of its medical experts to refute some of the suggestions made by the defense doctors and again rested. Some unimportant surrebuttal followed and the evidence was closed.

The Court limited the summations to eight hours for each side.

Remy, prosecutor for Marion County, opened for the State. His argument was a brief but telling résumé of the State's evidence. He denounced the asserted defenses as subterfuges and perjuries. "Madge Oberholtzer is dead," declared the prosecutor. "She would be alive today were it not for the unlawful act of these three men. They have destroyed her body, they tried to destroy her soul, and in the last few days they have tried to dishonor her character." In his peroration he cried, waving the dying declaration before the jury, "Madge Oberholtzer's story still stands untarnished. Her dying declaration is before you again with corroborating and supporting evidence from witness after witness, credible witnesses. It stands not only with the solemnity of the declaration of a person who faces certain death, it still stands, after all the evidence is in, most of it not even denied."

Holmes, Christian and Inman argued for the defense. The principal argument was made by Inman. Experienced and shrewd, Inman realized the atmosphere of prejudice in which the trial was being conducted and tried his best to get the jury to rise above it.

"Gentlemen of the jury," Inman began, "in all my connection with this remarkable case I have been conscious of the weight of responsibility which rested upon us all. It has not been a responsibility of law or of fact, but it has been a responsibility which an implacable element of public sentiment, without knowing or being concerned with the facts, has cast upon us. I have never for a single instant feared for the safety of our clients under the law. I have not feared for their safety under the facts. That these men should have been indicted for murder is a shame to the jurisprudence of Indiana, and to the law of this state, and I sincerely believe that such an indictment would not have been returned except that the state's attorney and those privately employed to reap the vengeance of hate, determined to respond to the wishes of the unreasoning element of hostility which aims to bring Stephenson to destruction."

Continuing, Inman put his heavy emphasis on the single proposition that offered a hope for acquittal. "The sole question presented here," said Inman, "is: Can suicide be murder? Can suicide be homicide? . . . This so-called dying declaration—this lawyer-made declaration designed as poisonous propaganda to be used in an effort to gain money—if it declares anything it is a dying declaration of suicide and not homicide. She, by her own concealment of taking the poison for six hours, made medical aid of no avail. She, by her own willful act of conduct, made it impossible for these men to save her life. The dying declaration was made by the girl for the justification of herself, to free herself from fault and place the blame on others, to put her right with her family and friends." Inman's plea was powerful— the strongest that could have been made under the law and the state of evidence.

Judge Cox and Ralph Kane closed for the State. Judge

Cox's arraignment of the defense was bitter. He declared that all of the witnesses called by the defense were per- jurers—"the slime of the serpent of perjury is over all of them." Directing his argument to a reply to Inman, he demanded, "Are you going to permit this unparalleled, this unequaled painter of words, this man of stately bearing and melodious voice, are you going to allow him to take the brush of scandal and write the scarlet letter on Madge Oberholtzer's tomb?" He declared that at his advanced age he had been reluctant to enter upon such a long trial and had done so only because he felt that the brutal murder of an innocent girl should be avenged by the law. In a voice choked with emotion, he concluded: "In the name of the law, in the name of virtuous womanhood, in the name of justice, I call upon you to write your verdict in a way that will put a stop to tragedies like this one."

The final and most convincing argument for the pros- ecution was made by Ralph Kane. It was aimed down to the level of the jury and presented in language they could understand.

"The theory of the law," Kane began, "maintained by the State in this case has been the law of England for more than 500 years, and it has been the law of this country ever since the English common law was brought to this coun- try. I don't care anything about germs. When these de- fendants unlawfully abducted Madge Oberholtzer, at- tacked her and dragged her to Hammond, they made them- selves criminals, and by that very act drove that poor girl, honored and respected in her community, loved by all, drove her into a position where she had lost all, where she was bereft of all she cherished, and forced her to take the poison of death. By those acts D. C. Stephenson and his cohorts became murderers just the same as if they had plunged a dagger into her throbbing heart. . . . What is the story, gentlemen? Why, it is the most scurrilous story in the history of the ages. . . . Don't let the defense befuddle

you about this story. Madge Oberholtzer told you a co-
herent story. She was drugged, of course. She didn't know
the exact route she took through the Union Station. But
the Pullman conductor identified Gentry and Stephenson.
So did the porter. They registered at the hotel. We didn't
have to call a handwriting expert, as Mr. Inman suggested,
to identify the writer of 'W. B. Morgan and wife.' We have
the man who held the pen. There he is!" cried Kane,
pointing his finger at Stephenson.

He took up the dying declaration. "These gentlemen,"
he said quietly, "don't like Asa Smith. Asa Smith was born
in Hamilton County. His mother sleeps in the churchyard
in Tomlinson neighborhood. He is one of the nation's
heroes. He came back from the battle of the Argonne, ter-
ribly wounded. He's no Stephenson. He's no Klinck. He's
no Gentry." Smith deserved credit, said Kane, for his foresight and care in taking Madge Oberholtzer's dying declaration.

"When the dread news came from the sick room," Kane
went on, "that the poor girl could not recover, and that
any evidence would have to be as a dying declaration, Smith
wrote it down, God bless him! He brought the evidence
into this courtroom which clinches this case and will send
these men to the place where they belong."

One after another, Kane raised barriers the defense
could never hope to hurdle. "There are some things that
you and I know," said Kane. "If Madge Oberholtzer had
gone willingly with Stephenson that night she would have
done it by prearrangement, and she would have worn a hat.
If I understand anything at all about women, when they
start on a 250-mile Pullman ride they take along their
clothes, their hats, their cosmetics, their lingerie and other
things.

"Another thing," continued Kane, "do you think she
would ever have had big, pug-nosed Gentry in the same
compartment if she had been conscious of what was hap-

pening? If she was a willing companion, why bring her home looking like she had been in a fight?" Here he seized a copy of the testimony of the girl's nurse and read: "Her left cheek was bruised; the lower half of her abdomen, the inside of her thighs and her legs down to her ankles—all were bruised." And then, with withering sarcasm, Kane said, "A willing victim, eh? Oh, gentlemen, she wasn't hurt. Oh, no. She just went along with Stephenson because she loved him." Glaring now at Inman, he thundered, "And that able, touted, newspaper-boomed criminal attorney Inman—if he had half as much sense as any one of you jurymen he wouldn't have the nerve to make such a flimsy argument."

He concluded with a slashing reply to Inman's attack upon the special prosecutors (Cox and himself), his charge that "blood money jingled in their pockets." Kane said, "Our reward is in the consciousness of having performed a duty. Can you honestly say that, Mr. Inman?" And then to the jury he solemnly added, "These fellows are guilty of murder, staphylococci or no staphylococci. I want you to demonstrate to Stephenson, to Gentry, to Klinck, and to Inman and Christian, if it can be done, that in Indiana the law is supreme. Put them away so others can be safe."

The ringing tones of Kane's impassioned plea had scarcely died away when Judge Sparks commenced the reading of his charge. He gave the jury fifty-seven separate written instructions. Eighteen of these were tendered by the State; twenty-seven were prepared by the Court. The defense tendered 161 separate instructions of which the Court gave twelve. Taken as a whole, the instructions—according to the later decision of the Supreme Court of Indiana—declared the law of the case accurately and fully.

Specifically, the Court charged the jury that under Indiana law it might, from the evidence, return any one of three verdicts: *i.e.*, murder in the first degree, for which the punishment could be death or life imprisonment; murder in the second degree, for which the specified punishment was life imprisonment; or manslaughter, for which the punishment could be imprisonment for not less than two nor more than twenty-one years.

Murder in the first degree was defined as the killing of a human being purposely and with premeditated malice, or in the perpetration of or an attempt to perpetrate a rape, arson, robbery or burglary; murder in the second degree as the killing of a human being purposely and maliciously but without premeditation; and manslaughter as the killing of a human being without malice, express or implied, or unlawfully upon a sudden heat, or involuntarily in the commission of some unlawful act.

The case went to the jury shortly before noon on November 14. The jury was out slightly less than six hours. By its verdict it found Stephenson guilty of murder in the second degree and that he should be imprisoned in the Indiana State Prison for and during the term of his natural life. Gentry and Klinck were found not guilty.

Judgment was entered on the verdict on November 16, and on November 21, 1925, the gates of the Michigan City penitentiary closed behind David Curtis Stephenson, erstwhile Grand Dragon of the Ku Klux Klan and, at the time of his indictment, the most powerful political figure in the State of Indiana.

AFTERMATH

Stephenson appealed his case to the Supreme Court of Indiana. Every adverse ruling of the Courts of Marion and Hamilton counties was assigned as error. It was argued with earnestness and great ability that Stephenson was prejudiced by remarks made by the trial Court in its rulings on the evidence; that incompetent evidence had been admitted; that the Court's instructions were erroneous and

insufficient; and that the verdict of the jury was not supported by the evidence. A majority of the court (three out
of five) ruled against Stephenson on every contention.[9]
One of the others, while agreeing that the verdict was fully
warranted by the evidence, considered there was prejudicial
and reversible error in some of the lower Court's instructions. The second dissenter held that the admissible evidence in the case was insufficient to justify a verdict of
second-degree murder.

This was, however, only the beginning of Stephenson's
fight to set aside the judgment of the lower Court, to obtain
a new trial or to secure a pardon or release on parole. In
all, he is said to have instituted more than forty separate
proceedings directed to these ends. It is perhaps significant
that, speaking generally, a completely new set of lawyers
appeared on each successive occasion. The allegations made
in one of these proceedings—an original petition in the
Supreme Court of Indiana for the ancient common-law
writ of *coram nobis* to compel a setting aside of his conviction[10]—is fairly typical of Stephenson's oft-repeated contentions.

He claimed that he was "framed" by Hiram Evans, Imperial Wizard, and other high officers of the Ku Klux Klan
because of his opposition to the official Klan following his
"resignation." These powerful and unscrupulous conspirators had used Madge Oberholtzer as a lure to ruin him.
The attorney Asa J. Smith had been paid a huge bribe to
compose the alleged dying declaration and obtain her signature to it. Stephenson, his attorneys said, did not take
the stand in his own behalf for fear of being shot[11]; that
had he taken the stand, he would have shown that someone
else (one of the "conspirators" against him) committed the
murder for which he was convicted.

Stephenson's final complaint was that because of fear and

---

9 *Stephenson* v. *State,* 205 Ind. 141; 179 N. E. 633.
10 *Stephenson* v. *State,* 186 N. E. 293.
11 Outside of Stephenson's statement there is not the slightest testimony to
support this claim.

threats (undescribed) he had signed his motion in the lower court for a new trial without reading it and before he had had an opportunity to acquaint his attorneys with the facts which he desired to have set up in that motion. The supreme court held it had no jurisdiction of the petition but remarked that Stephenson's allegedly insufficient motion for a new trial had contained 294 assigned grounds, "all of which were asserted vigorously and fearlessly by resourceful and intelligent counsel."

In May of 1927 Stephenson presented a petition to Governor Jackson for parole. On this he had built high hopes. He claimed, and with some truth, that more than any one man, he had been responsible for Jackson's election. The governor, before Stephenson's conviction, had recognized his importance in the distribution of patronage and other political perquisites. But a new day had dawned. The Klan had ceased to exist as a political factor. To a calculating politician, which Jackson was, a Klan connection was no longer an asset but a taint. So, forgetting past associations, the governor lined up with "the outraged citizenry" and promptly denied Stephenson's application.

The application for parole was repeatedly renewed. In connection with one such application, a well-known psychiatrist made an examination of Stephenson. His diagnosis and report to the parole board (September 10, 1942) was that Stephenson was a paranoiac and should be committed to a state institution for the insane.

In March 1950 Stephenson's persistence was rewarded. On the recommendation of the board of paroles he was released by Governor Schricker and paroled to his daughter, a resident of Tulsa, Oklahoma. He was later given permission by the board to reside in Carbondale, Illinois. On August 30 he disappeared. Newspaper accounts suggested that he might have met with foul play, but on November 15 he was discovered at work in a small printing shop in a Minneapolis suburb.

Stephenson had violated his parole by failing to report in

September, October and November. He was immediately
arrested and the Indiana authorities were notified. At their
request the governor of Minnesota signed a warrant for his
extradition, but his immediate return to Indiana was
thwarted by the issuance of a writ of habeas corpus. A ruling adverse to him in the lower Court was followed by an
appeal to the Supreme Court of Minnesota. Here Stephenson again lost, and in December 1951 he was returned to
the Indiana State Prison.

In passing, it may be remarked that the troubles of Klinck
and Gentry did not end with their acquittal on the charge
of participation in the murder of Madge Oberholtzer.
Stephenson's house in Irvington was later burned. Investigation disclosed that the fire was probably of incendiary
origin. Klinck, Gentry and one other were suspected and
indicted for conspiracy to commit arson. The case, however, was later dismissed for want of evidence.

Gentry, after the collapse of his clay-footed idol and his
own release from the toils of Indiana law, sought new and
greener fields. He moved to Wisconsin, where his genius for
getting into trouble continued to flower. In 1931 he was
accused of stabbing a Fort Atkinson tavern keeper in a
drunken brawl. He seems to have escaped trial on this
charge, but Nemesis caught up with him three years later
when he got on the wrong side of a love triangle and was
shot to death by a jealous rival. His murderer—who
pleaded guilty and was given a life sentence—enlarged the
court record with an attempted justification of his act,
which carried with it an estimate of Gentry from which
there can be but little dissent: "I am not in the least sorry
for the act I committed, as I feel I did a good deed for society
when I killed Earl Gentry."

When Stephenson realized that he had been abandoned
by Governor Jackson and when his other fair-weather political associates fell away, his disappointment and resent-
ment may be imagined. He sulked for a while and then

struck back. To one of the Indiana newspapers, which he considered had been fairer to him than the general run of the press, he wrote a letter telling of the existence of "two black boxes" in which, through the previous years, he had kept records, receipts and other papers which he said would reveal wholesale corruption in high places. Grand-jury investigations followed. Stephenson was released from prison under custody so he could procure the boxes and disclose their contents.

From the papers the boxes contained and leads the papers furnished, indictments were returned against the mayor of Indianapolis for violation of the State's corrupt-practices act and against six of the city's aldermen for accepting bribes. Governor Jackson and "Captain" George V. Coffin, Republican political boss, were indicted on Stephenson's charge that they had offered Jackson's predecessor in office, Governor McCray, a bribe of $10,000 to appoint a henchman of the Klan group as prosecuting attorney of Marion County. The mayor was convicted, sentenced to thirty days in jail and forced to resign. The aldermen paid small fines and resigned. Governor Jackson and Coffin evaded trial by a plea of the statute of limitations.

While the result of these disclosures and prosecutions suggests more smoke than fire, the larger consequence should not be lost sight of. By them the Klan was completely stripped of its pretense to superior political virtue and revealed for what it was: an evil thing, dominated for the most part by selfish, conscienceless hypocrites who preached a gospel of racial and religious hate to delude and organize a multitude in whose name and by whose help they might gain and wield supreme political power. Stephenson's conviction and its aftermath killed the Ku Klux Klan.

Was Madge Oberholtzer's story true?

The question is put because the persistent cry of Stephenson through the twenty-five years of his incarceration

that he was "framed" by the Southern branch of the Ku
Klux Klan and his political enemies seems to have lodged
doubt in many uninformed minds. Stephenson, a mas-
ter psychologist, evidently believed in the Hitlerian theory
that if you harp long enough on the same theme—true or
false—the mob will ultimately be brought to believe it.

Of the correct answer to the question, there can be no
doubt. Miss Oberholtzer's story, told to the family physician immediately after her return and told as her dying
declaration when she knew she was soon to face her Maker,
was accepted by twelve impartial jurors. Their verdict was
approved by the trial judge—a man of recognized integrity,
legal ability and fairness—and his judgment was affirmed by
the Supreme Court of Indiana. While there were two dissenting opinions, none of the supreme-court judges questioned the truth of the girl's declaration.

Her story was fully corroborated—by railway employees
at Indianapolis, by hotel employees at Hammond, and by
the wounds and bruises on her body for which her story
of the assault offered the only explanation.

Finally, the most conclusive circumstance in support of
her story is the fact that neither Stephenson, Gentry, Klinck
nor Shorty, the chauffeur, took the witness stand to deny
any part of it.

Was Stephenson proved guilty of murder?

This question is not so easily disposed of. Out of the
maze of legal charges and denials the jury found that
Stephenson drugged the girl and then forced her against
her will to accompany him to the train and into the drawing room; that he not only criminally assaulted her but
subjected her to almost unbelievably cruel and inhuman
treatment; that, as a direct consequence of his criminal
acts, she became distracted to the point that she took the
poison which ended her life.

The instructions of the Court specifically authorized the
jury to return a verdict of guilty of murder on such findings.

The question of whether the girl's suicide was the direct (proximate) result of Stephenson's acts was argued vigorously but unsuccessfully by Stephenson's able counsel as one of their major contentions in support of his motion for a new trial. It was again argued by another set of able lawyers appearing in Stephenson's behalf in the Supreme Court of Indiana. Four out of the five judges in that court held that the evidence justified the verdict of murder found by the jury.

Of course it can be argued, as Stephenson and his lawyers have argued it in more than a score of legal proceedings, that after the assault had taken place the girl was able to leave the train at Hammond and walk a block to the hotel, to drink a cup of coffee, to worry that she had no hat, to accompany Stephenson's chauffeur to a millinery shop to buy one, to get in and out of the automobile and to return to the hotel. It is further arguable that from the time she left the train she was a free agent and could at any time have summoned help or escaped from Stephenson and his agents; that she took the poison without his knowledge and outside of his presence; and that, in summary, her actions subsequent to the assault and before the taking of the poison showed a complete absence of fear of further bodily harm, irrationality or hysteria, and, therefore, the essential "causal connection" between the assault and the suicide was lacking.

Nowhere was this contention more vigorously asserted than in the appeal to the Supreme Court of Indiana. That Court, in its majority opinion, answered with equal vigor, supported by unimpeachable legal authority, that "When suicide follows a wound inflicted by a defendant, his act is homicidal, if deceased was rendered irresponsible by the wound and as the natural result of it."

"We should think," said the Court, "the same rule would apply if a defendant engaged in the commission of a felony such as rape or attempted rape . . . inflicts upon his victim both physical and mental injuries, the natural and probable result of which would render the deceased mentally irresponsible and suicide followed." The learned judges added that they saw no difference in law if, instead of the girl's actions as shown by the evidence, she had secured possession of the revolver and shot herself or had thrown herself out of the window of the car.

"The same forces," said the Court, "the same impulses, that would impel her to shoot herself during the actual attack or throw herself out of the car window after the attack had ceased, were pressing and overwhelming her at the time she swallowed the poison. . . . To say that there is no causal connection between the acts of appellant and the death of Madge Oberholtzer, and that the treatment accorded her by appellant had no causal connection with the death of Madge Oberholtzer would be a travesty on justice."

The Court concluded, "The evidence was sufficient and justified the jury in finding that appellant by his acts and conduct rendered the deceased distracted and mentally irresponsible, and that such was the natural and probable consequence of such unlawful and criminal treatment, and that the appellant was guilty of murder in the second degree as charged in the first count of the indictment."

The Court's opinion, which was widely publicized, met general but not universal approval. The dissent came not only from Stephenson's few remaining friends but also from well-meaning persons who, while they could recognize murder when the act of killing and death were in immediate relation, could not recognize it where there had been an intervening act of suicide. This is probably the reason why today you can find in Indianapolis people who followed the evidence in the Stephenson case and are ready to argue that, while undoubtedly Stephenson was guilty of a bestial criminal assault and deserved the extreme penalty for that crime, he was not guilty of murder.

III

The Trial of

SAMUEL INSULL
and
OTHERS

for the Use of the

MAILS TO DEFRAUD
(1934)

3

The Samuel Insull Case

THE SIGNIFICANCE *of the Insull case, as one of the out-*
standing causes célèbres *of the last half century, lies not so*
much in its particular facts as in its revelation of the com-
mercial practices of the time which sanctioned or tolerated
most, if not all, of the acts which the government charged
against the defendants as crimes. Even more significant is
the fact that long before the echoes of the resounding crash
of the Insull enterprises had died away there was legislation
on the statute books regulating the issuance of securities,
outlawing holding companies, governing stock exchanges
and, in general, giving assurance to the shorn lambs and the
lambs yet unborn that the same instruments would not be
employed to fleece them again. It is not an exaggeration to
say that the beneficent Federal Securities and Exchange
Act was reared on the ashes of the Insull empire.

OCTOBER of 1929 marked the beginning of the end of
an era in American life—an era in which the pur-
suit of false concepts had built the illusion that the
United States of America was a nation set apart to enjoy
perpetual prosperity and a constantly improving standard
of well-being—"a car in every garage; a chicken in every
pot." Business, undisciplined and unregulated, would go
on to new frontiers and undreamed-of destinies, carrying
with it to affluence all who possessed the wit or the luck to
buy shares in the right enterprises.

Samuel Insull was for thousands the sun-crowned prophet of this incredible age. For Chicago he was, to borrow a phrase, "Aladdin reincarnated."[1] This was the man who in forty short years had taken a conglomeration of small, inefficient electricity-generating plants and, by absorbing all of his competitors, developed the $200,000,000 Commonwealth Edison Company. Here was the man who had taught the world the secret of more and cheaper electric current—100,000-kilowatt turbines instead of 500-kilowatt generating plants; transmission lines that would carry light and power in terms of miles rather than feet. Here was the man who had taken over and rehabilitated the all-but-moribund Peoples Gas Light & Coke Company. Here was the man who supplied the power which ran the streetcars; who controlled the Chicago elevated lines and the electric interurbans entering the city from the north, south and west. Here was the man who had just completed a $20,000,000 setting for the Chicago Civic Opera. Here was the colossus whose restless energy and indomitable will brooked no bounds; whose ever-expanding Public Service Company of Northern Illinois, Midland United Company and Middle West Utilities Company already operated in thirty-nine of the forty-eight states of the Union and bade fair to monopolize the electric-power industry in America.

In the winter of 1928 Insull had organized the first of his two giant investment companies—Insull Utility Investments, Inc. Its stock in eight months went from $30.00 to $147.00 a share. In September of 1929 the second investment company—Corporation Securities Company of Chicago—was launched. The stocks of Corporation Securities Company had been taken at their offering prices and oversubscribed. Within a year there were over $100,000,000 of its securities in the hands of a trustful public. Even November's "Black Friday" and the wiping out of billions of

---

[1] Lloyd Lewis and Henry Justin Smith, *Chicago—The History of Its Reputation* (New York: Harcourt, Brace & Co., 1929).

paper values on the stock exchanges had not weakened the potent magic of the name "Insull."

The story of Insull's struggle to beat the depression was told at his trial. It was valiant but it failed. The end came in 1932. Corporation Securities Company, Insull Utility Investments, Middle West Utilities Company and Midland United Company went into the hands of receivers. Bankruptcy petitions followed. Only the three great operating companies—Commonwealth Edison Company, Peoples Gas Light & Coke Company and Public Service Company of Northern Illinois—escaped. Insull continued as their head and as one of the receivers of Middle West Utilities Company until June 6, when it was given out that he had resigned because of his advanced age and ill health. A few days afterward he sailed for Europe. There was at this time no charge or suggestion of misconduct.

By the end of June the depression had deepened. Every day brought its new batch of failures of old enterprises hitherto considered sound. In Chicago the Foreman National Bank, the twelve "Bain" and a score of other "neighborhood" banks, with deposits aggregating over half a billion dollars, closed never to reopen. The Chicago elevated lines and the Chicago, Aurora & Elgin interurban went into receivership. Companies like Atchison, Topeka & Santa Fe Railroad passed dividends after records of from twenty-five to fifty years of uninterrupted payments. Stocks reached new all-time lows.

America's supposedly indestructible business structure had collapsed. The inevitable investigations followed—investigations to fix on someone the blame for the shattering of a dream of an economic Utopia. Grand juries throughout the nation probed into the affairs of defunct banks to fasten a liability on officers or directors for shady investments, misappropriations of funds or the receiving of deposits while insolvent. A committee of the United

States Senate held public hearings and subpoenaed before it officials of the stock exchanges, economists and unemployed brokers and customers' men to tell of "pools," "pegged prices," "wash sales" and other stock-market manipulations and how far they had contributed to the debacle.

While there were as yet no specific charges against Insull, there was mounting criticism and plenty of gossip. Former employees who had invested complained that the "invitations" to them to buy the Insull stocks had really been commands—"buy or else." Erstwhile beneficiaries of the deposed monarch's bounty revealed that their annual contributions to the perennial Chicago Civic Opera deficits had actually been drafts they had to honor if they wanted to continue in royal favor. The financial editor of a Chicago daily, who in the halcyon days had praised and blessed everything that was Insull, suddenly discovered that holding companies, such as the one Insull had held out to the public as a bank for their savings, while not illegal, were none the less evil snares.

"A holding company," this editor wrote, "can do almost anything short of murder and keep within the law. It can elect its own officers and directors to high-salaried positions in the operating subsidiary. It can milk the latter for dividends that no prudent management would continue to pay. It can use the common stock of the operating company with its inflated and uncertain dividend as a supposedly solid foundation for its own bond issues. It can then use its own common stock still further removed from actuality as the foundation for a bond issue of a still higher holding company. It can take profits on financing deals and on engineering deals that the subsidiary might well do without. . . . This may be making a mountain out of a molehill to some financial minds but to us it is a basic matter of principle to any community that expects to make honesty its touchstone. It is not so much the damage done in the first instance, although that was enough to wreck thousands of lives, as the fact that when such things are done by men high in the life of the city they make it impossible to deal properly with the smaller fry who are more culpable only in degree."

The actual investigations of Insull's affairs began to take form in September. The receivers of Middle West Utilities Company and the two investment companies had engaged a well-known firm of public-utility accountants to examine the books and records of those companies so they might report their true condition to the Court. Specific items of information leaked out in advance of the formal report: The losses of Middle West Utilities security holders would run to over $700,000,000; those of Corporation Securities Company to $85,000,000. There had been a "cross loaning" of collateral between the Insull companies, and illegal preferences had been given to favored creditors. Millions had been taken out of the assets to pay questionable brokerage fees. There had been "secret syndicate lists" and huge secret profits to as many as 1,600 favored participants. Payrolls had been padded and loaded with relatives and friends of Insull.

Nineteen thirty-two was an election year. Franklin D. Roosevelt was the Democratic candidate for President. Among his other numerous pre-election pledges, he promised drastic new curbs on corporations—particularly holding companies—new legislation to insure full publicity as to the exact nature of security issues and regulation of the stock exchanges. In Chicago, John Swanson, the state's attorney of Cook County, was a candidate for re-election. He was quick to take advantage of the hue and cry against Insull and share in the front-page publicity. He appointed a staff of assistants to co-operate with the receivers in their investigations and to study the applicability of existing state criminal laws to the anticipated evidence of wrong doing. There had possibly, declared Swanson, been violations of the Illinois "Blue Sky" law; it was not impossible that the completed investigations would show huge embezzlements. The evidence in due time would be presented to a grand jury.

On September 23 the receivers disclosed the much publicized "secret syndicate list." It made the headlines. Insull had allowed his friends—social and political—to "get in" on Insull Utility Investments common stock at $12.00. It opened on the exchange at $30.00 and went on up to nearly $150.00. Two hundred and fifty thousand shares had been thus distributed. Selling at the opening price, the favored ones would have "cleaned up" $4,500,000. Among the favorites was one of Insull's old friends who had been appointed a receiver for Insull Utility Investments, and another who held a similar appointment in the Corporation Securities Company receivership. Both were removed by the Court.

On September 25 United States Attorney Green announced that the Federal Department of Justice had commenced a full-scale investigation into the affairs of the Insull companies.

On October 4, 1932, a Cook County grand jury returned indictments against Samuel Insull and Martin Insull (Samuel Insull's brother), charging them with embezzlements from Middle West Utilities Company and Mississippi Valley Utilities Investment Company.

On February 27, 1933, a Federal grand jury at Chicago returned an indictment against Samuel Insull and sixteen others, charging them jointly with a violation of Section 338[2] of the United States Criminal Code (using the United States mails to further a scheme to defraud). Included with Insull as codefendants were his son, Samuel Insull, Jr., Harold L. Stuart, eight others who had been either directors, officers or employees of Halsey, Stuart & Company or Cor-

---

2 Section 338 provides a penalty for its violation of a fine of one thousand dollars or imprisonment for not more than five years, or both.

poration Securities Company of Chicago, four who had been officers or employees of Utility Securities Company (an Insull security-selling organization), and an attorney and a certified public accountant who had approved the stock-offering circulars and annual reports of Corporation Securities Company.

A second indictment was returned on June 1, 1933, against Samuel Insull, Samuel Insull, Jr., and Harold L. Stuart, charging them with having, in contemplation of bankruptcy, illegally transferred property of Corporation Securities Company with intent to defeat the purpose of the National Bankruptcy Act and to prefer selected creditors in the distribution of the assets of the anticipated bankrupt.[3]

Insull, with his wife, was living quietly and inexpensively in Paris when he learned of the investigations and the efforts that were being made to indict him. Some Chicago attorneys, with whom he had long been associated, advised him to establish a domicile in Greece, which they said had no extradition treaty with the United States. Unwilling, as he later testified, to be crucified in a political campaign, Insull followed this advice, going first to Turin, Italy, and then to Athens.

He successfully resisted extradition proceedings and, despite the ever-increasing pressure of the United States upon the Greek government, remained unmolested and at liberty until December 5, 1933. On that date he was peremptorily ordered to leave the country not later than January 1, 1934. By successive modifications the date of the order of expulsion was extended, because of Insull's ill health, to March 15. On that day Insull disappeared.

The Greek government had not anticipated a secret departure and at once set afoot an inquiry to discover the

---

[3] Section 29 (b), Clause 6, National Bankruptcy Act, as amended (Title 11, Sec. 52 [b], Clause 6, U.S.C.A.). The penalty prescribed for violation of the section was a fine of not more than five thousand dollars or imprisonment for not more than five years, or both.

fugitive's whereabouts. All vessels which had sailed from Greek ports on the fourteenth and fifteenth were radioed to report a list of their passengers. Promptly the proprietors of a small Greek steamship line reported that Insull was a passenger aboard one of their ships—the *Maiotis*—bound for Egypt; that his papers were in order; and that he had left without notifying the authorities to avoid unnecessary publicity. The captain was ordered to return to port (Piraeus). He immediately complied. The ship's and Insull's papers were examined and found to be in order, and after six hours' detention the *Maiotis* with its passengers was permitted to resume its voyage.

The press flashed daily rumors of wireless negotiations between Insull and the Mediterranean countries—Egypt, French Somaliland, Ethiopia, Yugoslavia, Albania, Rumania and Turkey—for permission to land and establish residence. On March 22—a week after Insull's departure from Greece—the State Department had rushed a bill through both houses of Congress giving the United States government the right to arrest Insull in any country in which by treaty it had extraterritorial rights.

On March 29 the *Maiotis* put into Istanbul harbor for provisions. The United States ambassador, on direct orders from the State Department, demanded of the Turkish government that it arrest Insull. Although the extradition treaty with Turkey, adopted by the United States February 21, 1933, had not yet been ratified by the Turkish government, the latter promptly acceded to the demand and ordered Insull taken into custody. Extradition proceedings were hastily instituted. After a hearing lasting less than twenty minutes, Insull's extradition was ordered. The trial Court ruled that its order was unappealable, and on April 11 Insull, under heavy guard, was put aboard a Turkish ship from which he was shortly transferred to the American Export liner, the S.S. *Exilona*, bound for New York.

The *Exilona* docked at New York on May 8. Insull was

rushed to a Chicago-bound train and twenty hours later
was a prisoner in the Cook County jail. His bail on the
Federal charges was fixed at $200,000; on the state charges,
at $50,000. Sureties for the required amounts were pro-
cured, and on May 12 he was released.

Before entering St. Luke's Hospital for needed medical
treatment Insull made a brief statement to the press which
foreshadowed his defense to the accumulated charges
against him. He said: "I have erred but my greatest error
was in underestimating the effects of the financial panic
on American securities and particularly on the companies
I was trying to build. I worked with all of my energy to
save those companies. I made mistakes, but they were honest mistakes. They were errors in judgment and not dis-
honest manipulations."

The case of the United States of America *v.* Samuel Insull, *et al.,* for using the United States mails to defraud,
came on for trial October 2, 1934, before the Honorable
James H. Wilkerson. Judge Wilkerson's exceptional experience made him the ideal judge for this particular case.
He had served a term as United States attorney. In practice
he had defended some important criminal cases. Four years
as chairman of the Illinois Commerce Commission had
given him detailed practical knowledge of corporate organization, financing and management. In fourteen years' previous service on the Federal district bench he had tried
many important civil and criminal cases and acquired an
enviable reputation for integrity, ability, judicial poise and
impartiality.

Appearing for the Government were Leslie Salter and
Forest A. Harness, special assistants to the Attorney General
of the United States; the Honorable Dwight H. Green,
United States attorney for the northern district of Illinois;
and his first assistant, Leo J. Hassenauer. Salter and Harness had tried many cases for the government, among them

some prosecutions for violation of the Mail Fraud Statute.

The defendants, Samuel Insull and Samuel Insull, Jr., were represented by Floyd E. Thompson. Judge Thompson had completed a nine-year term as a justice of the Supreme Court of Illinois in 1928, when he retired to enter private practice. Earlier he had served for seven years as state's attorney of Rock Island County, Illinois. He specialized in trial work and was a sincere, able and effective advocate. His representation of the two principal defendants naturally threw on his shoulders the burden of the defense.

Appearing for the other defendants were Harry S. Ditchburne and Charles E. Lounsbury, John J. Healy, Frederick Burnham, James J. Condon, J. Fred Reeve and William H. Haight. Ditchburne and Lounsbury, who represented the defendants Harold L. and Charles B. Stuart, were able and experienced lawyers with extensive previous experience in the trial of criminal cases. Healy, Burnham, Condon, Reeve and Haight were all conscientious, alert and competent advocates.

A jury of twelve with two alternates was promptly selected. In residence they were about equally divided between Cook County (the Chicago metropolitan area) and the adjacent counties in the northern Federal district. Five were salesmen; two, retail grain dealers; one, a grocer; one, a farmer; one, a garage proprietor; one, a bookbinder; and one, a heating engineer. Two were unemployed.

The United States attorney for the northern district of Illinois, the Honorable Dwight H. Green, opened for the prosecution. The defendants, he said, were charged with an unlawful use of the United States mails—unlawful because the use was for the purpose of perpetrating a fraud.

Green read at length from the fifty-page, twenty-five-count indictment. Stripped of its repetitious verbiage, it charged that the defendants had devised a fraudulent scheme whereby, through false pretenses, representations and promises, they intended to and did defraud divers persons of their money and property by inducing them to buy at inflated prices the common stock of Corporations Securities Company of Chicago, an Illinois corporation, organized and controlled by the Insulls and Halsey, Stuart & Company. The scheme, it was alleged, contemplated a nationwide sales campaign through the medium of circulars, letters, telegrams, booklets, bulletins and oral representations, to be put out by the Insull-dominated Utility Securities Company, Corporation Syndicates, Insull, Son & Company, and selling and distributing groups named and organized by Utility Securities Company.

It was also charged that as part of their scheme to mislead and deceive prospective purchasers as to the true value of the common stock and to maintain a fictitious market for it, the defendants bought and sold large quantities of it on the Chicago Stock Exchange at inflated and fictitious prices and, for that purpose, used the funds of Corporation Securities Company of Chicago, Utility Securities Company, Middle West Utilities Company, and other Insull-controlled companies. The concluding charge was that, having devised this fraudulent scheme, the defendants, for the purpose of executing it, had used the United States mails to send letters and circulars to the persons whose money and property they proposed to obtain through their false pretenses, misrepresentations and promises. The twenty-five counts of the indictment were identical except for the allegations as to the matter mailed and the recipient.

Green then proceeded for the remainder of two hours to outline the specific evidence the Government expected to produce. He led the jurors through a bewildering maze of corporate names—operating companies, holding companies, investment companies, investment trusts, selling companies, syndicates, participating groups, stock-transfer agents, dividend disbursing agents, voting trustees—and a jumble of boxcar figures—a million shares of stock that went to Insull, a million more that went to H. L. Stuart, fifty million dollars here and fifty million dollars there—with market quotations, book values, estimates of liquidating value, bank loans of more millions, etc.

When Green had finished this confusing recital, the twelve good men and true had probably, because of its constant reiteration, grasped at least the Government's central theme—that some thousands of persons, among them schoolteachers, stenographers, clerks, janitors, elevatormen, and other "little people"—had been swindled out of over a hundred million dollars by the criminal machinations of a crowd of rapacious and ruthless stock-manipulating buccaneers, who had prostituted the United States mails for the accomplishment of their nefarious designs.

Over the protest of Special Assistant Attorney General Salter, who practically took over the prosecution of the case from this point, the defendants were permitted to reserve their opening statements until after the conclusion of the Government's evidence.

In rapid succession the Government called some eighty witnesses—receivers, receivers' employees, former employees of the bankrupt Insull companies, present and former employees of Halsey, Stuart & Company, representatives of Chicago and New York banks and brokerage houses—to identify books, records and correspondence deemed pertinent to establish its charges. These, when authenticated and received in evidence, became the basis for the testimony of a half-dozen expert accountants in the Bureau of Investigation of the Department of Justice that they had spent upward of two years fine-tooth-combing the documents so that they might produce and present to the jury summaries and charts to prove the guilt of the defendants.

Fifty or more witnesses, summoned from all parts of the United States, appeared and testified to their solicitation by agents of Halsey, Stuart & Company, Corporation Securities Company of Chicago, Utility Securities Company and others to buy the stock of Corporation Securities Company of Chicago, of their receipt of circulars, bulletins and letters, and of their reliance on these and oral representations made to them, which induced them to exchange their money for the engraved stock certificates which most of them still held.

Most of the *basic* facts produced by the Government—those going to the alleged existence of a scheme to defraud—were indisputable. They rested on public and corporate records and reports, circulars, contracts, letters and memoranda in the files of banks, brokerage houses, Halsey, Stuart & Company and the various Insull companies. The conflict between the Government and the defendants arose out of the constructions properly to be placed on those basic facts.

It will simplify this account to disregard the actual order of proof and present first these indisputable basic facts.

Samuel Insull for many years prior to June 6, 1932, had been the directing head of Commonwealth Edison Company and Peoples Gas Light & Coke Company, public utilities supplying electricity and gas to the city of Chicago, and Public Service Company of Northern Illinois, which supplied both electricity and gas to numerous municipalities and industries in the northern half of Illinois outside Chicago. He was chairman of the board of directors and a heavy stockholder in each of these corporations. All of the companies enjoyed complete monopolies in the territories they served and, through Insull's industry and admitted genius as a utility operator, had long before the great depression been developed into highly efficient organizations with premier credit, outstanding records of good customer and employee relations, and regular and liberal dividends to stockholders.

In the early part of the century, Insull also acquired sole or controlling interests in a number of small gas and electric properties in southern Indiana. As time went on, numerous other out-of-Chicago properties were purchased.

THE "INSULL EMPIRE"*

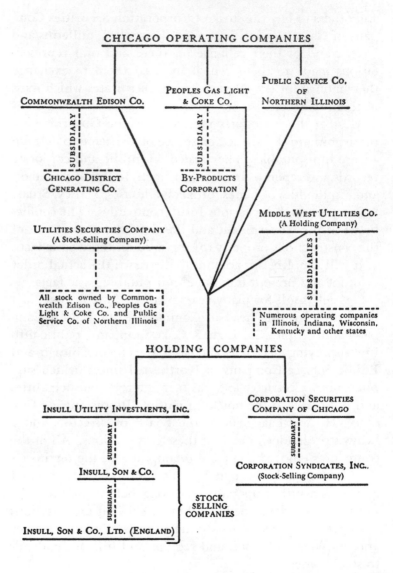

CHICAGO OPERATING COMPANIES

COMMONWEALTH EDISON CO.

PEOPLES GAS LIGHT & COKE CO.

PUBLIC SERVICE CO. OF NORTHERN ILLINOIS

SUBSIDIARY

CHICAGO DISTRICT GENERATING CO.

BY-PRODUCTS CORPORATION

MIDDLE WEST UTILITIES CO. (A Holding Company)

UTILITIES SECURITIES COMPANY (A Stock-Selling Company)

SUBSIDIARIES

All stock owned by Commonwealth Edison Co., Peoples Gas Light & Coke Co. and Public Service Co. of Northern Illinois

Numerous operating companies in Illinois, Indiana, Wisconsin, Kentucky and other states

HOLDING COMPANIES

INSULL UTILITY INVESTMENTS, INC.

CORPORATION SECURITIES COMPANY OF CHICAGO

SUBSIDIARY

INSULL, SON & CO.

CORPORATION SYNDICATES, INC. (Stock-Selling Company)

SUBSIDIARY

STOCK SELLING COMPANIES

INSULL, SON & CO., LTD. (ENGLAND)

* Chart does not include numerous other corporations which did not figure in the trial.

While separately managed, all of these were directed and a common policy was determined by Insull himself. The new uses and increasing demands for electrical power necessitated an almost continuous flow of new capital for the enlargement of these plants. According to Insull's later testimony, it was to meet this demand and acquire and develop other desirable properties that in 1912 he organized Middle West Utilities Company as a holding company in which to centralize these scattered properties. The expansion of Middle West Utilities Company during the ensuing twenty years was astonishing. By 1931 it served over 1,800,-000 customers in some 5,300 communities in thirty-nine out of the forty-eight states of the Union.

Shortly after the World War I armistice, Insull formulated plans for selling the stock of the three operating companies under his direct management (Commonwealth Edison Company, Peoples Gas Light & Coke Company and Public Service Company of Northern Illinois) to their customers and employees. The reason, according to his uncontradicted testimony, was to create a bulwark of popular opposition to a mounting sentiment for municipal and government ownership of public utilities.

The first step was the organization of a stock-sales department in Public Service Company of Northern Illinois. That company purchased its stock on the market and offered it for sale for cash or on easy installment terms. Regular employees of the company acted as solicitors and salesmen. The plan was soon extended to Peoples Gas Light & Coke Company and Commonwealth Edison Company.

In 1922 it was determined to remove these activities from the operating companies and concentrate them in a central agency, and Utility Securities Company was organized. All of the stock in this company was originally owned by Commonwealth Edison Company, Peoples Gas Light & Coke Company and Public Service Company of Northern Illinois. There were no individual stockholders, but the alleged activities of the officers of Utility Securities Company (several of whom were codefendants) loomed large in the Government's case.

In December of 1928 Insull organized Insull Utility Investments, Inc. Upon its organization, the Insull family—Samuel, Mrs. Samuel, Samuel, Jr., and Martin—turned over to it securities of Insull operating companies on which they placed a value—which was market value—of $9,765,000 and received in exchange 764,000 shares of the common and 40,000 shares of the preferred stock of Insull Utility Investments. Coincident with the exchange, Samuel Insull obtained an option to purchase 200,000 additional shares of the common stock at fifteen dollars a share. (This option was later exercised to his profit). Halsey, Stuart & Company exchanged at the same ratio Insull operating companies' securities (which it acquired from the Insull family for cash at its market value—approximately $4,500,-000) for common and preferred stock of Insull Utility Investments.

The Government made much of the fact that the Insull family's entire accumulation of Insull operating stocks represented a cost to it of $5,400,000; that when the family sold part of that accumulation to Halsey, Stuart & Company for $4,500,000 cash, it left its investment in the remainder something less than $1,000,000, which made the cost of the 764,-000 shares of Insull Utility Investments common which they received about thirteen cents a share.

Although at organization Insull Utility Investments common had a book value of $7.54, it sold on the Chicago Stock Exchange when listed for $30.00 a share. While its book value steadily increased through additional acquisitions and the market increase of the securities in its portfolio, the market on Insull Utility Investments consistently outran its book value. On August 2, 1929, it reached an all-time high of $147.00 a share. On October 4, 1929, when

Corporation Securities Company of Chicago was organized, it was selling on the Chicago Stock Exchange at $100.00 a share.

In the summer of 1929 Insull and Harold L. Stuart of Halsey, Stuart & Company conceived the idea of organizing still another investment company. The Government contended strenuously from first to last that the object of this second investment company was to provide a "dumping ground" for Middle West Utilities Company securities. That company, it contended, was proving a "white elephant." It was not earning enough to continue the payment of cash dividends on its common stock. Some of its senior securities bore excessively high rates of interest—six, seven and eight per cent. A reorganization was imperative and a controlled outlet for its stock necessary.

While these claims were denied by the defendants, the fact was undisputed that in June of 1929 Halsey, Stuart & Company, for the joint account of itself and Insull, commenced the accumulation through market purchases of a large quantity of Middle West Utilities Company stock.

The Government linked the reorganization of Middle West Utilities Company with these purchases by Halsey, Stuart & Company and Insull of Middle West Utilities stock and the later formation of Corporation Securities Company of Chicago in this wise: The Middle West Utilities Company's plan of reorganization, put forth in the summer of 1929, provided for the issuance of "rights" to the holders of the old common shares to subscribe to a new common stock at $200.00 a share. The outstanding notes and bonds bearing high interest rates were to be retired. New senior securities were to be issued at much lower rates. The new common stock (to be immediately split ten shares for one) was to be put on a regular stock-dividend basis so as to insure the retention by the company of its earnings to meet the constantly demanded improvement and extension of the company's properties. When the reorganization plan was published the old common stock was selling on the market for around $170.00 a share.

According to the Government's contention, stockholders could not under such a circumstance be expected to buy the new stock at $200.00 a share and Insull and his principal codefendants knew it. And so, said the Government, to make the new stock attractive and insure the success of the reorganization, Insull and Stuart began the accumulation of Middle West Utilities Company common to "run up the price." The price did go up—from $170.00 to $310.00 at the end of July when they had accumulated nearly $13,000,000 of the stock and ceased buying. Even then it didn't stop. On September 27, 1929, it reached $505.00.

There was an additional incident to the reorganization of Middle West Utilities of which the Government attempted to make much. This was a so-called "secret" or "preferred" syndicate list. The undisputed facts were that on August 17, 1929, about a month prior to the formal publication of the recapitalization proposal of Middle West Utilities Company, that company entered into an agreement with Insull, Son & Company (the stock of which was wholly owned by Insull Utility Investments, Inc.) by which Insull, Son & Company, for a consideration of $1,875,000, agreed to underwrite the subscription and payment of all of the new stock to be offered. Insull Utility Investments, Inc., guaranteed Insull, Son & Company's performance.

Insull, Son & Company thereafter entered into a so-called "Middle West Preferred and Common Stock Syndicate Agreement" with some 300 persons to participate in specific amounts and share proportionately in the risk and profit, if any, that might result from such underwriting. Insull's agreed participation was $2,600,000; Halsey, Stuart & Company's was $2,500,000; Samuel Insull, Jr., subscribed for something over $1,000,000. Other defendants were subscribers for smaller amounts.

The syndicate participants were called on to pay in cash six per cent of their respective subscriptions. The stock which remained unsold (not taken up by the common stockholders or sold to the public), amounting to $18,600,-000, was later sold, one half to Insull Utility Investments, Inc., and one half to Corporation Securities Company of Chicago, the new investment company. When the syndicate[4] was wound up in January of 1930, each of the syndicate subscribers was returned the amount he had advanced on his subscription, together with a "profit" of approximately twenty-five per cent of that sum. That profit to Samuel Insull, Sr., and Halsey, Stuart & Company was about $35,000 each.

Corporation Securities Company of Chicago, organized October 4, 1929, was a consolidation of two corporations: Corporation Securities Company (a more or less dormant corporation, all of the stock of which was owned by Halsey, Stuart & Company) and Western Securities Company (a recently organized company, all of the stock of which was owned by Samuel Insull, his wife, son and brother Martin). Halsey, Stuart & Company turned in to Corporation Securities Company (referred to in the testimony as Old Corp.) 152,270 shares of stock of Insull Utility Investments, Inc., for which it had paid approximately $3,400,000. Simultaneously, Old Corp. borrowed $3,500,000 from a Chicago bank on a note guaranteed by Halsey, Stuart & Company, and paid Halsey, Stuart & Company $3,400,000 for the Insull Utility Investments stock which it had received from it.

The Insulls had turned in to Western Securities Company in exchange for its stock 152,270 shares of stock of Insull Utility Investments. In the consolidation all outstanding shares of Old Corp. and Western Securities Com-

---

4 This is to be distinguished from the Insull Utility Investments syndicate earlier referred to. The Government offered no evidence with respect to that syndicate.

pany were surrendered to Corporation Securities Company of Chicago (referred to in the testimony as New Corp.) and canceled. New Corp. after the consolidation thus had as assets 304,540 shares of Insull Utility Investments common stock. It assumed the total liabilities of the old corporations, amounting to some $3,510,000.

Of the 7,000,000 shares of authorized common stock of the new corporation, 1,000,000 shares were issued to Halsey, Stuart & Company and 1,045,436 shares to the Insulls. The Insulls also received 45,436 shares of so-called three-dollar optional preferred stock. The greater number of shares issued to the Insulls was to balance the $3,400,000 paid out of the bank loan to Halsey, Stuart & Company, the intent being that the investments of the Insulls and Halsey, Stuart & Company in the new corporation should be equal. With the object of insuring continuing control of the new corporation, 1,000,000 shares of its common stock owned by the Insulls and a similar amount owned by Halsey, Stuart & Company interests were placed in a voting trust of which Samuel Insull, Samuel Insull, Jr., Martin J. Insull and Harold L. Stuart were trustees.

When the organization of Corporation Securities Company of Chicago was completed, Halsey, Stuart & Company had on hand some 557,000 shares of the new common stock of Middle West Utilities Company which it had acquired for the joint account of itself and the Insulls at a cost of $12,700,000. On October 14, 1929, ten days after its organization, Corporation Securities Company of Chicago recorded on its books the purchase from Halsey, Stuart & Company of this stock and accrued rights for $13,444,000, and its liability to pay Halsey, Stuart & Company that amount. The stock thus acquired was given a value on the new company's books of approximately $23,000,000, which represented its market value on October 14, 1929.

The Insull Utility Investments stock in the new company's portfolio, acquired from the Insulls and from Hal-

sey, Stuart & Company, was given a value on its books of
$30,000,000, which represented its market value on Oc-
tober 4, 1929.

In addition to being chairman of the board of directors
of Commonwealth Edison Company, Peoples Gas Light &
Coke Company and Public Service Company of Northern
Illinois, Samuel Insull was an officer or director (or both)
of Middle West Utilities Company, Insull Utility Investments, Inc., and Corporation Securities Company of Chicago. The affairs of Insull Utility Investments were directed by a small finance committee, those of Corporation
Securities Company of Chicago by a small executive committee, and Insull was the chairman of both committees.
Through the offices he held, or through his nominees, Insull also dominated Utility Securities Company, Insull,
Son & Company and Corporation Syndicates, Inc. (to which
reference will later be made). It was the Government's
contention that the numerous intercompany dealings of
which it complained were made possible solely by this in-
terlocking of the Insull interests.

The Government's expert accountants testified and attempted to demonstrate by exhibits that, by the manipulations it described, Halsey, Stuart & Company and the Insulls
got two million shares of the common stock of Corporation
Securities Company of Chicago for practically nothing;
that Corporation Securities Company of Chicago, through
Insull and Stuart, later sold similar common shares to the
public at twenty-five dollars a share; and had their scheme
not miscarried, Halsey, Stuart & Company and the Insulls
would have reaped a profit on their common stock of
$50,000,000.

The object of Corporation Securities Company of Chicago, according to the defendants' later testimony, was the
acquisition for their income and appreciation of sufficient
quantities of the stocks and securities of the Insull operating companies to insure their continued control by the In-

sull interests. In the Government's view the object was to provide a receptacle for and to protect the market on Middle West Utilities Company stock. The accomplishment of either object required money—vast amounts of it. The company immediately set about to raise that money. Within a year following its organization it offered and sold approximately 635,000 participation certificates or units (one share of preferred and one share of common stock), 1,250,-000 additional shares of common stock and $30,000,000 of interest-bearing "serial gold notes." The proceeds of these sales aggregated something over $110,000,000. It was the sale of the units and common stock which the Government contended was induced by fraudulent representations and concealments of the true financial condition of Corporation Securities Company of Chicago.

Pursuant to the recommendation of its executive committee Corporation Securities Company of Chicago, on October 19, 1929, announced the offering of 700,000[5] participation certificates or units at seventy-five dollars per unit. The preferred stock, while without par value, was given a preference in assets upon liquidation of fifty dollars a share. This gave the common stock an assumed value of twenty-five dollars a share. The preferred stock was designated a "three dollar optional preferred" because the holder had the option, if he cared to exercise it, of taking in lieu of cash a specific amount of common stock as a stock dividend.

While protesting that it was not selling the units and was not interested in their sale (its traditional business being the underwriting and sale of municipal and corporate bonds and notes) Halsey, Stuart & Company practically turned over its gigantic sales organization to Corporation Securities Company of Chicago. The two companies at the

---

[5] Approximately 65,000 of these either went to the Insulls in the original organization of Corporation Securities Company of Chicago or were purchased by officers and employees of Halsey, Stuart & Company.

time occupied the same offices. The sales branches of Halsey, Stuart & Company in the various cities of the United States were asked to furnish lists of former customers of Halsey, Stuart & Company who might be interested in the purchase of the units.

On October 19 and October 21 Halsey, Stuart & Company distributed bulletins to its salesmen, advising them that letters had been mailed to the persons whose names had been suggested inviting their subscription to Corporation Securities Company of Chicago units, and enclosing a circular which described the nature and purpose of the new offering. The bulletins directed the salesmen to get in touch with the selected customers and tell them that they might, due to Halsey, Stuart & Company's suggestion, receive an invitation to subscribe to the units; that Halsey, Stuart & Company made no recommendation and had no interest in whether they bought or not but wanted to let them know that the new corporation was jointly controlled by Halsey, Stuart & Company and the Insulls, and that Halsey, Stuart & Company had a major interest in the enterprise. It was stressed that subscriptions should be sent directly to Corporation Securities Company of Chicago.

Coincident with the above offering and mailings, and continuing until November 4 when the issue had been fully subscribed, Corporation Securities Company of Chicago, through the defendant Harold L. Stuart, bought and sold on the open-market exchanges approximately 62,000 of the units, which constituted eighty-three per cent of all of the open trading in them. The market price range during the period was from $65.00 to $100.00. The Government contended this was "market rigging" designed as part of the scheme to deceive and defraud investors.

Halsey, Stuart & Company's salesmen promptly got in touch with their customers to whom the offering literature had been sent. The Government produced many of these customers as witnesses who testified that these salesmen went far beyond the injunctions contained in the Halsey, Stuart & Company bulletins. According to their testimony this is what they were told by the salesmen: Get your subscriptions in while there is still time. The units are selling on the exchange at ten, fifteen or twenty points above the subscription price. The issue is bound to be oversubscribed, and if you want twenty-five shares you had better subscribe for a hundred. Everything Insull has ever touched has turned to gold. Halsey, Stuart & Company are in this and they would not be in it if it wasn't good. These units are "a fine," "a good," "a safe," "a sound" and "an interest-paying" investment. One witness, a former Halsey, Stuart & Company salesman, testified that he was told by one of his superiors in Chicago that the securities held and to be held by the Corporation Securities Company constituted "the jewels of the Insull empire."

The issue was oversubscribed by 125,000 units. Corporation Securities Company received approximately $46,000,000 as the proceeds of the sale. Halsey, Stuart & Company received for its services in aid of the sale one per cent of the issue, or 7,000 units.

The Government next directed its proof to establish that the sale of the units was effected through the fraudulent representations and concealments of the defendants. The circular that was mailed out by Halsey, Stuart & Company in connection with the subscription invitation came in for particular attack. The Government's witnesses claimed that the statement in the circular that the company would commence business with assets of $80,000,000—$30,000,000 cash and $50,000,000 in marketable investments at current market prices—was false and deceptive; that the company had been organized and commenced business on October 4, 1929 (which was nowhere stated) and at that time had nothing except 304,000 shares of Insull Utility Investments that had cost it $7,000,000 and a liability on an outstanding bank loan of $3,500,000.

In order to get its figure of $80,000,000, the accountants for the prosecution pointed out, the company had written up those 304,000 shares on the company's books to $30,400,000 and had written up the value of the 557,000 shares of Middle West Utilities Company stock from the $13,000,000, at which it had contracted to purchase it, to $23,000,000, and had figured as cash the amount it expected to receive from the sale of the units. The circular, the witnesses said, concealed the fact that the vast bulk of the Middle West Utilities stock which the company had committed itself to purchase was common stock which paid a stock rather than a cash dividend.

The Government's witnesses testified that the statements that Corporation Securities Company had $50,000,000 of marketable securities of companies whose resources were directly or indirectly in the public-utility industry were false because neither Insull Utility Investments nor Middle West Utilities Company shares fell truthfully within such a classification. They also contended that the statement in the circular that 2,000,000 of the 2,700,000 shares of common stock outstanding would be owned by members of the board of directors or institutions with which they were connected, and placed in a voting trust, was deceptive because by it the prospective investor was led to believe that the organizers of Corporation Securities Company of Chicago had contributed $50,000,000 to the company, whereas the concealed fact was that the stock had cost them practically nothing.

The oral representations made by the Halsey, Stuart & Company salesmen, for which the Government claimed the defendants were responsible, that an investment in the units was "good," "safe," "sound" and "interest-paying" were, the Government's accountants said, palpably false: With 700,000 shares of prior preferred outstanding, which required an annual cash outlay of $2,100,000 to pay its dividend, and a portfolio heavily loaded and to be more heavily loaded with Middle West Utilities common stock which paid no cash dividends, Corporation Securities Company's common stock was anything but a good, safe, sound and interest-paying investment.

The effect of the Government's direct testimony as to the alleged misrepresentations in the circular was seriously impaired by the skillful cross-examination of its principal witness by Lounsbury, one of the counsel for the Halsey, Stuart & Company officers who were defendants. Through clearly stated leading questions requiring categorical answers, it was developed that the "write-up" of the Insull Utility Investments stock which went into the portfolio of the new company was at its current market price; similarly, that on October 14, 1929, when the company entered into the contract with Halsey, Stuart & Company to purchase the 557,000 shares of Middle West Utilities Company stock which had been accumulated the previous summer, it too was charged on the books at a figure exactly the equivalent to the aggregate per-share price quoted on the open market.

The witness was also compelled to admit that in prevailing commercial practice it was customary, in the case of new stock offerings, to issue circulars which represented the financial status of the offering company as of the date of the completion of the proposed financing, and in the case of Corporation Securities Company after the units had been sold and the company actually commenced doing business, it would and did have more than $30,000,000 cash in hand and something over $50,000,000 in listed securities figured at their market value. It was also brought out in the cross-examination that all of the officers of Halsey, Stuart & Company who were defendants had voluntarily made sizable purchases of the units at their offered price because they believed they were a sound investment, and had held the stock to the end and taken large losses.

As against the defendant Samuel Insull, the Government

produced testimony that in December 1929 he exercised the option he had previously taken to buy 200,000 shares of Insull Utility Investments common at fifteen dollars a share, and within a week sold 42,000 of them to Corporation Securities Company at forty dollars a share, thus realizing a profit on the partial sale of over one million dollars.

The Government presented a great deal of testimony respecting Corporation Securities Company's first annual report—the three months' operations ending December 31, 1929. It stressed the fact that there were eight drafts of it made before it met with the approval of the officers and directors and went to the printer in its final form. It was shown that the first draft disclosed a net loss for the three months' operations of $174,000, and the final draft represented that there was a net profit of $630,000. To arrive at this alleged profit the company had in the final draft erroneously taken and considered as cash earnings the stock dividends it had received or which had been declared on Middle West Utilities Company common stock in its portfolio at the market value of the stock. Only nineteen per cent of the securities in the company's portfolio paid cash dividends. The company had also, according to the Government's testimony, charged to earned surplus rather than against current earnings an "organization expense," and the report nowhere disclosed the fact that this reorganization expense was nearly one million dollars. It was the Government's contention, supported by highly competent expert testimony, that under proper and generally accepted accounting practice, stock dividends, until sold and realized on, were in no sense income.

As to "organization expense," it was the Government's contention that under proper and generally accepted accounting practice, it should be charged against the income or earned surplus account to the extent of the capacity of those accounts to absorb the charge and the excess charged against capital surplus. It was the Government's claim that with the stock dividends eliminated as current receipts, and "organization expense" included with current expenses, the result of the first three months of Corporation Securities Company's operations was a deficit of $500,000 or $600,000.

The Government produced testimony to support its contention that the 1929 annual report was false and deceptive in other respects. The report stated: " . . . so far, however, the activities of Corporation Securities Company of Chicago have been confined to the purchase for investment of substantial blocks of stock in the following companies: Middle West Utilities Company, Insull Utility Investments, Commonwealth Edison Company, Peoples Gas Light & Coke Company and Public Service Company of Northern Illinois." This the Government said was deceptive because ninety per cent of the stocks it held were Middle West Utilities Company and Insull Utility Investments, and the remaining ten per cent of its holdings, divided among Commonwealth Edison Company, Peoples Gas Light & Coke Company and Public Service Company of Northern Illinois, did not justify the use of the adjective "substantial" as applied to these companies.

As was the case with the offering circular, this direct testimony was shaken by intelligent and skillful cross-examination. This time the examining advocate was Judge Thompson, counsel for the Insulls. One of the Government's principal witnesses was compelled to admit that recognized authorities on accounting, one of whom was a professor of accounting at the University of Michigan and author of a widely used text book and manual on accounting practice, considered organization expense as an intangible asset of a permanent character, which might have substantial value. The witness also admitted that the Federal government, for income-tax purposes, treated organization expense not as a charge against current revenue or current loss, but as a permanent asset.

From another of the Government's witnesses came the reluctant admission, which went both to the question of the proper treatment of stock dividends and organization expense, that while he believed his testimony as to the proper accounting practices accorded with the weight of opinion held by reputable accountants, he recognized that contrary views were held by others and the questions were controversial. The way was thus cleared for later affirmative defense to these two vital elements of the Government's case.

The Government's evidence showed that on March 31, 1930, Corporation Securities Company, by resolution of its board of directors, who were defendants, authorized the offering to the public of 1,250,000 shares of its common stock. On the same day it accepted the written proposal of Insull, Son & Company and Corporation Syndicates, Inc. (a wholly owned subsidiary of Corporation Securities Company) to purchase the 1,250,000 shares at $25.00 a share. The offer was conditioned on Corporation Securities Company listing the stock on the Chicago Stock Exchange. Also, on the same day, Insull, Son & Company and Corporation Syndicates, Inc., entered into a contract with Utility Securities Company by which they agreed to sell and Utility Securities Company agreed, subject to the above condition, to buy the 1,250,000 shares at $25.50 a share. Utility Securities Company further agreed to "maintain a market" on the common stock between $27.00 and $28.00, and on the units between $69.50 and $70.00. It was the Government's claim that these simultaneously executed deals gave Insull, Son & Company an unearned profit at the expense of Corporation Securities Company of $300,000.

Utility Securities Company immediately entered into participation agreements with other stock-selling houses to underwrite parts of the 1,250,000-share offering. There were 398 such participants with main or branch offices in the principal cities of twenty-one different states. The stock was listed on the Chicago Stock Exchange, pursuant to Corporation Securities Company's undertaking, on April 3 and trading in it commenced the following day.

An offering circular and a number of form letters were prepared by Corporation Securities Company and Utility Securities Company and distributed to salesmen and prospective investors. The Government's proof was directed to showing that these were fraudulent and deceptive because of their misrepresentations and concealments. Particularly it was contended that the circular, which contained an estimate of 1930 earnings, misrepresented the company's anticipated income as $7,100,000, of which $2,200,000 would be required for dividends on the outstanding preferred stock, leaving $4,900,000, or $1.42 as net earnings per share for the common stock. The truth, said one of the Government's witnesses, was the company would not have had an income of $7,100,000 because $6,000,000 of that figure represented not cash but stock dividends on Middle West Utilities Company and Insull Utility Investments common stock; and, while the circular did state that stock dividends were taken as income at market, it nowhere stated that these dividends constituted six sevenths of the company's estimated income and that the company was operating and would continue to operate at a cash loss.

Other form and individual letters issued by Utility Securities Company in what the Government styled a "high pressure" stock-selling campaign contained much that was claimed to be false and deceptive: Statements that Corporation Securities Company held *substantial* blocks of Middle West Utilities Company, Insull Utility Investments, Commonwealth Edison Company, Peoples Gas Light & Coke Company and Public Service Company of Northern Illinois stocks; that the stock of Corporation Securities Company offered the investor a means of diversifying his investments and sharing in the growth and prosperity of the nation's largest group of public utilities, again mentioning, together with Middle West Utilities Company and Insull Utility Investments, the three well-known operating companies; that stockholders "were kept constantly informed"; and that "earnings were expanding rapidly."

It was shown by the evidence that Utility Securities Company did high-pressure its salesmen. One of the Government's exhibits was a letter from one of the officers of that company to the manager of its San Francisco office, complaining of the poor showing made by that office. "Surely," read the letter, "there must be some clerk, stenographer, small merchant or janitor who could be interested to buy stock on the installment plan. Concentrate on this . . . our success has been in getting the small fellow to buy. . . . They are not like the big buyers who sell out at the least turn of the market."

The Government called two score of witnesses to testify that certain salesmen for the Utility Securities Company and its participating associates needed no such urging. According to these witnesses, the representations made were many, rose-colored and positive—"wonderful investment," "good, safe investment," "would pay six per cent," "could be relied upon to pay dividends," "anything Insull is good," "you can't go wrong," "you will always have something coming," "it will jump like a race horse." One prospect who hesitated because all of the money he had was what he had saved up to pay a debt shortly coming due was told to buy the stock because it would make him enough to pay the debt before it was due. A Chicago schoolteacher had no money; she was being paid in promissory "script." Utility Securities Company sold her the stock and accepted the script as payment. (When the receiver for Corporation Securities Company took over, it had in its assets $32,000 of this script.)

According to the Government, the efforts of Utility Securities Company and its salesmen were ably abetted by the performance of the stock market. The range of the common stock between April 4 and May 7 was between twenty-seven and twenty-eight dollars, and the units held steadily at around seventy dollars. But this, said the Government's witnesses, was all on the surface. Here is what went on about which the sheared sheep knew nothing: In April sixty per cent of all the transactions on the Chicago Stock Exchange in the common stock were made by Utility Securities Company, Insull, Son & Company, Middle West Utilities Company or Insull Utility Investments. In May the same companies figured in ninety-nine per cent of all of the transactions in the stock on the exchange. Of the units traded in, seventy per cent of all the trades in April represented purchases or sales by the Insull companies. In May that percentage rose to ninety-five per cent.

The offering was a huge success. The issue was oversubscribed by 104,000 shares. On May 7, 1930, Corporation Securities Company wrote a letter to Insull, Son & Company, acknowledging receipt from Utility Securities Company of $31,875,000 payment in full of the 1,250,000 shares of its common stock, and included a check payable to Insull, Son & Company for $299,748.50. This represented, so the letter said, one half of the "profit" on the transaction. The so-called profit had resulted from the sale of the stock by Corporation Securities Company to Insull, Son & Company and Corporation Syndicates, Inc., at $25.00 a share and the resale of it by those companies to Utility Securities Company at $25.50 a share.

During the first half of 1930, the securities of Corporation Securities Company and Insull Utility Investments held up well. This was due in part to general market conditions, but also, the Government claimed, to a continued rigging of the market by the defendants which created an illusion of activity in the issues and kept up their prices. Witnesses testified that in a volume of something over a million shares of Corporation Securities Company's stocks traded in on the Chicago Stock Exchange, transactions by and for Utility Securities Company, Middle West Utilities Company and other Insull companies accounted for over seventy per cent.

There was evidence, too, of what the Government witnesses called "wash" or "matched" sales—transactions in the names of "dummies" in which Utility Securities Company bought and sold the same number of shares on the same day for the same price, and there was no actual change of ownership. A broker employed by Insull and the Utility Securities Company to buy and sell Corporation Securities Company's common stock and units, testified that in midsummer, when the market commenced to slip, he called up one of the officers of Utility Securities Company and told him he did not see how the price could be held up unless they were prepared to "buy the company"; that he was likely to have a "bushel basket of the stuff" if he kept on buying. He said he was told to go ahead and buy—"there was nothing else to do"; "the price had to be maintained."

The Government also produced evidence that the cash assets of Corporation Securities Company were used to further these manipulations. One of its exhibits was an excerpt from the company's corporate minutes for September 8, 1930. It recited that Utility Securities Company had sustained a loss of over $250,000 in protecting the market, and the syndicate which it had formed to sell the stock had sustained a loss of an equal amount because of the slump in the market, and that Corporation Securities Company was sharing these losses by contributing $250,000 to Utility Securities Company. Another item of evidence was a corporate resolution showing that Corporation Securities Company gave its note to Insull, Son & Company for $6,585,000 for some 90,000-odd shares of Insull Utility Investments stocks which Insull, Son & Company had accumulated in its efforts to support the market on those issues.

For some time, before June of 1930, Samuel Insull had been negotiating with Cyrus Eaton, head of Continental

Shares, a large investment trust, for the purchase of a block of 160,000 shares of Commonwealth Edison Company, Peoples Gas Light & Coke Company and Public Service Company of Northern Illinois stock owned by the trust. The Government contended that Insull's interest was motivated by the consideration that possession by "outsiders" of such a large number of the shares of the underlying operating companies was a threat to their continued Insull domination.

The average market for the shares was about $300.00. Eaton started by asking $400.00 a share. Negotiation brought about an agreement for the sale of the stock at $350.00 a share, or $56,000,000: $48,000,000 payable in cash within three months and the balance in the common stock of Insull Utility Investments at $65.00 a share and the common stock of Corporation Securities Company at $25.00 a share. A deal was consummated on that basis on June 3, 1930. The Government made no claim of fraud or irregularity in this transaction, other than that Insull and his associates purchased this stock at an excessive price when they knew the corporation was "on dangerous ground" and did it solely for the selfish purpose of protecting their own interests.

The stock acquired from Eaton was allotted equally to Corporation Securities Company and Insull Utility Investments, each assuming one half of the purchase obligation. To assist in financing Corporation Securities Company's part of the commitment, it issued and sold to Halsey, Stuart & Company $40,000,000 of "serial gold notes" at $95.50 per $100.00 of face value and thereby obtained $38,200,000. In December 1930 it bought back 10,000,000 of these notes at the same price.

Despite its receipt of the proceeds of the sale of its serial gold notes and a continuing sale of its common stock, the bank loans of Corporation Securities Company steadily increased.

The Government produced its expert accountants and chartists who testified that at the end of the year 1930 the common stock of Corporation Securities Company had a liquidating value, which they held was its actual worth, of only $1.06 a share. These witnesses arrived at this figure by adding to the company's outstanding liabilities (principally bank and other loans) the face value of the preferred stock ($38,000,000), deducting that total from the market value of its assets and dividing the remainder by the number of outstanding common shares. Despite this so-called liquidating or actual value, the stock, the Government contended, through the defendants' deceptive market manipulations was selling on the Chicago Stock Exchange for $15.00 a share.

The evidence of the Government with respect to Corporation Securities Company's annual report for the year ending December 31, 1930, was substantially the same as that which was directed to the 1929 report: The income and expense were misrepresented; the company showed its income as $9,685,000—the Government's witnesses said it should have been shown as $2,877,000—the difference being accounted for because stock dividends were taken into the income account at market price and treated as cash. The company showed its expenses as $1,678,000, and the Government said they were actually $3,422,000—the difference being principally made up of items aggregating $2,800,000 representing losses on the sale of securities, which the Government said was a charge against income but which the company charged to a capital account. The result, said the Government, was that the company instead of having a profit for the year of $6,800,000 had actually sustained a loss of $550,000.

The so-called support of the market for the Corporation Securities Company's units and common stock continued through 1931. Government witnesses testified that during the year, of the 617,000 shares of Corporation Securities

Company stocks traded in on the Chicago Stock Exchange, Utility Securities Company and Middle West Utilities Company participated in sixty-five per cent of them; also, that there were many wash or matched sales—specifically, that from April 1931 to January 1932 there were 33,800 such transactions where there was no change of ownership in stock ostensibly bought and sold.

Throughout 1931 Utility Securities Company continued to push the sales of Corporation Securities Company common stock to individual investors. The stock was offered at progressively decreasing prices for cash or on a contract for a down payment and monthly installments. In addition to the representations which had accompanied previous offerings, a new form letter unqualifiedly recommended Corporation Securities Company common stock as a "sound security." This, the Government claimed, was palpable fraud: Corporation Securities Company at this time was not a sound security; on the contrary, on the basis of liquidating value it was absolutely worthless.

Early in 1931 there was a sequel to the Eaton purchase. As the Government contended, either because of an implied or actual threat that he was going to throw his large blocks of Insull Utility Investments and Corporation Securities Company stock on the market, those companies bought for cash, at market prices, the securities which Eaton had taken as part payment in the June 3, 1930, transaction. The claim of the Government was that this purchase, in view of the company's financial condition, was an unjustified depletion of its meager cash reserves, made solely to serve the selfish objects of the defendants.

On August 19, 1931, $8,000,000 of the serial gold notes fell due. The Government called witnesses to testify from Corporation Securities Company's books and records that on August 17 it sold to Halsey, Stuart & Company $1,500,-000 of like notes of a later maturity, and on September 30, 1931, sold an additional $535,000 to Chicago District Elec-

tric Generating Corporation—a corporation controlled by
Insull operating companies.[6] To make up the difference,
Insull, on his personal signature, borrowed $5,000,000
from the National City Bank of New York and collateral-
ized his note with securities which Corporation Securities
Company lent him from its portfolio.

Regular stock dividends were paid on Corporation Securities Company common stock throughout 1931. The seven-
ty-five-cent quarterly cash dividend on the optional preferred stock was paid in regular course in February, May
and August, but a question arose among the directors as to
the propriety or wisdom of paying the last quarterly dividend in November. The Government produced evidence
to show that Insull argued for payment on the ground that
to omit the dividend would collapse the market on both the
preferred and the common stock. His view prevailed and
the dividend, which required a cash outlay of $558,000, was
paid. On October 10, 1931, Corporation Securities Company borrowed $500,000 from Insull Utility Investments
on its demand note. The Government claimed this money
was used to pay the November 1 dividend on Corporation
Securities Company preferred.

By December 31, 1931, Corporation Securities Company
was in desperate straits. As the market tumbled all of the
banks clamored for more collateral. The National City
Bank of New York demanded that its loan be reduced, and
Insull satisfied it briefly by giving it $1,000,000 which he
succeeded in borrowing from General Electric Company.
He signed the note to that company personally, and Corporation Securities Company secured it with $1,250,000 of
collateral from its portfolio. While it lasted the calls of the
other banks for additional collateral were met. When some
of the banks objected to the stocks and other securities of
Insull Utility Investments and Corporation Securities Com-

---

[6] This left $24,033,000 of these notes outstanding, a condition which con-
tinued until the receivership.

pany, trades were made with Insull Utility Investments, Middle West Utilities Company and Insull, Son & Company to get the stocks of Commonwealth Edison Company, Peoples Gas Light & Coke Company and Public Service Company of Northern Illinois.

Day after day the market and liquidating value of the collateral sagged. Depreciation from book value at the end of the year was over $53,000,000. At the end of December, Corporation Securities Company common was selling on the market for $2.25 a share; its liquidating value was less than nothing.

Early in 1932 the company issued its annual report for 1931. The Government claimed it was fraudulent and deceptive. The company showed its income as $5,416,000. Most of that figure was made up of stock dividends taken into income at market value. The Government's witnesses testified that with these dividends eliminated and proper adjustments made for losses in the sale of securities—which the company had charged to a capital account—the company's actual income was $1,333,000. The company claimed its expenses had been $2,847,000. The Government's witnesses said that, because of the company's failure to charge as expense the discount it had taken on the sale of the serial gold notes, the expenses were $583,000 more than that. The company had charged this item to a capital account. The net of it, said the Government, was that Corporation Securities Company had misrepresented its net income or year's profit as $2,569,000, whereas, in fact, it had sustained a loss of over $2,000,000.

In 1932 the dividends on Middle West Utilities Company, Insull Utility Investments and Corporation Securities Company were passed. The effect was to all but run the stocks off the board. There was no market at all for the stocks of Corporation Securities Company. Insull Utility Investments common went to five dollars and eighty-seven cents a share; Middle West common to twenty-five

cents a share. Insull and his companies no longer supported the market. There was nothing left anywhere to
support it with. Utility Securities Company had no capital with which to finance installment sales and practically
ceased doing business. Middle West Utilities Company had
ten million dollars of notes coming due June 1. There was
no hope they could be paid or refinanced.

On April 16 a "friendly creditor" of Middle West Util-
ities Company filed a petition in the United States District
Court for a receiver. Two days later similar petitions were
filed against Insull Utility Investments and Corporation
Securities Company. When the receivers for Corporation
Securities Company took over its affairs they found no cash.
What they did find were miscellaneous securities of an ap-
proximate value of $50,000 and $32,000 of script which the
Board of Education of Chicago had issued to its unpaid
schoolteachers in lieu of cash. There was no equity in the
stocks which Corporation Securities Company had up as
collateral to its loans with the Chicago and New York banks.
Their market value was far less than the amount of the
notes which the banks held.

The Government closed its case with proof of the specific mailings charged in the different counts of the indictment. Each of the twenty-five persons named appeared and
testified they had received the enclosures described—letters,
offering circulars, annual reports, etc.—through the United
States mails.

On October 27, 1934, the Government "rested." It had
made a strong prima-facie case—a stronger case, indeed,
than many of the so-called mail-fraud cases to be found in
the Federal reports in which convictions have been sustained.

Separate motions on behalf of all the defendants except
the Insulls to direct the jury to return a verdict of not
guilty were made, argued at length and denied by the

Court. Statements by the various defense counsel of their expected proof followed, and Samuel Insull took the stand not only as a witness in his own defense but for everyone who had been indicted with him.

The calling of Insull as the first witness was sound trial strategy. He was the principal defendant. It was he the jury wanted most to hear. It was his "industrial empire" or "house of cards" (depending on the point of view) which had collapsed and caught in its ruins the thousands of little people for whom the Government's prosecutors had manifested so much concern. If Insull could not satisfy the jury of his innocence all his codefendants were in jeopardy. Each had played his role—major or minor—in the Insull tragedy. If, on the other hand, Insull could convince the jury there had been no crooked scheme and no intent to defraud anyone, but that he, like so many others, had been a victim of the most devastating economic debacle in American history, all the other defendants were in the clear.

The old man (he was seventy-five) took the witness stand, calm and assured. To the oath impressively pronounced by the clerk, "Do you solemnly swear . . . " he replied with a ringing "I do." He faced the jury and, under the skillful direct examination of his able counsel, told his story—one of the most remarkable ever heard in an American courtroom.

He was born in England in 1859. His father had been a dairyman and nonconformist preacher. Insull's education, while limited, had been sound; he had attended a good private school and had been well grounded in the fundamentals. He became, and throughout his life continued to be, an avid and purposeful reader. At fourteen he had gone to work as a junior clerk for a firm of London auctioneers and real-estate agents. His starting wage was five shillings a week—the American equivalent of one dollar and twenty-five cents. In four years he rose to the position of office manager. Under the tutelage of the head clerk, he had learned shorthand and how to run a typewriter.

When Insull was sixten he obtained an extra job—in the evening—as stenographer and secretary to the publisher of a magazine devoted largely to financial and political news and comment. When he was eighteen he obtained a position as secretary to a Colonel Gourard. This was the turning point in Insull's career. Gourard was the London representative of the great American inventor, Thomas A. Edison. This new position brought Insull into direct contact with the leading financiers, industrialists and statesmen of Britain. A more important contact, however, was a man named Edward H. Johnson, one of Edison's principal technical assistants, who visited London on some of the inventor's business. Impressed with Insull's intelligence, ability and industry, Johnson suggested him to Edison as a private secretary.

On February 28, 1881, Insull, aged twenty-one, became private secretary to Thomas A. Edison. He served Edison in that and other capacities for eleven years. At the end of the period he was Edison's most trusted adviser, held Edison's general power of attorney and, at his own discretion, handled all of the great man's financial affairs.

Edison's cash income was always uncertain and irregular; his expenditures in new ventures were tremendous. Insull, with amazing perspicacity, arranged to take most of his compensation for services in small interests in Edison's various enterprises. One of the enterprises in which Edison was interested was a machine works at Schenectady, New York, operated under the name of Edison General Electric Company. The company was not doing well. Its production techniques were bad and its output slow and meager. It was losing money. Edison requested Insull to represent him and, so far as it was possible considering other interests in the company, to take charge. His commission to Insull, which the latter told with evident pride, strikes a reader of the record as indicative of Insull's guiding business principle throughout his long and colorful life. Edison's parting word to him, testified Insull, was: "Now, you go back up there and run the institution. And whatever you do, Sammy . . . make either a brilliant success of it or a brilliant failure. Just do something." Insull, in an aside to the jury, said, " 'Sammy'—that was my nickname with Edison."

This, according to Insull, was his "first real independent opportunity in life." He made the most of it, which was a great deal. When he took over the job, the plant employed 200 men; when he left a few years later, there were 6,000 on its payroll. Insull was vice-president in charge of manufacturing and sales. The company had prospered and Insull's salary—commensurate with his accomplishments—was $36,-000 a year.

Through various consolidations Edison General Electric Company became the General Electric Company. Insull's place in the new setup was not to his liking. He had long since turned his face westward. He had formed some strong friendships with prominent and influential Chicago businessmen and, in 1892, moved to Chicago to become president of Chicago Edison Company. Insull's confidence in the development of a demand for electric power in Chicago and the Middle West, and in himself, was evidenced by his willingness to accept as president a salary of $12,000 a year, and by his investing all of his earnings, together with $250,000 he borrowed from Marshall Field, in the stock of the budding company.

Chicago Edison Company was an amalgamation of numerous small electricity-generating plants and served a relatively small segment of the city. There were many other disassociated generating units serving restricted territories. One of these—Commonwealth Electric Company—was at least as large as Chicago Edison Company. Insull envisioned the consolidation of all these companies into one electricity generating and distributing company which should serve all Chicago.

One by one the plants were acquired, until in 1907 they were all encompassed in Commonwealth Edison Company, to which the City of Chicago granted a forty-year exclusive franchise to distribute electric power within the present or future limits of the municipality. All of these acquisitions were financed through the sale of bonds secured by an open-end mortgage on the properties of Chicago Edison Company or Commonwealth Edison Company. Insull declared with pride that no investor in any of these, or any later securities issued by Commonwealth Edison Company —and these ran into the hundreds of millions—had ever lost a dollar.

Commencing in the late nineties, Insull began acquiring small electric properties outside Chicago—in Cook, Lake, DuPage, Kane and Will counties. In 1902 these were merged into Public Service Company of Northern Illinois. Thereafter, other independent electricity generating and distributing units were purchased until, in 1934, the company had expanded to serve a territory of over 6,000 square miles in the northern half of Illinois. As was the case with Commonwealth Edison Company, these properties were acquired and developed through issues of bonds and stocks on which there had never been a default in either principal or interest.

To serve Commonwealth Edison Company, Public Service Company of Northern Illinois and other electric-utility properties in which he had become interested, Insull, again with money raised by bond issues or other securities, constructed huge generating plants—larger than any hitherto built in the world—to serve through long transmission lines the various distributing stations of these companies. This, said Insull, meant lower production costs, lower rates to consumers, more efficient service and increased profits. He told of the much-discussed and generally abused "power pool," an interrelation of these gigantic generating plants designed to provide an adequate, dependable and uninterrupted flow of electric current to distributing stations anywhere in Chicago and northern and central Illinois. He took credit and accepted full responsibility for the idea and its fulfillment and declared that, "It has contributed more to the wealth of this part of the Mississippi Valley—again and again—than all of the losses ever made in any of the securities I have issued which are not good today."

Insull told how he had become associated with Peoples Gas Light & Coke Company. While he personally had but a small financial interest in the company, he was induced in 1913 by some of his friends who were more heavily interested to become the chairman of its board of directors. The pre-emption of practically all of his time for the performance of his duties as chairman of the Illinois State Council of Defense prevented any active participation in its management during the period of World War I. The armistice found the affairs of the company in a desperate plight—to use the language of the witness, it was "within about two jumps of the sheriff." Bills for supplies were long overdue. It was in default for more than a million dollars in real and personal-property taxes. There was no money for needed rehabilitation and extensions of service. The company had no credit. Receivership was seriously contemplated. A separate By-Products Corporation, for which he was able to raise the money, was organized, and gas was manufactured and supplied to the company much more cheaply than had been the case before. By an aggregate of small loans—many of them from interested individuals—the pressing obligations were met and the company gradually worked its way back to solvency.

Again with pride the old man testified that the stock then rose from a low of $20.00 to over $400.00 a share at the crest of the big bull market, and while the company was under his management no creditor or investor in its securities had lost a dollar of principal or promised interest. Nor, he added, for that matter had there been, prior to the fatal depression year of 1932, a default in either principal or interest in Middle West Utilities Company, Insull Utility Investments, Midland United Company or any of the hundreds of millions of securities with which his name had been associated.

Insull told of the education and preparation of his only son, Samuel, Jr., to enter into and carry on after him the great enterprises which he had created or developed. The younger Insull had taken the Sheffield scientific course at Yale and had graduated with degrees of Bachelor of Science and Mechanical Engineering. He had spent better than a year abroad studying the equipment and operations of utility properties in Britain and western Europe. After his return to the United States in 1920 he served an apprenticeship of "general drudgery" in many different capacities until he had become thoroughly familiar with the engineering and operating departments of Commonwealth Edison Company, Peoples Gas Light & Coke Company and Public Service Company of Northern Illinois. "In short," concluded the elder Insull, "if I might speak as an expert rather than as a father, he is, to my mind, one of the most remarkably informed young men of his age engaged in the utility business today." It was not until early 1929 that Insull, Jr., was brought into close contact with the interrelated organizational and financial problems of the Insull properties.

Insull revealed that in 1926 he had declined an offered appointment by Prime Minister Stanley Baldwin of England to become chairman of a royal commission to study and advise on the development of electric power in Great Britain. He was, he said, sorely tempted. He was sixty-seven years of age. He could have sold out, rich, and returned to his native land and to a position of great dignity and comparative ease. He had not done it. He was an American citizen, naturalized in 1896, and felt a sense of obligation to the city which had given him his opportunity, to his stockholders who had trusted him and to the men around him who through forty years of struggle had brought his enterprises to their present fame.

Insull told of his knowledge of and association with the other defendants. He made no attempt to evade or shift responsibility. On the contrary, even when actions had been taken without his particular knowledge, he declared they had been properly taken to carry out his previously outlined plans or general policies. In a reference to two or three of the defendants who had been connected by the Government's proof only as secretaries or amanuenses, he declared, with some emotion, "Gentlemen, if I feel some embarrassment sitting here in this chair, I feel it infinitely greater for these young men who had no responsibility in this situation, and for whose welfare I have almost as much concern as for the defendant who bears my name."

His association with the defendant Harold L. Stuart, he testified, dated back to 1907, when Halsey, Stuart & Company had undertaken the sale of a large issue of Commonwealth Edison Company securities which, because of their then unseasoned character, other Chicago banking institutions had declined to handle. Since that time, he had placed most of his financing—running in total to over two billion dollars—with Halsey, Stuart & Company. He stated emphatically that rumors that he had ever been financially interested in this company were baseless; he had never owned or controlled a dollar's worth of its stock.

Insull told of the organization of Insull Utility Investments, Inc. As an incident to the big bull market of 1926–1929, there was a perfect rash of new investment trusts organized for the declared purpose of acquiring and holding the common stocks of Class A operating companies, and the thousands of shares of Commonwealth Edison Company, Peoples Gas Light & Coke Company, Public Service Company of Northern Illinois and Middle West Utilities Company acquired and being acquired by these investment trusts offered a serious threat to their present Insull control. To meet that threat, so testified Insull, he organized Insull Utility Investments, Inc., as an "investment company" which he and representatives of Halsey, Stuart & Company would control. The company, through its own issues of securities, would buy and hold for income and appreciation sufficient of the stocks and other securities of the so-called operating companies to insure continued Insull domination.

He stressed that in the exchange of the stocks of Commonwealth Edison Company, Peoples Gas Light & Coke Company, Public Service Company of Northern Illinois and Middle West Utilities Company for Insull Utility Investments stocks he had not received a dollar of cash. He further declared that when Insull Utility Investments common stock, in its first open sales after listing, sold on the Chicago Stock Exchange for thirty dollars a share he did nothing to boost the price but, on the contrary, stated publicly that it was too high. This, he said, had the opposite effect to what he had intended—it was taken by the speculation-mad public as an indication that Insull, for ulterior purposes, was belittling the real value of the stock. In the general market boom the stock went to $147.00, but in October, when it was exchanged for Corporation Securities Company common, had eased off to $100.00.

Insull told of the option he had taken at the organization of Insull Utility Investments to buy 200,000 of its common shares at fifteen dollars a share. He exercised the option in December of 1929 and sold part of the shares to Corporation Securities Company of Chicago at a profit. The market price per share was then sixty-five dollars; he sold it to Corporation Securities Company at forty dollars. The effect, he said, was to divide his market profit with the company. The balance, which was the bulk of the purchase option, he held "to the end."

He testified to the accumulation of Middle West Utilities

Company stocks during the summer of 1929 and the purpose of it. Again it was a question of insuring continuation
of control. The stock was discussed and considered as suitable for the portfolio of a new investment company, should
it be decided later to form one. It was acquired as quietly
as possible so as not to run up the price. From the start it
was understood that the purchases were for the joint account of Halsey, Stuart & Company and Insull, and, if a
new investment company was not formed, each would take
and pay for half of the stock. Furthermore, testified Insull,
the stock was bought because of the firm confidence he, his
brother, his son and Halsey, Stuart & Company all had in
its present and potential value—a confidence he still retained.

There was nothing sinister, declared the witness, in the
reorganization of Middle West Utilities Company. Its fixed
interest charges were high—above the current market. The
prior-lien preferred stock, which was callable, could be
refunded at much lower rates of interest. The division of
the stock—ten shares of new for one of old—was in line with
prevailing corporate practice to split high-priced shares and
bring them down to a point where they would be attrac-
tive to more investors. Stock, rather than cash, dividends
were not unusual; the cash earnings of the company were
thus conserved for continuously required expansion, and
those earnings "plowed back" into the business represented
increased equity value which could and should be evidenced by new dividend stock.

Insull told of the formation of Corporation Securities
Company of Chicago. The purpose of putting a majority
of the shares in a voting trust was to "insure control of the
company resting with the people who formed it." He received stock for the securities he turned in—not a cent of
cash. The Middle West Utilities Company stock which he
and Stuart had acquired was turned over to the new company at cost, notwithstanding the fact that the market price

had almost doubled. There was no "profit" either to himself or to Stuart.

As to the much-discussed offering circular of the "units," Insull testified that while he had no hand in its preparation he had approved it, and every statement in it was correct. The statement of its assets had been based on the condition after completion of the new financing which was strictly in accordance with usual market practice.

The witness declared that "the tremendous and unexpected break in the stock market" within five days after the offering was not believed by him, any more than by John D. Rockefeller and President Hoover, to presage a general business collapse. On November 24, 1929, he had attended a conference of the nation's leading business executives at the White House where the view was expressed that the fall in stock prices was merely a temporary market condition, and the President urged on all those in attendance that they should "go home and conduct their businesses as usual, and proceed with their expansion plans just as if nothing had happened."

Insull testified that he knew all about the first annual report. While he had not prepared it, he had gone over it carefully. He had approved the charging of organization expense to paid-in surplus rather than against income because that in his opinion was in accordance with sound accounting procedure. The treatment of stock dividends as income was "supported by a very large number of accounting people, . . . by the legislative branch of the government, and . . . can be absolutely justified. . . .

"Providing the method of charging [the stock dividends] is clearly stated," said Insull, "I can see no reason why it should not be charged at the market price if you want to charge it that way or at the price [shown on the books] of the issuing company if you want to charge it that way." He added that the reorganization of Middle West Utilities Company contemplated from the beginning that dividends on the common stock should be paid in additional common stock.

There was never at any time, said Insull, any criticism by bankers who were lending money to Corporation Securities Company, or by insurance companies who were investing in the securities of that company, of the accounting methods that were used in stating the financial condition of the company. There were never, at any time, any representations made that dividends on the common stock of Corporation Securities Company would be paid otherwise than in additional common stock; no other plan was ever considered.

The reorganization of Middle West Utilities Company, declared Insull, was a gigantic undertaking—the largest in his experience. It was necessary and in accordance with current practice to form an underwriting group or syndicate. The one formed in the case of Middle West Utilities Company was international in scope: There were participants in Canada, Great Britain and Europe. It was contemplated the syndicate participants would make a profit. The compensation they actually received was small in proportion to the risks assumed and the vast amount of money involved.

When the issue of 1,250,000 shares of Corporation Securities Company's common stock was put out in March of 1930, business conditions, said Insull, were reasonably good. The market had made a strong recovery. Electric-power consumption (one of the recognized indices of business conditions) was steady. The predictions of bankers, investment houses and economists were "buoyant." Insull shared these beliefs. Every statement in the offering circular, he declared, was true. He had never, he said, authorized anyone in connection with the sale of the stock to say that Corporation Securities Company's portfolio contained "the jewels of the Insull empire" or that the stock was the best buy on the market.

He told of the Eaton purchase. He admitted the purpose which the Government had ascribed to it. Such a quantity of stock in outside hands was "a menace to the Insull management." The purchase price was admittedly high, but at the time he thought it was justified. Events proved he was mistaken. Others made the same mistake and suffered for it—none more than he had. "Hindsight is always better than foresight."

The $40,000,000 serial-gold-notes issue, Insull testified, was arranged while he was in Europe, but he approved it.

Insull told of market conditions in late 1930 and early 1931—how the market slumped in December and the depreciation in the Corporation Securities Company's portfolio exceeded $45,000,000; how it rallied in the first forty-one days of the new year and there was an appreciation in the same portfolio of $86,000,000. Everybody, declared the witness, then thought the depression had run its course.

It was recognized as customary, said the witness, to "support the market" on new issues of securities. After the initial offerings he and his associates felt the market prices did not reflect the intrinsic value of the stocks and that "a large number of people [who had bought the stock at higher prices] might be seriously affected . . . by the market drop . . . and it was necessary to help them." He added that the demoralizing effect of a continued drop in the investment stocks, which reflected a relative drop in the stocks of the operating companies, meant serious interference with his ability and that of his associates to finance either the investment companies or the operating companies. They, therefore, gave protection to the market—"stood between it and its extreme demoralization."

There was nothing unusual in this, said Insull. Private interests responsible for large investments do it. The United States government did it on government bonds. As to the Government's evidence of what it called "wash" or "matched" sales, or transactions in stocks where there had been no actual change of ownership, he knew nothing about them; he had heard about them for the first time in the courtroom. As to trades that had been made in the names of nominees or "dummies," Insull declared that was a common practice "then and now" on both the Chicago and New York stock exchanges, indulged in for perfectly legitimate reasons, one of which was to prevent the circulation of rumors that the stock was either being systematically boosted or raided by some organized interest.

In a similar effort to try, against the downward trend, to sustain the prices of Corporation Securities Company stocks, Insull said he approved the payment of the November 1 cash dividend on the preferred. To have passed the dividend would have further demoralized the market. The amounts received by any of the defendants who owned preferred were incidental and infinitesimal.

By the winter of 1931 the financial skies, admitted Insull, were pretty black. There were increasing evidences that the panic was worldwide. Economic conditions in all the European countries were bad. Trouble was brewing in Germany. The drain on the Bank of England for gold had forced Britain to go off the gold standard—an event that shook the business world to its foundations. Insull had borrowed on his personal credit from the National City Bank of New York five million dollars which he turned in to the treasury of Corporation Securities Company. In December he had borrowed another million from General Electric Company, which was used to reduce the National City Bank loan.

By mid-December the company had no further collateral with which to continue margining its loans. An arrangement, called a "stand-still agreement," was worked out with most of the banks, by which they agreed to take no action on their claims before June 1. This, in the hope that a rise in the market after the first of the year (such as had occurred in 1930 and 1931) would give the collateral already pledged a requisite security value. The turn of the year brought no relief; on the contrary, stocks plunged to lower depths. "Blue chips" such as General Electric, General Motors and United States Steel sold for one tenth of their 1929 highs.

Insull said he continued the hopeless struggle until April of 1932. He had exhausted his resources and his credit. First, Middle West Utilities Company and then Corporation Securities Company and Insull Utility Investments went into receivership. He avoided personal bankruptcy by turning over to his creditors everything he had—a remnant of securities, $1,000,000 life insurance (against which $500,000 had been borrowed) and his 4,000-acre Lake County estate. Mrs. Insull had signed away her dower rights in the latter.

Contrary to his own wish Insull had been named as one of the three receivers for Middle West Utilities Company. Things ran along until June, when he resigned as chairman of the board of the three operating companies and as joint receiver of Middle West Utilities Company. He was tired, sick and discouraged. On June 14, 1932, with no protest from any quarter, he sailed from Quebec for Europe.

Insull testified the first information he had that there were any investigations of his conduct afoot was in September, when he read of it in a Paris edition of a Chicago paper. Later he had received a telegram from John Swanson, state's attorney of Cook County, asking him to return to Chicago. He had ignored it, he said, because of a conviction that Swanson was trying to make capital out of his misfortunes, and he didn't propose to be crucified in a political campaign. For this same reason he left Paris, going first to Turin, Italy, and then to Athens.

There was no secrecy, he testified, about any of it. He and his wife registered and traveled under their own names. When he arrived in Greece he had less than four

thousand dollars. While there he learned he had been
indicted by a grand jury in Cook County. The Greek
authorities refused to extradite him. There was never an
attempt made to extradite under the Federal indictment
for the crime for which he was now being tried. He had
repeatedly, he said, declared his intention of returning to
Chicago and facing his accusers after the 1932 elections
were over. At the present time he had no property of any
kind and no income; he was dependent entirely on his son
for food and shelter. He had paid his counsel no fees. His
defense had been provided by friends whose names he did
not even know.

An effective cross-examination of Insull would have
taxed the resources of a much cleverer man than Special
Assistant Attorney General Salter. As with many cross-
examinations of intelligent and resourceful witnesses, the
cross-examination of Insull, when finished, left a doubt as
to whether it should have been undertaken at all.

Salter inquired as to the annual salaries Insull received
from the various companies he served. They aggregated
nearly $500,000. Insull readily admitted the figures and
added, "Yes, and I was worth every penny of it; the laborer
is worthy of his hire." He added, however, that he had contributed a large part of it to the Chicago Civic Opera Association and other charitable and cultural enterprises in
which he was interested. The alleged profit he and Stuart
got out of the issuance to themselves of two million shares
of Corporation Securities Company of Chicago stock was a
"paper profit"; they had held it to the end and realized nothing. So, also, with his Insull Utility Investments and other
stocks. They represented the reward of a lifetime of hard
work. He had retained them all. Now they were all worthless.

He was questioned about specific statements in the offering circulars and annual reports. He reiterated his
direct testimony. Every statement in them was correct. No
one but a jaundiced-eyed prosecutor could read into the

statement that two million common shares of Corporation
Securities Company owned by the directors had been
placed in a voting trust the implication that they had
paid $50,000,000 for them. It had not been necessary to
fasten a stock dividend on the common stock in order to
sell it. The condition of the market and public confidence
in any Insull enterprise were such that the stock could have
been sold without any promise of dividends. For similar
reasons, he could have sold the stocks of Corporation Securities Company had it been represented that the entire portfolio was to consist of Middle West Utilities Company securities. He admitted he had put on stock-selling campaigns
among his employees—"even the coal passers participated."
But it was all voluntary, said Insull, because they had made
money out of their previous purchases of Insull stocks; they
did it because they wanted to and because they had confidence in the new issues and in him.

Insull had made a remarkable witness. John Healy, attorney for one of the codefendants, a former state's attorney
and a lawyer of sincerity and outstanding ability, summed
up the general impression when he declared in his argument: "I have sat in the prosecutor's chair, and I have sat
on the defendant's side of the table, and in my almost fifty
years of experience I have never seen a more remarkable
exhibition on the witness stand than you gentlemen wit-
nessed when Samuel Insull was upon that stand. This old
man, now on the rim of the dying day, with the courage of
a lion, fought for the only thing he has left—his honor and
his good name. And I say to you, gentlemen of the jury,
that he could not have given that exhibition if there had
not been in his heart a consciousness of innocence. No
crook, no scoundrel could have withstood the withering
cross-examination of my friend Salter if there had been any
falsehood in his make-up."

The defense's evidence which followed Insull's testimony
was anticlimactic. All the defendants, except three or four
that Insull's testimony had completely relieved of all re-

sponsibility for the acts charged by the Government, took
the stand in their own defense. None of them contradicted Insull in any respect. Some of them, notably Harold
L. Stuart and Clarence T. MacNeille, corroborated him
completely. Others sought to minimize their connections
with the acts charged or their responsibility for them.

Salter's cross-examination of MacNeille served to high-
light the controversy between the Government and the
defense as to proper accounting methods in the treatment
of organization expense, stock dividends, losses on sales of
securities and portfolio depreciation. The net result was
not damaging to the defense. What it had sought to get
over to the jury all through the trial was that there were
alternative theories for the treatment of these items, and
the defendants could not be validly charged with crime
because they had selected those which made the best-look-
ing balance sheet. A number of certified public accountants—partners and employees of well-regarded firms—supported the defendants in their claims that, so long as all
the facts were disclosed, there was nothing reprehensible
in the way in which the particular charges had been made.

Samuel Insull, Jr., was one of the last witnesses. He was
thirty-four years old, the only son of Samuel Insull. He was
a widower (his wife had died the previous March) and had
one child, a boy three years of age. His counsel, appre-
hending the prosecution, showed what he had received
from the various Insull companies as salary. He had never
received any payment for services rendered Corporation
Securities Company or Insull Utility Investments. The
total he had drawn from all other companies in 1929 was
$67,000. That amount, he said, was fixed in contemplation
of the demands made on him for civic and charitable contributions, which consumed more than half of it. Inci-
dentally, the jury was told that Grace of the Bethlehem
Steel Company received an annual salary of over $1,500,-
000, and Avery of Montgomery, Ward over $400,000.

Young Insull told of the organization and purpose of Insull, Son & Company. It was a complement to an English company of the same name, engaged in the selling of Insull securities abroad. The American company owned all the stock of the English company, and the American company, in turn, was wholly owned by Insull Utility Investments.

He paralleled his father's testimony as to the various offering circulars and annual reports—they were all factually accurate. The market during the unprecedented situation following the big break in 1929 had to be supported; otherwise "it would have gone through the floor." Corporation Securities Company had not been organized as a "dumping ground" for Middle West securities. Middle West Utilities Company was a great property; its possibilities for development and appreciation were unlimited. He thought so before the crash in 1929; he still thought so. He had profited by participation in the Middle West Utilities syndicate in 1929, but he had lost over $16,000 by his participation in a similar syndicate which underwrote an Insull Utility Investments offering in 1930, and, incidentally, he had paid this loss in cash. The failure of Corporation Securities Company and Insull Utility Investments had been due solely to the market collapse.

He presented a chart to show by well-known and recognized formulas for determining worth by a multiple of net or gross earnings that Commonwealth Edison Company, Peoples Gas Light & Coke Company and Public Service Company of Northern Illinois (which were the underpinning of Corporation Securities Company and Insull Utility Investments) were intrinsically worth between $250.00 and $300.00 a share in 1931; by the same calculations Middle West Utilities Company common was worth $20.00 a share. Could their portfolios have been given these values in 1931 and 1932, both Corporation Securities Company and Insull Utility Investments would have been solvent. He added, for illustrative emphasis, that the market value of the combined Chicago Loop banks in 1929 was $1,250,000,000; in October of 1931 it was around $300,-000,000. Yet all of these banks, he said, save one, weathered the storm and were operating and thriving today.

Salter's cross-examination of the junior Insull, while vigorous, searching and at times sarcastic, did not weaken the direct testimony. Like his father, the son made an excellent witness.

Some of the defendants supported their defense with character witnesses—men who had known them in their business, civic and charitable activities, and who testified their reputations for honesty, integrity and as law-abiding citizens were good. One such witness, so testifying for the defendant Harold L. Stuart, was George Cardinal Mundelein, who added that His Holiness the Pope had awarded Stuart the highest decoration the Catholic Church could bestow on a layman. George Craig Stuart, Bishop of the Episcopal Church for the Diocese of Chicago, Robert Maynard Hutchins, chancellor of the University of Chicago, and Joel D. Hunter, head of the United Charities of Chicago, testified in behalf of young Insull. Newspaper publishers, civic leaders, lawyers and prominent businessmen appeared for various other defendants. Significantly, Samuel Insull called no such witnesses—a circumstance which won for him one of the rare plaudits bestowed on any of the defendants by the Government prosecutors.

On November 16, 1932, the defendants "rested." There was a brief and, so far as it added anything to what had gone before, an unimportant rebuttal, and the Government closed. Renewed motions for directed verdicts were argued and overruled, and on the nineteenth the closing arguments were begun.

Harness made the opening summation for the Government. It was a carefully prepared, well-arranged résumé of the Government's evidence, clearly and effectively stated. Counsel for the several defendants followed. Judge Thompson, in behalf of the two Insulls, completed the summing up for the defense. His argument, which held closely to the record, faced courageously every damaging fact in the Government's case. Every charge and every item of proof offered to sustain it he contended had been met and answered by the testimony of Samuel Insull and the corrobation supplied by other witnesses and documents.

Thompson reviewed Insull's career—from his humble beginnings in London as an auctioneer's clerk at a wage of one dollar and twenty-five cents a week to head of the greatest aggregation of public-service ultilities in the world—an accomplishment not the result of luck or intrigue, but of forty years of hard work, organizing genius and conscientious direction. He reminded the jurors of Insull's many civic and charitable contributions—his leadership of the Illinois State Council of Defense during World War I, his gifts of time and money to the Chicago Civic Opera, the Century of Progress, to hospitals and charities. "Why," declared Thompson, "during the forty years that intervened between the World's Columbian Exposition and the Century of Progress, Samuel Insull was as much a part of Chicago as Lake Michigan!"

A crime, declared the advocate, was made up of two elements: the act, and the intent with which the act was done. Homicide with intent to kill was murder; homicide through accident or in self-defense was not a crime. So here, people had invested their money—large sums of it— in an enterprise put forward by Insull and his associates. But had the whole undertaking been organized and projected as a scheme to defraud? That was the question before them.

The facts—the positives and the negatives—were marshaled to give the jurors the answer. Thompson posed and answered a series of vital questions: Had the twelve men

ever heard of a scheme to defraud where the central idea
of it had not been to get somebody's money and put it in
the pockets of the schemers? Here there was no evidence
that any of the defendants personally received or profited
to the extent of a dollar. Had they ever heard of such a
scheme where the schemers had not tried in every way to
cover up their tracks? Here there was no such attempt.

Everything they did, continued Thompson, was spread
on the record. Every book, every letter, every scrap of paper had been made available to the Government's agents
in their long, two-year investigation. Why, if this had been
a scheme to defraud, did not Insull and Stuart and the
other defendants who served Corporation Securities Company milk its treasury for fat salaries? None of them had
ever drawn a dollar. Why, if this had been a crooked
scheme, had not Insull and Stuart unloaded their own
holdings of Corporation Securities Company stock when it
was riding high in the market? They did not unload it;
they held it through to the end. Why did many of these
other defendants, the close associates of Insull and Stuart,
invest their own money in the units and common stock of
Corporation Securities Company at the offering prices?

Thompson said there could be but one answer: With the
full knowledge they (the defendants) had of all the facts,
they believed they were good investments. If Insull and
Stuart were solely interested in making money, why, in
October, after they had a profit of over $10,000,000 on the
Middle West Utilities Company stock they had bought the
previous summer, had they not abandoned any idea of a
new investment company, unloaded the stock and divided
the profit? The answer had been given by both Insull and
Stuart: The idea of Corporation Securities Company was
not primarily to make money for them, but to insure their
continued operating control of Middle West Utilities and
the other Insull companies.

Through forty years, declared Judge Thompson, Insull

had given everything of the genius, ability and industry he possessed to the building up of these great Chicago and Middle West properties. Hundreds of millions of dollars had gone into the enterprises. Thousands of people had invested their money in them. Management of the businesses had involved thousands of transactions and required the effort and co-operation of thousands of employees. And yet, in all that time, there had never been a default on a single obligation; never the slightest suggestion of irregularity or wrongdoing. Do crooks build up that sort of record, asked Thompson? Do the masters of such enterprises, if they have chicanery and trickery in their minds and hearts, associate with themselves the Fields, the Byron Smiths and the Louis Fergusons, who stand for everything that is honorable and worthy in the business life of Chicago?

Why had the Government brought this charge against Insull? Thompson's answer was that the very greatness of the man was responsible. Insull's name had become a symbol—the symbol of an era, a tragic era in which people had gone speculation wild and money mad, in which millions of dollars had been risked and lost. Something, figured the Government, had to be wrong somewhere. Of the many failures in the depression, this one of Insull's was the worst because it was the biggest. There must be someone to blame. So the Government had indicted Insull and sixteen of his associates and, for the past two years, had devoted all the tremendous resources of the Department of Justice to an effort to discover evidence of a scheme to defraud.

The effort, said Thompson, had signally failed. The Government had not only not proved its case beyond a reasonable doubt, but its own evidence and that of the defendants had demonstrated the innocence of the accused. There had been no misrepresentations. There had been no concealments. There had been no misappropriations of money. There had been no unlawful rigging of the market. Money had been lost, yes. Who had got it? The greatest economic cataclysm in modern times—"Old Man Depression"—had got it. And it had got Insull and everything he had.

Judge Thompson reviewed the Government's evidence which had been particularly directed against Insull, Jr., and declared that he had completely cleared himself of every charge or suggestion of wrongdoing. He told of the place which young Insull had already made for himself in the business, civic and cultural life of Chicago—his aid and work for the United Charities, the Rosenwald Museum, Loyola University, the Children's Memorial Hospital; how, even in 1932, after the crash of the Insull fortunes, he had been honored by the Chicago Junior Association of Commerce as their 1931 selection of the outstanding young business and civic leader of Chicago.

Judge Thompson summed up the entire defense in a brief but telling conclusion: "Gentlemen, you saw this old man on the stand; you saw this young man on the stand. You have heard their testimony telling you the story of this tragic period in their lives and in the lives of other people in this country. You have had a description here of an age in American history which we hope never will be repeated. I say we are trying that age. The test is whether or not these men shall be made a horrible example; whether they shall be convicted because of a situation in which they lived. . . . These men have suffered. They have already paid the price of bad judgment in 1929—foolishness if you want to call it that—but there is no proof here of dishonesty. Whatever juggling the Government's witnesses may want to do with the figures, there is no proof here that anyone had any wrongful intention or motive. There is proof that these men believed implicitly in the business venture in which they were engaged, and they poured their own fortunes and their own good names into it."

Special Assistant Attorney General Salter and United States Attorney Green made the final summations for the Government. It is quite obvious from the record that the Government underestimated the effect of both the evidence offered by the defendants and the arguments which their very able counsel had based on it. There was little or no attempt on the part of the prosecutors to analyze or answer the contentions put forth by the defendants in answer to the Government's charges. Both Salter's and Green's arguments were, rather, restatements of the charges and the Government's evidence, interspersed with numerous well-adjectived characterizations of some of the defendants.

Salter devoted a considerable amount of his allotted time to a discussion of the "good character" testimony produced by certain of the defendants. Ordinarily, a prosecutor regards such testimony as more or less expected routine and, outside of a general observation on the ease with which such testimony can be obtained, says little about it. For some unapparent reason, the special assistant attorney general saw fit to castigate the defendants who had called such witnesses. In view of the high positions of the defendants in the business and professional world, and the exceptional standing of some of the witnesses called to attest to their reputation, the wisdom of such a course would seem open to question.

Insull, Sr., had called no such witnesses, a circumstance which prompted Salter to declare: "I want to say just one word in fairness to Mr. Insull. He sits here and takes it on the chin. I have to admire him for it. Don't you think for a minute that he could not have marshaled as many and as influential friends as these other defendants, and if he wanted to embarrass them he could have brought such people here to testify to his good reputation. But he didn't do it, and I have got to pay him a tribute for not doing it." If jurors pay any attention to the evidence of the commu nity as to the regard in which accused persons are held—and the persistence with which such evidence is resorted to would indicate that they do—the admission by the Government that Samuel Insull, Sr., could match the character witnesses produced by his codefendants could scarcely have done him any harm.

Salter concluded his argument with a plea to the jury to enforce the mail-fraud statute. "Remember this, Gentlemen," he said, "you are passing upon a state of facts here based upon the most wonderful act of Congress that has ever been passed for the protection of the public, the protection of investors from exploitation. This is a wonderful statute. . . . It is the only statute in all the statute books of federal law that would in any way fit the facts in this case. But wonderful as this law is, Gentlemen, it isn't worth the paper it is written on if you men, as citizens called into the jury box, do not enforce it by a verdict of guilty if you believe the evidence warrants it. You must breathe the breath of life into that law or it is worthless. . . . And so, I say to you, Gentlemen, this case presents to you a challenge to your integrity, . . . a challenge to your honesty, . . . a challenge to your devotion to the duty of a public trust."

It was one o'clock in the afternoon of Saturday November 24, 1934, when Judge Wilkerson began his long charge to the jury. It was a masterpiece of impartial statement. He analyzed the indictment and set its issues plainly before the jury. The indictment itself, he said, was only the Government's accusation; it was not evidence. Without indicative emphasis, he described and defined the presumption of innocence and the law's requirement that the Government's proof to warrant conviction had to exclude a reasonable doubt.

Proof of a criminal intent, he charged, was an essential part of the Government's case. That intent or the lack of it could be proved either by direct or circumstantial evidence. The fact the defendants had risked and lost their own money in the enterprise charged as fraudulent was no defense, but might properly be considered in determining their intent. Dispassionately, and with proper reservation that all the facts in the case were for the jury and it only to decide, he reviewed the evidence—the various items claimed by the Government to constitute false representations, the testimony of the various defendants respecting them and their participation in them. The defendants, he charged, should be convicted if they knowingly conceived and attempted to execute a scheme to defraud; they could not, however, be convicted for honest mistakes or bad judgment.

He summarized the conflicting evidence as to the proper methods of accounting for organization expense, stock dividends and depreciation. The defendants, he said, could not be convicted for selecting an unapproved or wrong theory of accounting, provided the method used and the facts stated did not misrepresent or conceal the true financial condition of the company, and were not made for that purpose. The test was: Was there an intent to deceive? The defendants had been charged with wrongful market operations. Here, too, the question was one of intent. Such transactions by or on behalf of the company as had been for the purpose of protecting investors against losses which they might otherwise have sustained through fluctuation in market prices were legitimate and proper. To that end a company might purchase its own stock. If, on the other hand, the jury found the purpose of the market purchases had been to create an inflated price for the stock in order that it might be held out to prospective purchasers as a price which had been paid on the exchange in a bona-fide transaction and the purchasers were thereby deceived, then that fact was to be considered with all of the other evidence in the case in determining the ultimate fact—whether the defendants had conceived and attempted, by use of the United States mails, to execute a scheme to defraud.

When the Court had concluded its charge both prosecution and defense counsel openly expressed their complete approval and acceptance of it—an unusual and deserved tribute to a conscientious and able judge.

It was 2:30 P.M. when the jury retired. In a little over two hours it returned with a verdict of not guilty as to all of the defendants. The jurors on a poll affirmed the verdict and were discharged. The Government's "big case" was over.

AFTERMATH

The troubles of Samuel Insull and his son were not ended with the verdict of acquittal in the mail-fraud case.

On March 12, 1935, the old gentleman and his brother Martin were put on trial in the Criminal Court of Cook County on the charge that they had embezzled $66,000 from Middle West Utilities Company. There was no substantial evidence to sustain the charge and, after a brief trial, a jury returned a verdict of not guilty as to both defendants. A week later the Cook County prosecutor dismissed the remaining state indictment.

Meanwhile, the Federal government had determined on one more serious attempt to fasten criminal guilt on Insull, his son and Harold L. Stuart. On June 11, 1935, it brought to trial in the Federal district court in Chicago the indictment which charged that these three had, in contemplation of the bankruptcy of Corporation Securities Company of Chicago, illegally transferred its property with intent to prefer selected creditors and defeat the purpose of the Bankruptcy Act.

There was a new set of prosecutors. The Honorable Dwight H. Green had been succeeded as United States attorney by the Honorable Michael L. Igoe.[7] Three special assistants to the attorney general—S. E. Whitaker, David V.

---

[7] Now a judge of the United States District Court for the Northern District of Illinois.

Cahill and Forest A. Harness—took over the presentation of the Government's evidence.

The Honorable John C. Knox of the United States District Court for the Southern District of New York had been specially assigned to hear the case. Floyd E. Thompson again appeared for the Insulls, and Ditchburne and Lounsbury for the defendant Stuart.

Specifically, the Government's contentions were: The Corporation Securities Company had gone into bankruptcy on April 18, 1932. The payment on November 1, 1931, of a dividend aggregating $558,000 on its preferred stock, the transfers out of its portfolio during November and December of large amounts of securities as additional collateral for its outstanding bank loans, its borrowing on December 22, 1931, of $1,000,000 from General Electric Company and delivering to that company $1,250,000 of securities as collateral, and its transfers in January of 1932 of various amounts of cash from one bank creditor to another were all illegal "preferences" made in contemplation of bankruptcy. The victims of these preferences, said the Government, were the holders of the $24,000,000 of outstanding serial gold notes, to secure which no proportionate, or any, amount of collateral was ever deposited.

The defense did not dispute the facts as to the dividend and the transfers of collateral and cash. It did dispute, and vigorously, the Government's contention that the actions were taken in contemplation of bankruptcy. On the contrary, it was contended that in a developing panic—which proved to be the worst in American history—the defendants had sought by every means at their disposal to avoid bankruptcy and save the company for the benefit of its creditors and stockholders. The bankruptcy proceeding had not been a voluntary one, but had been forced upon them by conditions over which they had no control.

At the close of the Government's case, defense counsel moved the Court for a directed verdict. Judge Knox, after a full argument, advised the jury that "the proof offered by the Government is not of a quality which would, if the case were submitted to you, enable you to find the defendants guilty beyond a reasonable doubt," and directed it to return a verdict of not guilty. Such a verdict was returned and formally read and entered of record.

Insull's troubles in the criminal courts were finally over, but civil litigation to which he was a party continued to harass him until shortly before his death in 1938.

All of Insull's codefendants in the government cases returned to their respective niches in the community life of Chicago, unharmed either by the prosecutions or the publicity ballyhoo which accompanied them. As this is written, only seventeen years later, the parts they played in the Insull tragedy have been well-nigh forgotten, and memory's view of Samuel Insull, like that of many another who for a brief moment has occupied one of the seats of the mighty, grows dimmer in time's lengthening shadows.

There are some who cannot forget their losses in the utility magnate's last gigantic financing effort, and to these the name Insull is still an anathema. Others, who remember and acknowledge the consequences of his business genius in the upbuilding of the Chicago metropolitan area, his unselfish and masterful leadership during World War I as chairman of the Illinois State Council of Defense, and his many contributions to Chicago's cultural development, are inclined to set these against his sole misadventure, and strike a final balance in his favor.

IV

The Trials of

ALGER HISS

for

PERJURY

(1949-1950)

4

The Alger Hiss Case

IT MAY *require a more remote perspective than is now available to evaluate properly the full significance of the Alger Hiss case. The history of the rise and spread of communism establishes that it flourishes best in the barren soils of destitution, discontent and hopelessness. It was not, therefore, surprising in the early 1930s, when the United States was suffering from the most devastating economic collapse in its history, that communism as an economic theory made considerable headway among the more unfortunate victims of the apparent failure of the free-enterprise system. The solid citizenry of the country was not particularly disturbed either by the noisy ranting of soapbox agitators, the Red parades, or the open discussions on public platforms and in college classrooms of the theory of communism and its current application in Russia. . Free speech and free assembly were constitutional rights—parts of the democratic process. There was general confidence that our tested American institutions were in no danger from this or any other foreign ideology.*

The Second World War intervened. Russia, the discarded partner of the Axis, became the ally of Britain and America. She contributed gloriously to the defeat of Nazism. The United Nations was born. The era of enforced perpetual peace was at hand. Our armies demobilized. Almost before it could be realized, the picture changed. With the collapse of Germany the mask of the Muscovite was dropped. Russia, by its repeated acts of duplicity, ruthlessness and aggression, stood revealed as the enemy of

197

*the free nations—a totalitarian state bent on subjecting the
entire world (by infiltration and the fomenting of revolu-
tion, if possible; by external force, if necessary) to its domination under a communistic form of government. America
suddenly awoke to the realization that her very existence
as a democratic state was threatened by a powerful, mil-
itant and utterly unscrupulous enemy.*

*Then in 1947 and 1948 came the series of revelations
that climaxed in the Hiss case, and American complacency
was shocked as it had not been since the treason trial of
Aaron Burr. If women like Elizabeth Bentley (American-
born Vassar graduate) and men like Harry Dexter White
(former Assistant Secretary of the Treasury and coauthor
of the Bretton Woods Monetary Plan), Henry Julian Wadleigh (American Oxford scholar and trusted official of the
State Department), and Alger Hiss (Johns Hopkins cum
laude, Harvard Law School magna cum laude, and State
Department official who had risen to be a Presidential
adviser at the Yalta Conference and secretary-general of
the San Francisco Conference to formulate the charter of
the United Nations)—if people such as these, beneficiaries in
the fullest measure of American democracy and the American way of life, had become dedicated Communists and
spies for Soviet Russia, how far had the American body
politic already been infected and corrupted by communism? The question is still being asked.*

*The verdict of a jury of his peers branded Hiss as a per-
jurer. American public opinion has overlaid that scar with
a brand more sinister—traitor!*

THE SPECIFIC charge against Alger Hiss was that he
had committed perjury in testimony given before a
Federal grand jury in 1948. The case, however, held
far greater implications than the usual prosecution for perjury in an ordinary civil or criminal proceeding; for, if Hiss
was guilty of the perjury charged, he was *ipso facto* guilty

of espionage—specifically the delivery ten years earlier of secret and restricted documents of State to a foreign power. The bar of the statute of limitations had precluded his indictment for the more serious offense.

The first scene of the Hiss tragedy, for such indeed it is, was the Washington hearing room of a congressional committee—the House Committee on Un-American Activities. The date of the action was August 3, 1948. The committee had been aroused from a long period of relative inactivity by the widely publicized disclosures of one Elizabeth Bentley, a confessed former Soviet agent, made after a Federal grand jury, on the strength of her testimony and others', had returned an indictment against the twelve members of the directing board of the American Communist party, charging them with a violation of the so-called Smith Act (teaching and advocating the overthrow of the government of the United States by force and violence).

Miss Bentley had appeared before the House committee on July 31 and in sworn testimony had implicated as attached or unattached members of Communist "spy rings" more than a score of persons presently or formerly employed in various departments of the government. Such of these as could be reached were summoned to appear before the committee. As other names were disclosed, more subpoenas were issued.

On August 2 a subpoena was issued and served on one Whittaker Chambers. The following day he appeared before the committee, and the oath was administered to him. He gave his full name as David Whittaker Chambers and his business as a senior editor of *Time* magazine. He stated calmly that from 1924 to 1937 he had been a paid agent of the Communist party. He asked, in order that his motives in joining and later breaking with the party might be made clear, that he be allowed to read a prepared statement. This statement touched the fuse which, burning its length with an ever-increasing intensity, finally exploded into one of the most sensational trials of modern times.[1]

Chambers' statement was that he had joined the Communist party in 1924. He had not been, he said, "recruited" but had "become convinced that the society in which we live, Western civilization, had reached a crisis of which the First World War was the military expression, and that it was doomed to collapse or revert to barbarism"; that he felt as an intelligent man that he must do something. "In the writings of Karl Marx," read the statement, "I thought I had found the explanation of the historical and economic causes. In the writings of Lenin I thought I had found the answer to the question, What to do?"

The statement proceeded:

In 1937[2] I repudiated Marx's doctrines and Lenin's tactics. Experience and the record had convinced me that communism is a form of totalitarianism, that its triumph means slavery to men wherever they fall under its sway, and spiritual night to the human mind and soul. I resolved to break with the Communist party at whatever risk to my life or other tragedy to myself or my family.

Describing his activities, Chambers declared that two days after the Hitler-Stalin pact he went to Washington and reported to the authorities what he knew about the infiltration of Communists into the United States government. He added:

The heart of my report to the United States government consisted of a description of the apparatus to which I was attached. It was an underground organization of the United States Communist party developed, to the best of my knowledge, by Harold Ware, one of the sons of the Communist leader known as "Mother Bloor." I knew it at its top level, a group of seven or so men, from among whom in later

---

1 Alistair Cooke has given to his complete and splendid analysis of the Hiss case the major title, *A Generation on Trial*. (*A Generation on Trial: U. S. A. v. Alger Hiss.* New York: Alfred A. Knopf, 1950.)

2 Chambers afterward corrected this to 1938.

years certain members of Miss Bentley's organization were apparently recruited. The head of the underground group at the time I knew it was Nathan Witt, an attorney for the National Labor Relations Board. Later, John Abt became the leader. Leo Pressman was also a member of this group, as was Alger Hiss, who, as a member of the State Department, later organized the conferences at Dumbarton Oaks, San Francisco, and the United States side of the Yalta conference.

While all the persons named as members of the Soviet "apparatus" or underground were well-known figures in Washington officialdom, Alger Hiss was by far the most important. Chambers had done little more than identify him.

Hiss was born in Baltimore, Maryland, in 1904. His father was a respected, well-to-do merchant. Alger Hiss obtained his early education in the Baltimore public schools, Baltimore City College and the Powder Point Military Academy at Duxbury, Massachusetts. He matriculated at Johns Hopkins University and graduated with high honors. He entered Harvard Law School, where his scholarship record was conspicuously brilliant. He was elected to the coveted membership on the editorial board of the *Harvard Law Review* and was graduated *cum laude*. On the recommendation of Professor (later United States Supreme Court Justice) Frankfurter, he became secretary to Supreme Court Justice Oliver Wendell Holmes.

In 1929 he married Priscilla Fansler Hobson, who had been previously married and divorced. Mrs. Hiss was a graduate of Bryn Mawr and had taken postgraduate work at Yale.

When Hiss's year with Justice Holmes was up, he engaged for a brief period in private law practice. In 1933 at the solicitation of his old Harvard schoolmate Lee Pressman, then assistant to Judge Jerome Frank in the newly organized Agricultural Adjustment Administration, Hiss came to Washington and became a member of the law department of the agency.

In 1934 Hiss was appointed legal assistant to the Senate Munitions Investigating Committee, of which Senator Gerald P. Nye was chairman. The appointment was generally credited to Pressman's influence. Hiss's record in this engagement was highly creditable. He was, according to his superior, a painstaking, indefatigable investigator of the facts and an implacable cross-examiner.

Hiss had been "loaned" by the AAA to the Nye Committee, but shortly after his work there had been finished he entered the office of Solicitor General Stanley Reed (later a justice of the United States Supreme Court) as an assistant.

In 1936, at the request of one of his former Harvard law professors, Francis P. Sayre, then Assistant Secretary of State, Hiss entered the State Department, to work under Sayre in the Trade Agreements Section. In 1940 he was named assistant to Stanley Hornbeck (also a former Harvard professor), then head of the State Department's Far Eastern Division. In 1942 he became a special assistant in the Public Relations Division of the State Department.

Early in 1944 Hiss was named deputy director of the newly created Office of Special Political Affairs and, within the year, succeeded to the directorship of that agency. In August of the same year he served the Dumbarton Oaks Conference as executive secretary and worked with Secretary of State Hull, Harry Hopkins and others on the first draft of the United Nations Charter.

When Cordell Hull resigned as Secretary of State and was succeeded by Edward Stettinius, Hiss at the latter's suggestion was appointed a Presidential adviser. It was in that capacity he attended the Yalta Conference. His importance in this association is evidenced by the fact that he was one of the thirteen signatories to the so-called Yalta Agreement. The impression created by Hiss on his top-level contacts at Yalta secured his designation in 1945 as secretary general of the San Francisco Conference to form the United Nations.

In January of 1946 Hiss attended the London session of

the United Nations General Assembly as principal adviser to the American delegation. Here he came into association with John Foster Dulles (later United States Senator from New York), who was chairman of the board of trustees of the Carnegie Endowment for International Peace, and it was on Dulles' nomination that in December of 1946 Hiss was elected president of that institution at an annual salary of $20,000. The position was one of high responsibility and honor. Hiss's immediate predecessor in the presidency had been Nicholas Murray Butler, long-time president of Columbia University. Butler had succeeded the endowment's first president, the Honorable Elihu Root, a distinguished former Secretary of State.

Newspaper reporters lost no time in advising Hiss of Chambers' accusation. Hiss acted with equal promptness. He at once dispatched a telegram to the chairman of the House committee in which he demanded the opportunity to appear immediately before the committee and deny Chambers' charges under oath.

Hiss appeared before the committee in its open session two days later. After being sworn he read a prepared statement in which he declared:

I am not and never have been a member of the Communist party. I do not and never have adhered to the tenets of the Communist party. I am not and never have been a member of any Communist-front organization. I have never followed the Communist party line directly or indirectly. To the best of my knowledge none of my friends is a Communist. . . . To the best of my knowledge I never heard of Whittaker Chambers until in 1947, when two representatives of the Federal Bureau of Investigation asked me if I knew him. . . . I said I did not know Chambers. So far as I know I have never laid eyes on him, and I should like to have the opportunity to do so.

He admitted knowing Henry Collins, Lee Pressman, Nathan Witt, John Abt and Charles Kramer (all mentioned by Chambers as Communist associates of Hiss), but he declared his associations with any of them since he had left the Department of Agriculture in 1935 had been occasional and infrequent. With the exceptions indicated, he branded Chambers' statements as "complete fabrications" and called on his record in government service to speak for itself.

Following the reading of his prepared statement, Hiss was rather extensively, but deferentially, questioned by members of the committee. He was asked as to his education, his various official employments, his associates and associations. He was shown a newspaper picture of Chambers. After looking at it closely Hiss said he would not want to swear that he had never seen the man, and would very much like to see Chambers face to face.

He admitted that in 1947 he had been visited by two FBI agents who put questions to him not unlike those which would be suggested by Chambers' testimony. He also admitted that when he returned from the London meeting of the United Nations General Assembly, James Byrnes, then Secretary of State, told him that he (Byrnes) had heard that Hiss was suspected by some members of Congress of being a Communist. Byrnes added that the situation was serious and he thought Hiss should immediately take the matter up with J. Edgar Hoover, director of the Federal Bureau of Investigation, and offer himself for questioning.

Hiss continued: He had gone to the bureau, as Secretary Byrnes directed, and in the absence of Hoover had given Hoover's principal assistant full information as to all of his past and present associations and organization connections.

Several members of the committee openly expressed their satisfaction with Hiss for his prompt appearance before them and his "forthright statements," and it is quite apparent from a reading of the record that a substantial majority felt that he had cleared himself of Chambers' charges. One member of the committee, however, was not wholly satisfied. The Doubting Thomas was Congressman (now Senator) Nixon of California.

The committee did not, as Hiss apparently expected, arrange at once for a confrontation of Hiss and Chambers. Instead, on the seventh of August, its subcommittee[3] summoned Chambers to appear before it, this time in private session, in a room in the Federal courthouse in New York City. Under questioning, mostly by Nixon, Chambers was led to add many details to his previous testimony. He readily and positively identified newspaper photographs of Hiss as the Alger Hiss he had known and previously referred to. He elaborated upon Hiss's connection with the Communist party—that as a member of the underground neither Hiss nor his wife had a party card, but both paid promptly their party dues to Chambers, and Chambers in turn handed them over to one J. Peters, the "head of the entire underground . . . in the United States."

Chambers was then questioned with great particularity as to the Hisses and his associations with them—their various residences in which he had visited them, their house furnishings, their family life, habits and hobbies as he had observed them, and items of personal and family history which they had told him. Under this examination Chambers supplied the subcommittee with a mass of particulars, among them that Mrs. Hiss's maiden name was Priscilla Fansler and that she came of a Quaker family from Great Valley, near Paoli, in Pennsylvania. Once while they were driving beyond Paoli Mrs. Hiss showed him the road down which her old home lay. Hiss called his wife by the nicknames "Dilly" and "Pross," and she usually referred to her husband as "Hilly." Mrs. Hiss's son by her former marriage was named Timothy Hobson and was usually called "Timmie."

Chambers told the committee that at one of their resi-

---

3 Congressmen Mundt, Nixon, Hébert, McDowell, Vail and Rankin.

dences the Hisses had a cocker spaniel, and when they took
vacations they sometimes boarded the dog at a kennel on
Wisconsin Avenue. He had known the Hisses when they
lived on 28th Street at a location and in a house which he
described. Later they moved to a house on P Street where
the Chamberses stayed with them several nights. He said
that one of the Hisses' hobbies was ornithology; that they
would get up early in the morning and go to Glen Echo
to watch the birds, and once they saw to their great excitement a "prothonotary warbler." Chambers said Hiss
once told him that when he was a small boy in Baltimore
he used to take his little express wagon and walk to Druid
Hill Park, some considerable distance out of the city, where
he filled up bottles with spring water, which he brought
back and sold to their neighbors in Baltimore.

Chambers further told the committee that Hiss had an
old, dilapidated Ford roadster, which he (Chambers) once
drove, and he remembered that the windshield wiper
would not work, and you had to operate it by hand. As he
remembered it, the Hisses got a new car—a Plymouth—in
1936, and Hiss told him he wanted to give the old car to
"some poor organizer." With Chambers' and J. Peters' permission Hiss had delivered it to a motor sales agency, the
proprietor of which was a trusted Communist. Chambers
gave, as nearly as he could remember it, the location of the
agency. Chambers was finally asked if he would be willing
to submit to a lie-detector test. He replied promptly that
he would.

The wealth of detail given by Chambers lent credence to
his charges. As Congressman Nixon said later, it showed
either that Chambers had known the Hisses intimately or
that he had without apparent motive made a remarkably
thorough investigation of Hiss's life for the purpose of
testifying against him.

The next meeting of the committee, called for the purpose of further interrogating Alger Hiss, was also a private

one. It was held August 16 in the old House Office Building in Washington. In the nine days which had intervened since its last meeting the committee had not been idle. Wherever it had been possible the committee's investigators had checked the details of Chambers' testimony. They had found corroboration for many of the items.

An entirely different atmosphere prevailed at the meeting of August 16 from that which had surrounded Hiss on his first appearance. The committee had been definitely impressed by the new Chambers disclosures and felt it was called on to subject Hiss to considerable further interrogation. The newspapers had carried stories of the "secret session" at which Chambers had been privately examined by the subcommittee. Hiss, in his turn, had become resentful and suspicious.

The session opened with a mildly phrased understatement by Congressman Nixon that the conflicting testimony of Hiss and Chambers had forced on the committee the responsibility of "resolving" the question of which of the two was telling the truth. It was for that reason, said Nixon, that the committee desired "to go into a number of items" which had a "direct bearing" on that problem.

In his answers to a barrage of ensuing questions, Hiss declared he could not recall anyone by the name of Chambers or Carl[4] with whom he had ever been connected. He was shown two other newspaper pictures of Chambers and asked if he could identify the person shown.

Hiss reiterated his former testimony: "The face has a certain familiarity." Then he added, "It is not . . . a very distinctive or unusual face. . . . I am not prepared to say I have never seen the man. . . . I cannot recall any person with distinctness or definiteness whose picture this is, but it is not completely unfamiliar."

---

[4] Chambers had told the subcommittee that the only name he had ever given Hiss was Carl; that it was not customary for Communist agents to give their last names to fellow workers.

One of the committeemen asked, "Would your answer be any different if the individual had stayed overnight in your house on several occasions?"

Hiss answered, "I would find it very difficult to believe that that individual could have stayed in my house when I was there on several occasions overnight, and his face not be any more familiar to me than it is."

To specific questions Hiss answered that he had two children—his stepson, Timothy Hobson, aged 22, and his son, Anthony Hiss, aged 7. His wife's maiden name had been Priscilla Fansler, and she was first married to a man named Hobson. She had been born in Evanston, Illinois, but had spent most of her early life just outside Philadelphia not far from Paoli.

When Hiss was asked to give the names of his house servants during the period 1934 to 1937 he countered with the statement, made rather contentiously, that the question before the committee was the determination of credibility as beween him and a confessed former Communist, that Chambers either could not or would not tell the truth, and that he had a feeling the details of his personal life which he gave honestly could be used to his disadvantage "by Chambers then ex post facto knowing the facts." He said he did not wish "to make it easier for anyone who, for whatever motive I cannot understand, is endeavoring to destroy me."

Congressman Nixon replied to the ex-post-facto contention by reminding Hiss that Chambers had already testified, that he had given many details which could be corroborated by third parties, and that the questions asked and to be asked of Hiss related to matters which Chambers had already placed on the record. Despite the obvious cogency of Congressman Nixon's statement, Hiss repeated throughout the hearing that he was being prejudiced by being asked for details which would aid Chambers in building up his case against him. That this attitude of Hiss's did him no good is apparent from a reading of the record.

Members of the committee other than Nixon, hitherto silent, commenced to take a hand in the questioning, and their inquiries took on a definite cast of unfriendly skepticism.

Pressed by questions as to how it would be possible for a man to have stayed in his house on several occasions overnight and he not remember him, Hiss adhered to his previous answer that he was not prepared to base an identification on a photograph, but would want to see the man and hear his voice. Then, without any prompting question, he introduced a new angle.

"I have written," said Hiss, "a name on this pad in front of me of a person whom I knew in 1933 and 1934, who not only spent some time in my house, but sublet my apartment. That man spent certainly more than a week, not while I was in the same apartment. I do not recognize the photographs as possibly being this man. If I hadn't seen the morning papers with an account of statements that he knew the inside of my house, I don't think I would even have thought of this name. I want to see Chambers face to face and see if he can be this individual. I do not want and I don't think I ought to be asked to testify now that man's name and everything I can remember about him. I have written the name on this piece of paper."

Hiss added that the man was not named Carl or Whittaker Chambers; that he could not state definitely the address of the apartment he leased, but it was the apartment he lived in from June 1934 until September 1935.

Under further questioning Hiss testified that the name of the man he had written down was George Crosley. He described him as a shortish man, not noticeably heavy, with blondish hair, very bad teeth and a voice of "low and rather dramatic roundness." Hiss said this man was a free-lance writer of magazine articles. He met him while he (Hiss) was engaged with the Nye Committee and had seen and talked to Crosley as he had seen and talked to dozens of other representatives of the press. As he remembered it, after they had taken the apartment on P Street, Crosley one day mentioned to him that he was thinking of bringing his wife and baby to Washington, and Hiss offered to let him have the apartment he was living in on 28th Street. Crosley and his wife and baby had spent two, three or four consecutive nights in the P Street house with the Hisses, because the arrival of Crosley's furniture was delayed.

Hiss was asked what kind of an automobile this Crosley had. Hiss answered that he had none, but that (Hiss) had sold him an automobile.

"I had an old Ford," Hiss said, "and I threw it in with the apartment. . . . He wanted a way to get around and I said, 'Fine, . . . I have another car,' and . . . I let him have it along with the rent. I think I charged him exactly what I was paying for the rent, and threw the car in in addition."

Hiss's recollection was that he did not give Crosley a bill of sale for the car but turned over to him the District of Columbia certificate of title which he had. He was asked if the Ford had a windshield wiper. He gave as his best recollection that it had one which you had to operate yourself. The new car which they had when they turned over the old Ford to Crosley was, according to Hiss's recollection, a two-door Plymouth.

In reply to questions put by Congressman Nixon, Hiss testified that by way of nicknames his wife called him "Hill" or "Hilly" and that he called her "Prossy." He denied that he ever called her "Dilly." He said that he and his wife spent their vacations during two summers with a friend just outside of Chestertown, Maryland. He admitted having owned a brown cocker spaniel which they sometimes boarded at kennels while they were away.

He was asked as to his hobbies, and promptly answered, "Tennis and amateur ornithology."

Congressman McDowell asked him if he had ever seen a prothonotary warbler.

Hiss replied quickly and brightly, "I have, right here on the Potomac. Do you know that place? . . . They come back and nest in those swamps. Beautiful yellow head, a gorgeous bird. . . . " He would have continued, but Congressman Nixon directed him into other channels. Hiss had at least definitely confirmed Chambers' report of his enthusiasm for prothonotary warblers.

Hiss told of his boyhood venture in collecting spring water at Druid Hill Park and selling it in Baltimore. He did not remember ever driving Crosley to Pennsylvania, but he did remember driving him to New York City once. He could not remember if Mrs. Hiss was along, but if she had been they would have gone by way of Paoli.

Crosley, testified Hiss, remained in the 28th Street apartment until the lease expired in September of 1935. He saw him several times after that and made him a couple of small loans. Crosley never repaid the loans or paid any rent. He did bring over a rug which he said some wealthy patron had given him, and he gave it to Hiss as a payment on account. Hiss said he did not press Crosley for the money, that he concluded he was a dead beat and had played him (Hiss) for a "sucker." Then, according to Hiss, Crosley faded out of the picture and out of his mind.

At the conclusion of the hearing Congressman Nixon asked Hiss if, in view of the existing situation, with him and Chambers giving positive and diametrically opposed testimony, he would be willing to submit to a lie-detector test. He added that the same question had been put to Chambers, who had agreed to it. Hiss hedged. Should he answer now? The scientific value of the lie detector was open to question. Would the committee want to rely on something that was not scientific? Who would administer it? When Congressman Nixon answered that the committee had got in touch with Professor Leonarde Keeler, "probably the outstanding man in the country," Hiss still hesitated. He wanted time to consider. He would take the matter under advisement.[5]

---

[5] The test was never given, but Hiss's refusal was to be weighed and counted against him in the second of his trials.

The committee now concluded that it had accomplished all that was possible through the separate questioning of Chambers and Hiss and decided on their immediate confrontation. On the evening of August 16 both were notified by telegram to appear before the committee in secret session the next afternoon at a designated suite in the Commodore Hotel in New York City.

The committee was called to order about 5:30 P.M. The hotel suite consisted of a living room and a bedroom. Chambers had arrived first and had been ushered into the bedroom. Hiss, when he arrived, was admitted to the living room. Congressman Nixon directed one of the committee's investigators to bring in Chambers. Chambers was brought into the living room. Both men were asked to stand.

"Mr. Hiss," said Nixon, "the man standing here is Mr. Whittaker Chambers. I ask you now if you have ever known that man before."

Chambers, at Hiss's suggestion, was asked to open his mouth, to speak, to read something. At one point Hiss said, "I think he is George Crosley, but I would like to hear him talk a little longer." Chambers continued his reading.

"The voice," Hiss said, "sounds a little less resonant than the voice of the man I knew as George Crosley, the teeth look to me as though either they have been improved upon or that there has been considerable dental work done since I knew George Crosley, which was some years ago. I believe I am not prepared without further checking to take an absolute oath that he must be George Crosley."

Chambers was then asked by Congressman Nixon if he had had any dental work of a substantial nature since 1934. Chambers replied that he had and, at Hiss's suggestion, gave the name and address of his dentist. Still Hiss was not willing to make a positive identification of Chambers as the George Crosley he said he had known. He asked the privilege of personally questioning Chambers, which was granted. Under Hiss's examination Chambers declared that he had never gone under the name George Crosley and had not sublet an apartment from Hiss on 28th Street, but that with his wife and child he had spent some time in the Hisses' former apartment on 28th Street after the Hisses moved to P Street..

Hiss thought he saw an inconsistency in Chambers' answers and asked him to reconcile them.

Chambers calmly replied, "As I have testified before, I came to Washington as a Communist functionary, a functionary of the American Communist party. I was connected with the underground of which Mr. Hiss was a member. Mr. Hiss and I became friends. To the best of my knowledge Mr. Hiss himself suggested that I go there [to the 28th Street apartment] and I accepted gratefully." He added in answer to further questions that he stayed there about three weeks and brought no furniture to the place.

After this positive declaration, Hiss interrupted. "I don't need to ask Mr. Whittaker Chambers any more questions," said Hiss. "I am now perfectly prepared to identify this man as George Crosley."

Hiss was asked to name three persons whom the committee could subpoena who could identify Chambers as George Crosley. After some hesitation, Hiss named three. (Subsequent investigation disclosed that one of these three was dead, another could not be located, and the third declared that he had no recollection of a man named Crosley.)

In answer to further questions Hiss added that his identification of Chambers was "positive" and "complete." Chambers, in answer to the direct question, said that he positively identified Hiss as a member of the Communist party at whose home he stayed.

At this point Hiss, in a definitely hostile manner, arose and approached Chambers. "May I say," Hiss said, "for the record at this point that I would like to invite Mr. Whittaker Chambers to make those same statements out of the presence of this committee without their being privileged for suit for libel?" Turning to Chambers, he added, "I challenge you to do it and I hope you will do it damned quickly."

It looked as thought a disturbance was threatened. The chairman declared a short recess.

When the committee resumed, Hiss asked the chairman "to be good enough to ask Mr. Chambers for the record his response to the challenge I have just made to him." Acting Chairman McDowell replied that the inquiry in his opinion was not pertinent to the matter under investigation. Hiss rejoined, "I thought the committee was interested in ascertaining truth."

This aroused the ire of the committee, and Congressman Nixon and the chief investigator for the committee commenced a bombardment of Hiss that from that time on lacked all the usual amenities of an official hearing. Hiss was virtually accused of deliberately misleading the public by his original declaration that so far as he knew he had never set eyes on Whittaker Chambers.

Hiss repudiated any such intention and repeated that he had never known Chambers under the name of Chambers or Carl. He denied he had ever paid Communist party dues to Chambers, or J. Peters, or Henry Collins. He admitted that Chambers—known to him as Crosley—was the man to whom he gave the Ford car; that he had eaten several meals in Chambers' house, and that possibly he had had lunch with him at other places.

The committee set August 25 as the date of the public hearing for the confrontation of Hiss and Chambers. The forthcoming session was widely publicized. One of the larger assembly halls in the old House Office Building had been assigned for the hearing. Long before the convening hour it was filled to suffocation with press representatives, officeholders, and such of the public as were important or fortunate enough to gain admission.

The chairman of the committee, Congressman J. Parnell Thomas, called the meeting to order. Chambers and Hiss were both present—the latter with his lawyer. It was obvious from the start that it was Hiss and not Chambers who was under fire. The questions of Congressman Nixon and Chief Investigator Stripling, with which the hearing led off, were directed to Hiss and unmistakably hostile.

Whether by prearrangement or instinctively, Hiss's answers were cautious and repeatedly hedged about with those well-known escapements from a subsequent perjury charge: "so far as I can remember," "according to my best recollection," "I would not be sure, but I think," and so forth. With one of these limitations, he identified Chambers as a George Crosley he had met in 1934 and had last seen in 1935 or 1936. Confronted with old leases and utility-company records, Hiss had to admit that his previous recollection of the date of the expiration of the 28th Street apartment lease was faulty; it was the end of June 1935, rather than the last of September 1934 or 1935.

He was made to repeat his testimony concerning the old Ford car: that he had given it to Chambers in May or June of 1935 *after* he had purchased the new Plymouth. He was faced with records of the local traffic bureau which showed that he had purchased the Plymouth September 7, 1935. Nixon pressed him for a positive answer that he had *given* Chambers the Ford. Sensing some sort of a trap, Hiss replied that "to the best of his recollection" he definitely *gave Crosley the use* of the car. He was reminded of his previous testimony that he had *given* Crosley the car. Hiss quibbled: If that was in the record, that was what he said. After dozens of pages of the record had been read back, Hiss made a further amendment: "He *gave Crosley the use* of the car," but whether he "gave him the car outright," or "whether the car came back," he did not know. Even these last amendments were prefaced with the protective "to the best of my recollection."

The next shot was of larger caliber. Hiss was shown a

photostatic copy of a bill of sale of a 1929 Ford, dated July
23, 1936, from one Alger Hiss to the Cherner Motor Company, and confronted with the motor company's record
that on the same day it had transferred and delivered the
car to one William Rosen. The photostatic copy not only
bore the signature "Alger Hiss" but purported to have
been signed and sworn to by him before a notary public.
Hiss was asked if the signature was his. Again he hedged.
He disliked the idea of swearing to a signature on a photo-
stat; he would prefer to see the original. The notary was
produced. He was an employee in the State Department.
Hiss recognized him and conceded the signature was his.
He was then asked if, with his memory refreshed, he could
now recall the transaction which resulted in the transfer of
the Ford. His back against the wall, Hiss could only falter,
"I have no present recollection of the disposition of the
Ford." One outspoken member of the committee was
prompted to exclaim, "You are a remarkable and agile
young man, Mr. Hiss!"

When the committee ended the examination, Hiss attempted to shift the spotlight and heat to Chambers. He
presented the committee with a memorandum of questions
he wanted the committee to propound to Chambers. He
wanted to know the present and past addresses of Chambers, his various aliases, and he wanted a catalogue of
Chambers' various employments with the Communist
party, a list of his writings, whether he had ever been convicted of a crime, and if so, the particulars—"where, when
and for what"—whether he had ever been treated for mental disease, where, when, and to whom he had been married, how many children he had, and where his wife presently resided.

Hiss also wanted the committee to inquire as to the circumstances under which Chambers had come in contact
with the committee and to make public all memoranda
which he might have handed to any representative of the
committee. Hiss's concluding request was that the com-

mittee put it up to Chambers whether he was willing to
repeat the statements he had made before the committee
under conditions where they would not be privileged so
that Hiss might test his veracity in a suit for slander or libel.

Chambers under oath answered without hesitation or
reservation all of Hiss's questions which the committee put
to him. He gave the details of his family life and all of his
former addresses. He withheld, with the committee's permission, his present address for reasons, he said, of his own
and his family's security. He told of his activities and employments with the Communist party, of his Communist
associates, including Hiss, and of the books and articles he
had written. He denied that he had ever been convicted of
any crime or had ever been treated for mental illness. He
declared that he had not volunteered his testimony; he had
appeared before the committee in response to a subpoena.
He was not asked to nor did he answer Hiss's challenge to
repeat his testimony under conditions where he could not
claim immunity on account of privilege.

On the twenty-eighth the committee made public what
it termed an interim report of its espionage hearings. As to
the Hiss-Chambers imbroglio, it reported that the verifiable portions of Chambers' testimony had "stood up
strongly"; that the verifiable portions of Hiss's testimony
had been "shaken badly"; that Hiss's vague and evasive testimony as to the Ford car raised a doubt as to the other portions of his testimony; "that on 198 occasions Hiss qualified
his answers to questions by the phrase 'to the best of my
recollection' or similar qualifying phrases," and that the
confrontation of the two men and the attendant testimony
of both witnesses had definitely shifted the burden of proof
as to which was telling the truth from Chambers to Hiss.

On August 27 Chambers appeared and participated in a
nationwide radio program, "Meet the Press." In answer to
the direct question of one of the interlocutors, he declared,
"Alger Hiss was a Communist and may be now." Hiss had

invited the attack and Chambers had thrown down the gage. The charge had now been made, openly and to a nationwide audience. There was no question of privilege. The only possible defense to an action for slander or libel, if one should be brought, was that the charge was true and was published for good motives and justifiable ends.

Days went by and Hiss did not bring suit. The newspapers kept the thing alive. Was Hiss going to sue? What was he waiting for? A Washington paper put it pointedly: Hiss had brought the situation upon himself; it was up to him "to put up or shut up."

Finally on September 27[6] Hiss filed an action against Chambers in the Federal court in Baltimore for defamation of character; damages claimed, $50,000.[7] Hiss's lawyers proceeded vigorously to prepare the case for trial. Availing themselves of the liberal Federal Rules of Procedure, the lawyers had Chambers summoned to a pretrial hearing in Baltimore. Only the principals, their lawyers and stenographers were present. The press knew nothing about it. Under the unrestricted questioning of Hiss's lawyers, prompted by suggestions from information in hand, Chambers was taken through every year of his life since boyhood. Every fact or incident, discreditable or embarrassing (and there were many such facts) was put on the record. Chambers was shaken. As he later declared, it looked as though Hiss was determined to destroy him.[8]

Chambers, however, had what is spoken of in the vernacular as "an ace in the hole." Back in 1938 he had left for "safekeeping" with a nephew in Brooklyn a batch of incriminating documents—copies of secret State papers— which he had secured from his inside connections in the State Department but had not turned over to his outside Soviet contacts. Following a recess in the pretrial hearing

---

6 Hiss explained the delay: His lawyer had been in Europe and had just returned on September 14.

7 Increased by later amendment to $75,000.

8 Before the commencement of the first trial both Chambers and Hiss had resigned from their important and lucrative employments.

Chambers went to Brooklyn and retrieved the package. It contained forty-seven typewritten copies of State Department documents, five rolls of microfilm, four memoranda sheets in Hiss's handwriting and several papers in the handwriting of Harry Dexter White.

When the pretrial examination was renewed Chambers bided his time until he was asked directly if he possessed any documentary proof to support his charge that Hiss was a Communist. Then, with a pretense of nonchalance, he produced the package which contained all of the material he had reclaimed from his nephew Levine, except the five rolls of microfilm and the memoranda in the handwriting of Harry Dexter White. There was no blinking the devastating character of the exhibits. At the suggestion of Hiss and his lawyers, Judge W. Calvin Chestnut—before whom the civil action was pending—was called into consultation. There was general agreement that the pretrial hearing should be suspended and the exhibits turned over to the Federal Department of Justice. Representatives of the department sealed the documents and pledged the principals, lawyers and court reporters to secrecy pending future action.

The secret was kept until the first of December, when a news article appeared in one of the Washington papers that some startling information had been developed in the pretrial hearings and that the matter was now under consideration by the Department of Justice. That was enough to galvanize the newspaper bird dogs into action. Hiss, Chambers, the lawyers, Judge Chestnut and Justice Department officials were bombarded with questions. Although all of these refused extended comment, a word here and a word there prompted one reporter to wireless Congressman Nixon (in the Caribbean on a vacation cruise to South America) that important new evidence had been produced by Chambers in the Hiss-Chambers slander suit—and what was his committee going to do about it? Nixon replied, asking that Stripling, the committee's chief investigator, be

directed to investigate and report to him at once; committee hearings, added Nixon, would be reopened, if necessary.

Stripling moved in a straight line. He at once got in
touch with Chambers and asked him if he had withheld any
evidence from the committee. Chambers admitted he had,
but he declined to give further information for fear that
he might subject himself to a proceeding for contempt of
the Baltimore court. Congressman Nixon was advised. He
made immediate arrangements to return by air to Washington.

Without waiting for Nixon's arrival, the committee
acted. Chambers was served with a subpoena *duces tecum*
to produce any documents or material still in his possession.
At his request two of the committee's investigators accompanied him to his Maryland farm. Chambers piloted them
to his back porch on which lay a number of squashes and a
pumpkin. A section of the pumpkin had been neatly removed, the seed and loose tissues had been scraped out and
the plug replaced in the shell. In the presence of the investigators Chambers removed the plug and from the interior
produced the five rolls of microfilm. These were immediately christened by the newspapers the "pumpkin
papers."

With the dramatic disclosure of the "pumpkin papers"
the Hiss-Chambers controversy again took the front pages
of the press. There were suggestions, probably emanating
from the House committee, that the Department of Justice,
under administrative direction, was not anxious to air the
matter.[9] Whatever the fact, with the House committee

---

9 A brief collateral note is here necessary. The Eightieth Congress (1946-
1948) was Republican. The composition of the House Un-American Activities Committee, while made up of members of both parties, was predomi-
nantly Republican. The Republicans had made Communist and "fellow
traveler" infiltration into government offices and the allegedly "soft" attitude
of the administration toward them a campaign issue in the 1948 Presidential
election. The House Un-American Activities Committee was undoubtedly
used as a sounding board for this theme. The Democrats, in opposition,
branded the charges of communistic influence in the government as ridicu-
lous and insincere—to use the much quoted phrase of President Truman, a
"campaign red herring" to obscure the real issues.

clamoring for the production of all documents, the department was forced to choose between surrendering them to the committee or keeping them under its control through a grand-jury investigation. Accordingly, on December 4 the New York special grand jury, idle since the preceding October, was reconvened. Hiss and Chambers and their wives were called before it and subjected to lengthy examination. So were numerous other witnesses.

The House committee held numerous sessions, but with the so-called Baltimore evidence impounded with the grand jury its scope was limited. It made the most of the evidence and information it had. Undersecretary of State Welles and Assistant Secretaries Sayre and Peurifoy were called before it. Both positively declared that in no circumstance could any documents be removed from the State Department. The release of the microfilmed information in 1938 would have been in the highest degree prejudicial to the national interest. The documents filmed were "restricted" and extremely confidential, some of them so much so that even now, ten years later, they could not with safety be made public. To have delivered them to a foreign power would have meant putting such a power in possession of means whereby it could break the government's most secret codes. There was no excuse, they said, for copying State Department documents or preparing handwritten memoranda concerning them, even for interdepartmental use, much less for passing them outside the department.

Meanwhile the Federal Bureau of Investigation had been working frantically to link Hiss to the typewriter on which the copies produced by Chambers had been typed. It was readily determined that the documents had been written on an old-model Woodstock typewriter. There had been no Woodstocks in the section of the State Department where Hiss was employed. It was ascertained that Hiss at one time had had a Woodstock. The Hisses were asked to supply specimens of the typing that had been done on this machine. They declared that after the lapse of ten years they were unable to find any. However, from leads developed in questioning the Hisses, the FBI agents did turn up two such specimens—one, a letter from Hiss to his insurance company, and the other, a letter from Mrs. Hiss to the headmaster of the private school which her son "Timmie" Hobson then attended. Expert comparison of the specimens with the grand-jury exhibits demonstrated conclusively that all had been written on the same machine.

On the fifteenth of December Hiss was again summoned before the grand jury. He was examined by United States Attorney John F. X. McGohey:

Mr. McGohey: Mr. Hiss, you have probably been asked this question before, but I should like to ask the question again: At any time did you, or Mrs. Hiss in your presence, turn any documents of the State Department or of any other government organization, or copies of any other government organization, over to Whittaker Chambers?

Mr. Hiss: Never; excepting, I assume, the title of certificate to the Ford.

Q. In order to clarify it, would that be the only exception.?

A. The only exception.

A Juror: To nobody else did you turn over any documents, to any other person?

A. And to no other unauthorized person. I certainly could have to other officials.

Mr. McGohey: Now, Mr. Hiss, Mr. Chambers says he obtained typewritten copies of official State documents from you.

Mr. Hiss: I know he has.

Q. Did you ever see Mr. Chambers after you entered into the State Department?

A. I do not believe I did. I cannot swear that I did not see him sometime, say, in the fall of '36. And I entered the State Department September 1, 1936.

Q. Now you say possibly in the fall of '36?

A. That would be possible.

Q. Can you say definitely with reference to the winter of '36? I mean, say, December '36?

A. Yes, I think I can say definitely I did not see him.

Q. Can you say definitely that you did not see him after January 1, 1937?

A. Yes, I think I can definitely say that.

After this testimony Hiss was confronted with the typewriter evidence and asked to explain how the documents had been copied on his typewriter. He professed complete amazement. "Until the day I die," said he, "I shall wonder how Whittaker Chambers got into my house to use my typewriter."

The grand jurors' reaction was of a different character. They promptly returned an indictment against Hiss charging him with willful perjury.

On December 16 Hiss appeared before a Federal district judge and was arraigned. He pleaded not guilty. Pending trial he was released on a $5,000 bail bond.

THE FIRST TRIAL

The case of the United States of America *versus* Alger Hiss was called for trial May 31, 1949, five and a half months after the indictment. Appearing for the government were John F. X. McGohey, by Thomas F. Murphy, Assistant United States Attorney, and Thomas J. Donegan, special assistant to the attorney general. Hiss was represented by Lloyd Paul Stryker and Edward C. McLean and their associates Harold Rosenwald and Harold Shapero. District Judge Samuel H. Kaufman presided.

Murphy, a six-foot-four, solidly built, determined, and serious-looking man, was the veteran of many Federal criminal trials; none, however, of the importance of the one for which he had now been made responsible. Donegan had taken a leading part in the grand-jury proceedings which had resulted in the indictment against Hiss.

Now that Max Steuer had passed on and Samuel Liebo-witz had been elevated to the bench, Lloyd Paul Stryker was probably the best-known criminal lawyer at the New York bar. He had a flair, perhaps a little overdone, for the dramatic, but he was indefatigable in the preparation of his cases; he was a thorough and, when the occasion demanded, ruthless cross-examiner and an orator of no mean ability.

McLean had taken an active part in the investigation of the collateral aspects of Chambers' testimony. Rosenwald, a classmate of Hiss's, had participated in the taking of the pretrial depositions of the Chamberses in the libel suit and was intimately familiar with that record.

Judge Kaufman was a comparatively recent appointee to the Federal bench. His previous experience, both as practitioner and judge, had run in the direction of civil rather than criminal cases. The Hiss trial was his first really major assignment.

The business of selecting a jury proceeded with unusual dispatch. Within two and a half hours some forty or more veniremen had been called and examined. All had read or heard of the case. Many had formed fixed opinions which made them vulnerable to challenges for cause. Others, not wanted by one side or the other, were eliminated through peremptory challenges. The ten men and two women finally chosen declared themselves without preconceived ideas or prejudices, and were sworn to make a true deliverance between the Government and the prisoner at the bar.

Murphy's and Stryker's opposed positions of prosecution and defense were detailed in their opening statements. Reduced to the barest outline, the prosecution's promised evidence was that (1) Hiss had twice perjured himself before the grand jury—once, when he swore that he had never given any secret documents to Whittaker Chambers and, again, when he swore that he had never seen Chambers after January 1, 1937; (2) the fact that Hiss had lied would be proved by the testimony of Whittaker Chambers that he had seen Hiss in 1938 and that Hiss had then given him secret documents of State; and (3) Chambers' testimony would be corroborated by the production of four memoranda in Hiss's handwriting and typewritten copies of forty-seven original secret State documents, all dated in the first three months of 1938, forty-six of which copies it would be conclusively shown had been typed on a Woodstock typewriter owned by Mr. or Mrs. Hiss. Mindful of the legal requirement that one cannot be convicted of perjury except by the testimony of two witnesses or by one witness and corroborating facts or circumstances, Murphy concluded his opening with the bald statement, "When you have heard all of this testimony . . . if you don't believe Chambers, we have no case under the Federal perjury rule."

Stryker in his opening pounced on Murphy's closing admission and rang the changes on it. Murphy was right, declared Stryker. The entire case depended on Chambers. If the jury did not believe him, that was the end of the matter. And the defense, continued Stryker, would establish beyond peradventure that Chambers and not Hiss was the liar. This it would do by (1) exhibiting to the jury the honorable and notable career of Hiss, (2) showing his sterling reputation for truth and loyalty, as certified to by the most trustworthy people in America, (3) Hiss's unqualified denial of all of the charges made against him by Chambers, and (4) proving that Chambers—the man of many aliases, the confessed Communist, spy and traitor to his country—was an infidel, a perjurer, a cheat and a moral leper, "unclean" and utterly unworthy of belief.

Murphy, presenting the Government's case, was the ideal prosecuting attorney: assured but unpretentious, deliberate but not hesitant, methodical, quiet-spoken, courteous. The first few witnesses were as to more-or-less formal matters: literal proof of the allegations of the indictment as to the answers of Hiss before the grand jury which were charged as perjury, and the records of utility companies which fixed with definiteness the exact locations and dates of the various Washington residences of the Hisses from June of 1934 to November of 1943. Murphy then called his star witness, Whittaker Chambers, to the stand.

Chambers' appearance was not particularly prepossessing or inspiring. He was ill-groomed, leaden-faced and apparently indifferent to the effect of his testimony on the jury. It was this latter quality, further manifested by the unemotional and frank confessions of his many previous derelictions and the simple account of his repudiation of communism and his remarkable effort to rehabilitate himself as a man and a loyal citizen, that lent credence to his equally unemotional recital of the facts which wove the tangled web around Alger Hiss.

Chambers testified he was born in Philadelphia in 1901 but moved to Long Island, New York, while still a child. He attended the Lynbrook Grammar and Rockville High schools, but his schoolwork was interrupted with short terms of employment. He had very little parental supervision and practically no religious upbringing. When he was seventeen he ran away from home and for two years lived a precarious existence, much of the time in highly discreditable surroundings. When he was nineteen he returned to New York and enrolled for a liberal-arts course in Columbia University.

In his junior year at Columbia he got into difficulty over writing and publishing in a campus magazine a playlet entitled "Play for Puppets," which was deemed by the faculty blasphemous and immoral. He left Columbia in his junior year, drifted around the country for a while and in the summer of 1923, with two student companions, worked his passage to Europe and traveled for several months in Germany, France and Belgium.

On his return to America he re-entered Columbia (by misrepresentation in his application, it was later to appear). He had for some time been studying Fabian socialism and in 1924 joined the Communist party. As his first party

activity he got a job with the *Daily Worker*—collecting unsold copies of the publication from the newsstands—and
eked out a shabby living with what he got from the paper
and what he earned as a night attendant in the New York
Public Library.

He began to write articles for the *Daily Worker* as early
as 1924. In 1926 his work was interrupted because of the
suicide of his brother. This, according to Chambers, paralyzed all his efforts for several months. He not only abandoned his job with the paper but ceased active association
with the party. In 1927, however, he returned to the *Daily
Worker*, first as the paid editor of "Workers' Correspondence" and later as foreign editor. He described the latter
job as rewriting the foreign cables as they appeared in the
metropolitan dailies so as to give them a "class slant." By
self-study and his European travel he had acquired a proficiency in German and had done a number of highly
praised literary translations, among them Felix Salten's
Bambi.

Following a clash with some of his associates in 1929,
Chambers left the *Daily Worker* for good and became a
free-lance writer. Several of his stories, all with a definite
communistic tinge, were published in *New Masses* and
were widely commented on for their literary quality. In
1932 Chambers, aided by Communist influence, became the
editor of *New Masses*, a position he held until 1934, when
he resigned to become an active member of the Communist underground.

Continuing his direct-examination testimony, Chambers
described the various party underground "units" or "cells,"
their locations, membership and activities. He first met
Hiss, he testified, in the spring or summer of 1934. He
identified him in the courtroom—"sitting over there beside
his wife, Priscilla." The place of the meeting was a Washington restaurant, and Hiss was introduced to him by Harold Ware and J. Peters—both Communists. Hiss was then,

according to Chambers' recollection, in the law department of the Agricultural Adjustment Administration. After that, by party direction, he saw Hiss every two or three weeks—always at his home, never at his office. Hiss lived at that time at 2831 28th Street. He told of moving his family from Baltimore to Washington and of their occupying the Hisses' 28th Street apartment (without payment of, or agreement to pay, rent) from some time in May until the lease expired at the end of June 1935. The Hisses had in that interim moved to 2905 P Street N.W. and Hiss had become one of the counsel for the Nye Munitions Committee.

According to Chambers, it was at this time that Hiss commenced to secure secret and restricted documents from the State Department. These were specified papers requested by him in the name of the Nye Committee which dealt with munitions and the munitions trade. Hiss gave them to Chambers who photographed them and turned over the developed films to J. Peters. The originals were then returned to Hiss and, by him, to the State Department.

In January or February of 1937, so testified Chambers, he introduced Hiss to Colonel Bykov, the "head of the underground apparatus with which I was then connected and with which Alger Hiss would also be connected." The Russian colonel spoke German but no English. Chambers, speaking German fluently, acted as interpreter between the colonel and Hiss. Soviet Russia, said Bykov, was gravely threatened by the rising tide of Fascism; documents from the United States State Department would be of great help to the Soviets; they were particularly interested in information from diplomatic sources affecting Germany, Italy, the Far East and Japan. Would Hiss undertake to procure this information? Hiss, according to Chambers, gave ready assent.

The transmission of documents, further testified Chambers, commenced soon afterward. He described how Hiss brought the papers home every night, how copies of them were made on the Hiss typewriter, how both the originals and copies were photographed, how the originals were returned to Hiss, and how the typed copies and photographic negatives were turned over to Chambers and by Chambers to Bykov. This arrangement continued, swore Chambers, until April 1938, when he ceased to work with the Communist party.

Shortly after he broke with the party, Chambers said, he delivered an envelope containing typewritten copies of a number of State Department secret documents, several microfilms, and some memoranda in Hiss's and Harry Dexter White's handwriting to his wife's nephew Nathan Levine, a New York attorney, for safekeeping. He said he retrieved them intact in November of 1948 for production at the pretrial hearing in the defamation suit. Forty-seven cellophane-wrapped, typewritten copies of documents, four handwritten memoranda and two strips of microfilm were produced by Murphy and identified by Chambers as having been contained in that envelope.

So much for Chambers' main story. The balance of his direct examination was directed to corroborating details. Chambers described Hiss's various Washington residences and their interiors and furnishings. He repeated the testimony he had given before the House Un-American Activities Committee about Hiss's disposition of his old 1929 Ford, but by the Court's ruling he was not permitted to tell his entire conversation with Hiss concerning the transaction. He described a trip he took in the summer of 1937 with Mr. and Mrs. Hiss to Peterboro, New Hampshire, to see Harry Dexter White—the incident was impressed on his memory because they stayed overnight there at a tourist home called Bleak House and saw a local stock company perform Goldsmith's *She Stoops to Conquer*.

Chambers further testified that at about the beginning of the year 1937 Hiss received, through him, an Oriental nine-by-twelve Bokhara rug as "a present from the Soviet people in gratitude for the work of American Communists." In the fall of 1937, said Chambers, Hiss gave him $400 in cash with which to buy a new automobile.

It was Christmas 1938, declared Chambers, when he saw Hiss and his wife for the last time. It was at their home at 3415 Volta Place N.W. He told Hiss he had definitely broken with the Communist party and urged Hiss and his wife to do likewise. Hiss refused and said it was a pity Chambers was quitting because he had been informed that a new and important post was about to be offered him.

After his break with the party, said Chambers, he concealed himself "through fear of assassination or kidnaping at the hands of Soviet agents." He spent some time in Florida. In 1939 he secured a position with *Time* magazine as a book reviewer. In this organization he rose rapidly until, at the time of his first appearance before the House Un-American Activities Committee, he was a senior editor. When he resigned in 1948 he was getting $30,000 a year.

After he resigned his position with *Time* he retired to his dairy farm in Westminster, Maryland, which he had purchased in 1940. It was in that year that he had suffered a nervous breakdown which incapacitated him for several months. Subsequently he embraced Christianity—first as an Episcopalian and later as a Quaker.

Repeating his testimony before the House Un-American Activities Committee, Chambers testified to his having in 1939 got in touch with Adolf A. Berle, one of the Presidential advisers then in charge of State Department security, and disclosed to him his knowledge of the Soviet underground cells in Washington. In this interview, he said, he named six persons as members of the Soviet underground, among them Alger Hiss and Donald Hiss (Alger's brother).

The cross-examination of Chambers was aptly characterized by some of the press as "ruthless" and, in certain instances, as "brutal." But if the belligerent Stryker had counted on terrorizing or paralyzing Chambers by loud-

voiced questions, freighted with charges of disgraceful conduct and embellished with insulting and provocative
characterizations, he must have found the result disappointing. The ex-Communist seemed utterly emotionless. He
admitted calmly, and usually with no attempt at justification, that while a Communist, and later, he had perjured
himself and that he had stolen, cheated and otherwise
breached the moral code. However, on the vitals of his
story—Hiss's treachery and perjury—he was unshakable.

The ordeal lasted for the better part of four days. The
examination can be only broadly sketched. Chambers was
asked if he knew what an oath was and to define it. No
lexicographer could have found fault with his definition.
Wasn't he, during his service with the Communist party,
an underhanded enemy of his country, bent on its destruction? He admitted, without hesitation, that he was. When,
in October 1937, he secured a job with the Federal National Research Project, had he not taken an oath to support and defend the Constitution of the United States? He
had. Had he not then perjured himself and taken the oath
merely to get the job? "Of course," replied the imperturb-
able Chambers. Had he not been an atheist and while at
Columbia written a "Play for Puppets" which blasphemed
Christ and held up Christianity as "a sadistic religion"?
Perfectly true, said Chambers. Had he not stolen books
from the public library? He had not, but he had taken some
books from Columbia University Library which he had
failed to return. Had he not lived in a "wretched dive" in
New Orleans, with a prostitute known as "one-eyed
Annie"? He replied that he had indeed lived in a wretched
dive and that one of the inmates was a prostitute known
as "one-eyed Annie," but he had never "lived with her."
(Chambers at this time was seventeen years of age.) Had he
not lived with a prostitute named Ida Dales and had he not
taken her to his mother's home? All of that, said Chambers,
was correct, except that Ida Dales was not a prostitute. He
admitted Communists regarded marriage as a "bourgeois,

middle-class institution" and for their own purposes preferred to have party members outside the marriage relation.

Chambers, under further cross-examination, admitted
having translated and written several pieces of pornographic literature, identifying among others a poem contributed to a "slightly erotic magazine."

Chambers acknowledged without hesitation that he had
gone under many aliases—among them J. Charles Adams,
Charles Whittaker, Arthur W. Dwyer, Lloyd Cantwell,
Breen and Carl. Asked specifically if he had ever used the
name "Crosley" he answered that he did not remember
ever having done so but that it was possible; that he did not
believe either Mr. or Mrs. Hiss had ever known him by
that name or any other name than "Carl."

Stryker brought out the fact that in 1940 Chambers had
deliberately left a typewriter (a Remington) on an elevated
or subway train to "get rid of it"—the suggestion (confirmed on redirect examination) being that it had reminded
him of his discreditable past.

The cross-examination further developed that Chambers'
maternal grandmother had died insane, after having been
committed, and that his brother, after trying to get him to
enter into a "suicide pact" and after several threats to do
so, had killed himself by inhaling illuminating gas, and
that Chambers had been "immobile" for several months
after that event.

Stryker spent a great deal of time in going over the
shorthand and stenotyped transcripts of Chambers' previous testimonies before the House Un-American Activities
Committee, the New York grand jury and representatives
of the FBI. He developed six or seven instances of indubitable contradictions of Chambers' direct testimony.

Chambers admitted, without embarrassment, that in
these respects he had lied or had withheld part of the truth.
He admitted that in 1939 when he told Berle of his and
other Communists' connections with the so-called under-

ground "cells," he had not told him about Colonel Bykov or that he (Chambers) had conspired with Hiss to abstract secret papers from the State Department; and, further, that he had not told the truth when he swore before the House Un-American Activities Committee that he had told Berle all he knew. He admitted also that he had perjured himself when he testified before the grand jury in October 1948 that he had no knowledge of espionage.

Stryker examined Chambers in great detail about his concealment of the typewritten copies, memoranda and microfilms with his nephew and their subsequent production. By showing that Chambers was alone in the Levine kitchen for a matter of several minutes, he attempted to raise the inference that the envelope left with Levine in November 1938 had not contained the papers; that the papers had been secured long after 1938 and slipped into the envelope by Chambers.

Stryker ridiculed the idea that when Chambers broke with the Communists he was in fear of his life. He made Chambers admit that, while he was presumably afraid of foul play when he last visited the Hisses to beg them to follow his example and leave the Communist party, he nevertheless remained to supper and nothing happened to him. Also, that while professing to hide from these would-be assassins and protecting himself with an ever-ready loaded revolver, he had, unarmed and alone, made several trips to Baltimore and New York.

Asked on redirect examination the reasons for his admitted perjuries in withholding information on espionage from the House Un-American Activities Committee and the New York grand jury, Chambers said there were two reasons: He had wanted to disclose in part and paralyze the Communist conspiracy and, at the same time and so far as he could, protect the persons involved with him in that conspiracy.

"Any revelation involves injury," said Chambers, "but

there are degrees of injury and I sought to keep them from the ultimate consequences of what they had done. I was particularly anxious not to injure Mr. Hiss any more than necessary because of past friendship and because, by common consent, he had been a very able man. Rather than reveal the extent of his activities, I chose to jeopardize myself."

Murphy developed that Chambers had five official sources from which he secured confidential and restricted information: Hiss, Henry Julian Wadleigh,[10] Ward Pigman,[11] Vincent Reno,[12] and Harry Dexter White, deceased.[13] He repeated that all of the documents and microfilms which he had identified on his direct examination came from Hiss and from no other source.

On recross Stryker, in an examination teeming with sarcasm, ridiculed Chambers' testimony that he had perjured himself to avoid injuring Hiss. Chambers stoutly maintained that it was much less harmful to Hiss to charge him with having been a Communist than to charge him with having been a Soviet spy.

At the end of seven days of grueling examination Chambers left the stand "as serenely unperturbed," to quote a phrase from one newspaper, "as when he had answered to his name in response to Mr. Murphy's first question."

Murphy proceeded next to offer proof of "facts or circumstances" to corroborate Chambers' story of his relationship with Hiss.[14]

---

[10] Later called by the Government as a witness.

[11] Chemist in the United States Bureau of Standards. He denied before the grand jury that he had ever known Chambers.

[12] Mathematical expert at the United States Proving Ground at Aberdeen, Maryland.

[13] Former Assistant Secretary of the United States Treasury and coauthor of the Bretton Woods Monetary Plan. Shortly after Chambers testified, White appeared before the House Un-American Activities Committee and denied the charges of Chambers and Elizabeth Bentley that he was or had ever been a Communist. He succumbed to a heart attack a few days after his appearance before the committee.

[14] The order in which the witnesses were called following Chambers has been disregarded.

To lay the foundation for expert opinion that the type-written copies of documents produced and identified by Chambers had been written on the Hiss typewriter, four witnesses appeared to identify letters and papers which had been written on the Hiss machine. A record keeper at the University of Maryland produced a letter of inquiry written by Mrs. Hiss in April 1937 concerning her enrollment for a course in inorganic chemistry. The headmaster of a Washington school identified a letter written by the Hisses in September of 1936 regarding their son Timothy's admission. A former classmate of Mrs. Hiss at Bryn Mawr identified a three-page typewritten report from Mrs. Hiss, dated May 18, 1937, concerning her administration during the year 1937-1938 of the presidency of the Washington Bryn Mawr Alumnae Association. A representative of an insurance company produced a typewritten letter he had received from Alger Hiss in 1933. All of these were received in evidence as standards of comparison with the typewritten copies produced by Chambers.

A custodian of records at Columbia University produced the school's records to show that in 1927 Mrs. Hiss had taken an English and typewriting course and had satisfactorily passed the school's proficiency test.

An employee of the Eastman Kodak Company testified that one of the microfilms produced by Chambers had been manufactured by that company in the last half of 1937. A representative of the Dupont Company swore that the other microfilm had been made by that company either in 1936 or 1944. A laboratory technician from the Federal Bureau of Investigation testified that the photographs of the documents produced by Chambers had been made on a Leica camera owned by a man named Felix Inslerman of Baltimore. Inslerman had been previously identified by Chambers as a trusted Communist who did most of the secret photography for the underground.

Mrs. Chambers' nephew Nathan L. Levine took the stand to corroborate Chambers' testimony that in 1938 he had turned over to him for safekeeping a large, brown, sealed envelope. He testified that he had put it in back of a closet in a dumb-waiter shaft in his mother's home in Brooklyn, and it was still there, sealed and covered with dust, on November 14, 1948, when Chambers called for it and he returned it to him. He also testified that while he cleared up the dust in the bathroom, Chambers had the envelope and was alone in the kitchen—a point of which Stryker attempted to make much in his later argument.

On June 15 Murphy commenced the tedious process of identifying as copies of official State documents the typewritten papers which had been produced by Chambers. Two witnesses were used for this purpose: Eunice Lincoln, Assistant Secretary of State Sayre's private secretary and an employee of the State Department for more than thirty years, and Walter H. Anderson, chief of the State Department's Records Branch. Miss Lincoln testified she thought the four handwritten memoranda which had been produced by Chambers were in Hiss's handwriting.

Murphy had followed a prosecutor's approved technique for presenting a mass of documentary evidence. To capture and hold the jurors' attention, the Chambers copies had been "blown up" into photographic enlargements five feet high and four feet wide, and placed on an easel of even larger dimensions. Beginning with the enlargement at the top of the pile, the witness was handed a document identified as an original from the State Department files and asked to read it aloud so the twelve jurors could follow and compare it with the enlarged copy on the easel. This course was pursued until all the Chambers copies had been compared. It took the better part of a day and a half to demonstrate that the papers produced by Chambers were substantially exact copies of the government's original secret files. One of the documents, by consent of all parties, was withheld from the jury and the public "for reasons of national security."

The documents were, for the most part, cables from top-level State Department officials in European and Asiatic capitals recording pre-World War II diplomatic maneuvers by the United States and foreign nations in those areas and exchanges of highly confidential information concerning foreign policy between high-ranking officials in the diplomatic service.

However much the defense had belittled or would attempt to minimize the importance of these documents, a jury of twelve ordinary men and women could not but be awed by their recital. Regardless of whether the damage done by their release had been great or small, they were after all secret documents stolen from the government's files by the agents of Soviet Russia. It was proved beyond all doubt that the documents were confidential and restricted. The witness Anderson identified the code markings on each one to establish that fact beyond cavil.

McLean conducted the cross-examination of Anderson. The examination was intelligent and yielded one valuable nugget for the defense: Security regulations in the State Department were not nearly so strict in 1938 as they were in 1948; copies of the so-called secret documents were distributed to at least fifteen different agencies of the government, where a total of 236 persons might have had access to them; other copies remained in the code room in unlocked files for several days before they were destroyed; and no check was maintained to see that all copies made were either returned to the cabinets or destroyed.

To climax the evidence on the documents an experienced questioned-document examiner from the Federal Bureau of Investigation was called to state his opinion, with supporting reasons, that the four handwritten memoranda were in Alger Hiss's handwriting and that all the Chambers copies but one had been typed on the same Woodstock typewriter on which the specimens traced to the Hisses had been written. Before the expert could state his opinion as

to the four handwritten notes, Stryker was on his feet to
admit that they had been written by Hiss. The witness
then proceeded to demonstrate by photographic and sectional enlargements the unquestioned similarity of type and
impression peculiarities in forty-six of the forty-seven
Chambers copies and the exemplars—positive identities,
among others, of misalignments, bruised letters, battered
serifs (the "tails" on the ends of some letters), letters off
footing and off-spacing between letters.

To corroborate Chambers' testimony that in the fall of
1937 Hiss had given him $400 cash with which to buy a
new automobile the prosecution called a vice-president of
the First National Bank of Washington, who testified that
on November 19, 1937, Mrs. Hiss had withdrawn $400 from
her and her husband's joint account and after the withdrawal there was only $40.46 left on deposit. He was fol-
lowed by an official of a Randallsville, Maryland, motor
company, who swore that his concern sold and delivered a
Ford sedan to Mrs. Chambers on November 23, 1937. The
price paid was $486.75 and an older Ford was traded to
make up the full purchase price.

To corroborate Chambers' testimony about the Soviet
gift to Hiss of the Oriental rug about the first of the year
1937, a well-known New York rug dealer took the stand
and testified that on December 29, 1936, an interior decor-
ator named Schoen bought four such rugs and on his order
they had been delivered to Dr. Meyer Shapiro, an associate
professor of fine arts at Columbia University. The price
paid for the four rugs was $1,476.71. Professor Shapiro
followed Schoen in the witness box and testified that in
December of 1936 Chambers had asked him to advance him
the money with which to buy four Oriental rugs. He had
advanced the money and commissioned Schoen to buy
them. When he received them, he turned them over to
Chambers. Chambers, the witness testified, repaid the loan.
If this transaction appeared unusual, it was explained by

the further testimony of Dr. Shapiro that he and Chambers were close friends; they had been classmates at Columbia and Shapiro had accompanied Chambers on his jaunt to Germany and Belgium in 1923.

To corroborate Chambers' testimony of his having made a trip with the Hisses to Peterboro, New Hampshire, in August of 1937 to visit Harry Dexter White and his having seen there a performance of *She Stoops to Conquer,* an Edith Stearns testified that she had been the managing director of the Peterboro players and that play had been produced by the company in Peterboro between August 10 and 15, 1937. She was followed by a State Department employee who produced records showing that Hiss was on vacation leave from August 2 to August 14.

A representative of the Federal Bureau of Investigation testified he had accompanied Chambers on a tour of Washington and that Chambers had located and readily identified the various Hiss residences which had figured in his testimony. Photographs of the places had been taken and identified by Chambers' signature. They were received in evidence.

The twenty-seventh witness called by the Government was Esther Chambers. She was a little woman, dark-complexioned, spectacled, plainly dressed and without make-up. She was visibly nervous throughout her examination and spoke so low at times that she could scarcely be heard. She told of her early life and education, her study of painting, her employments and her marriage in 1931 to Whittaker Chambers. She and her husband now worked on their dairy farm in Maryland, and, among other chores, she said she milked eighteen cows and took care of forty head of cattle.

She admitted knowing of Chambers' membership and activities in the Communist party. She had never been a party member herself, but she had been sympathetic to the cause. She had seen Mr. and Mrs. Hiss on many occasions.

She identified them in the courtroom. The Hisses and the Chamberses, she said, had been very close friends. They had made excursion trips and celebrated holidays and anniversaries together. In the summer of 1935 they had spent ten days in one another's company in a cottage at Smithtown on the Delaware River. Mrs. Hiss had taken care of the Chamberses' baby while Mrs. Chambers painted. She had painted a portrait of Mrs. Hiss's son Timothy and given it to her for a present. She had also, Mrs. Chambers said, given her one or two other paintings.

Under Murphy's easy questioning she detailed the furnishings in the various Hiss homes—the pattern and color of the wallpaper, a chintz bedspread bought by Mrs. Hiss at a sale, the purple window draperies and the various articles of furniture. Mrs. Hiss, said the witness, called her husband "Hilly" and he called her "Pross." The Hisses called her "Lisa" and her husband "Carl." She added, "We never had a last name."

Mrs. Chambers testified they had gone under various names—Cantwell, Dwyer and Breen—but never under the name of Crosley.

Stryker's cross-examination of Mrs. Chambers was as ruthless as his examination of Chambers had been. Practically every question carried an accusation. Before her marriage hadn't she been associated with the Garment Workers' Union? Hadn't she participated in street riots and been a disturber of the peace? Didn't she know that her husband, as a Communist, was dedicated to the overthrow of the government of the United States by violent means? Hadn't she masqueraded under false names and deceived and abused the confidence of decent people?

Mrs. Chambers followed her husband's technique: She admitted without hesitation or explanation the facts charged.

Stryker did succeed in hopelessly confusing her on the dates of the various occurrences about which she testified.

She accounted for her contradictions by the simple statement that she never had been very good at remembering
dates.

With good trial strategy Murphy closed the Government's case with his best witness, excepting Chambers. This
was Henry Julian Wadleigh. Named in various accusations, Wadleigh had been summoned before the House
Un-American Activities Committee to answer whether he
was or had ever been a Communist and to tell what he
knew of Soviet espionage. There he had asserted his constitutional privilege against self-incrimination. This in
itself had been one of the sensational highlights in the
committee's hearings.

Under Murphy's quiet interrogation, Wadleigh testified
he was a native American, the son of an Episcopalian minister and a graduate of Oxford and London universities. In
the early 1920s he had returned to America and taken postgraduate work at the University of Chicago. He obtained
a government position, first with the Federal Farm Bureau,
then in the Agricultural Department; and, in March of
1936, he had entered the Department of State. He said
that, while he "collaborated with the Communists for a
certain period," he was never a party member. He admitted, however, that shortly after he entered the State
Department, he commenced to select what looked like important diplomatic correspondence ("rich finds" was his
expression) and to turn it over to two Soviet agents known
to him as "Carpenter" and "Zimmerman." Zimmerman
was identified as a copywriter on the *Daily Worker*. It was
Carpenter, testified Wadleigh, who introduced him to
Chambers, to whom he also gave secret and restricted documents. Wadleigh would have testified that Chambers, in
1937, gave him an Oriental rug as a token of Soviet appreciation, but Stryker's vehement objection was sustained by
the Court.

Outside of perhaps showing that Wadleigh was something of a "smart aleck," Stryker's cross-examination accomplished nothing.

Wadleigh's testimony was a serious blow to the defense. He was the only witness to corroborate Chambers on the existence of a spy ring and an organized Soviet plot to obtain access to secret documents of State. His admission that he abstracted the papers from his department and gave them to Chambers not only corroborated the latter's story that Wadleigh was one of the Soviet's sources of information, but lent credence to the rest of Chambers' story. Perhaps of greater significance, in view of Hiss's announced defense, was the fact that here was a man who, while he had not attained to the eminence of Hiss, had a comparable background of breeding and education and was not above lending himself to the treacherous practices which were charged against Hiss.

Two more relatively unimportant witnesses testified briefly on minor points, and the Government rested its case.

The defense was introduced with a parade of "character witnesses"—men who had known Hiss and were familiar, before the date of the indictment, with his reputation for integrity, veracity and "loyalty to his government." The impressive array included Dr. Harry Hawkins, former chief of the State Department's Trade Agreements Section; Charles Darlington, an ex-assistant chief of the same section; John W. Davis, famous New York lawyer and, in 1924, the Democratic candidate for the Presidency; Charles Fahy, an ex-Solicitor General of the United States; retired Admiral Arthur Hepburn, naval delegate to the San Francisco Conference of the United Nations; Felix Frankfurter and Stanley Reed, associate justices of the Supreme Court of the United States; Calvert Magruder, a judge of the United States Court of Appeals of Massachusetts; Charles E. Wyzanski, a Federal district judge in Massachusetts; Dr. Stanley Hornbeck, former head of the Far Eastern Division of the State Department; and Gerard Swope, General Counsel of the International General Electric Corporation. United States Ambassador at Large Philip Jessup and Governor Adlai Stevenson of Illinois gave their testimony by deposition. With varying emphasizing adjectives, each of these testified that Hiss's reputation in the respects indicated was good.

To meet the prosecution's testimony that Chambers had taken a trip with the Hisses to Peterboro in August of 1937, the defense called a director of a summer camp at Chestertown, Maryland, who testified that Timothy Hobson and Ruth Fansler (a niece of Mrs. Hiss) enrolled for the camp about July 1, 1937; that while they were there the boy met with an accident in which he broke his leg, and during the first half of August both Mr. and Mrs. Hiss lived in a near-by apartment and went to the camp frequently to see Timothy and help teach him to use his crutches.

A prim, elderly lady from Hancock, New Hampshire, testified that she operated Bleak House, a tourist home in Peterboro, at the time Chambers testified he was there with the Hisses and that she had never seen either Mr. or Mrs. Hiss before she met them in Stryker's office the evening before.

A man named Boucot testified that in 1935 he rented a cottage at Smithtown on the Delaware River to the Chamberses, under the name of Breen, and the only woman he ever saw in the cottage after that was Mrs. Chambers.

A next-door neighbor of the Hisses (when they lived on 30th Street) testified that he dropped in on them frequently at almost any hour of the day or night and had never encountered either Mr. or Mrs. Chambers. He also testified that he visited the Hisses a number of times after they moved to Volta Place and on these visits never met either of the Chamberses.

A Washington building contractor testified to exterior alterations he had made in the 30th Street and Volta Place residences of the Hisses in 1946. This testimony was to establish that Chambers had misdescribed the houses as they appeared in the 1930s.

One of the more important witnesses for the defense was Claudia Catlett, a Negro woman, who had been the Hisses' maid while they lived at the P Street and 30th Street residences and during part of the time they were at Volta Place. Under McLean's questioning she testified she had seen Whittaker Chambers on one occasion, when he called at the P Street apartment and announced himself as "Crosby." She swore she had never seen Mrs. Chambers. The next time she saw Chambers, she said, was in the spring of 1949 when he was with some FBI men. Chambers then asked her about the furniture and rugs the Hisses had, where the kitchen was and where "Timmie" slept. Her most startling testimony concerned the Hiss typewriter. Either when the Hisses moved from P Street to 30th Street, or when they moved from 30th Street to Volta Place, Mrs. Hiss, she said, had given her an old typewriter for the children to play with, and her daughter Burnetta had later used it in her schoolwork.

On cross-examination she said she could not tell what kind of a typewriter it was. She admitted some FBI men had come to see her early in 1949, and she had told them she did not remember anything about any typewriter. She said that at that time she didn't remember; that she first remembered about the typewriter sometime later in 1949 when one of her sons told her they had got a typewriter from the Hisses.

The testimony of Mrs. Catlett was followed by that of her two sons, Raymond and Perry. Raymond Catlett (who was more often called "Mike") testified that he had done house and yard work at the Hiss residences and had never at any time seen Mr. and Mrs. Chambers. He swore that "one time" when the Hisses moved they gave him some old clothes and a typewriter; it was a Woodstock and "it was broke"—the keys were jammed, a wheel was broken off, the ribbon would not work and "it wouldn't type good." A Woodstock typewriter was produced by the examiner and Catlett testified it was the typewriter he had been talking about. He said that when the typewriter had been given to him he took it to the place where the Catletts lived on P Street; his sister-in-law had it for a while, and then his sister Burnetta "got hold of it." He also told how he assisted McLean to find the typewriter; how he talked with many people about it and finally located it in the possession of an expressman named Lockey.

On cross-examination Murphy pressed Catlett for details. Despite all his efforts he could not get him to fix even approximately the date when he got the typewriter. He admitted that in May of 1949 he had been visited by some FBI men who asked him about the typewriter. He said he told them nothing, but reported to Donald Hiss that the "government" men had been inquiring about the typewriter. Donald Hiss, he said, had given him forty dollars to use in trying to find the typewriter.

On redirect it was brought out that after the typewriter had been found Catlett was again interviewed by agents from the Federal Bureau of Investigation. They questioned him, he said, from four-thirty until nine o'clock, and one of the agents, a man named Jones, told him the typewriter was worth $200 and they would give him that if he would get it for them.

Perry Catlett testified that he also had worked for the Hisses off and on as a handy man. He corroborated his mother's and brother's statements that the Hisses had given them a typewriter. He fixed the time: It was when the Hisses moved from 30th Street to Volta Place (this would have been December 1937). He said the machine was in "pretty bad condition" and he took it to a repair shop on the corner of K Street and Connecticut Avenue to have it repaired.

Ira Lockey, in whose possession the typewriter was finally found, was the next witness called. He testified he had got the typewriter from a woman named Marlow, in payment of a moving job he had done for her. He wanted it for his daughter so that she could type some of her homework on it. On April 16, 1949, he testified, he sold the typewriter to Counsel McLean for fifteen dollars.

One Edward E. Edstrom, a resident of Valley Stream, Long Island, testified he had gone to school with Chambers in Rockville, Long Island, when they were boys. Chambers had always been untidy in his dress and careless of his person. He always needed a haircut. He did peculiar things such, for instance, as walking in the creek with his shoes on, to cool his feet. Chambers, he said, had passed off an obscene composition as his own, and it later turned out it was stolen from the earlier work of a French writer. He had written a class prophecy which was rejected by the school authorities as unfit. He wrote a second one which was deemed acceptable, but when he came to deliver it he had maliciously substituted the first one.

On June 23 Alger Hiss took the stand in his own defense.

The commencement of his examination was dramatic. To a series of questions, voiced by Stryker in his most impressive manner, the former diplomat answered with equal impressiveness that he was not and never had been a member of the Communist party, a fellow traveler or a Communist sympathizer. He denied that he had ever "furnished, transmitted or delivered" any "restricted, secret or confidential documents of the State Department of any kind, character or description whatever" to Whittaker Chambers or any other unauthorized person.

Stryker then took the witness in great detail through his school and later career—his confidential association, as secretary, with Supreme Court Justice Oliver Wendell Holmes, the confidential nature of his later assignments to the Agricultural Adjustment Administration, the Nye Committee, the Solicitor General's office, the State Department, as executive secretary of the Dumbarton Oaks Conference, as an adviser to the President of the United States at Yalta

and, finally, as secretary-general of the San Francisco Conference on International Organization, which led to the
formation of the United Nations.

Under further direct examination Hiss told of his first
meeting and subsequent relations with Chambers. It was a
repetition of the testimony given before the House Un-
American Activities Committee. He denied Chambers'
testimony of his having met Bykov and of Chambers thereafter visiting him regularly every week or two to pick up
copies of State papers for transmittal to Bykov.

Hiss flatly contradicted the testimony of Chambers that
he and his wife had made a trip with him to Peterboro,
New Hampshire, during the first half of August 1937; they
had been continuously at Chestertown during all of that
period. He further denied that he or Mrs. Hiss had ever
visited the Chamberses at Smithtown or had ever celebrated any holidays or anniversaries with them.

He slid over the 1929 Ford incident with the statement
that from inquiries he made he found the car had a trade-in
value of only twenty-five dollars; that he had intended to
get a new car in the spring and told Chambers he could
have the use of the old car.

He admitted that while the Chamberses visited at the
P Street house or lived in the 28th Street apartment Mrs.
Chambers painted a picture of "Timmie." About the Oriental rug, he declared Chambers gave it to him sometime in
the spring of 1936, while the Hisses were living on P Street;
that Chambers said it had been given to him by a wealthy
patron.

Hiss denied Chambers' testimony that he had given or
lent him $400 in November of 1937 with which to buy an
automobile. He admitted Mrs. Hiss withdrew $400 from
their joint bank account on November 19, 1937, but said
she took the money out of the bank and used it in cash
purchases for additional furniture which they needed in
the Volta Place house.

He admitted the initials "A. H." on two of the Government exhibits produced by Chambers were in his hand-writing; also, that the specimens of typewriting identified by the Government as standards of comparison had been written either by him or Mrs. Hiss on the Woodstock type-writer.

Hiss told of his first learning of the charge made against him by Chambers before the House Un-American Activi-ties Committee and of his prompt demand on the commit-tee to be heard in denial, and he added that neither then nor at any later time before the committee or the grand jury had he refused to answer any question put to him on the ground of possible self-incrimination. He gave his version of what he had testified to before the committee during his confrontation of Chambers.

He testified further that when Chambers, in response to his challenge, publicly repeated his charge that Hiss was a Communist, he instituted a civil action for defamation and proceeded promptly to force the case to a determination by a pretrial examination of Chambers; that when Chambers produced the typewritten copies and memoranda, he in-sisted they be immediately turned over to the Department of Justice.

He had testified, he said, before the grand jury that he was under the impression he had the Woodstock type-writer while they lived on P Street and for a part of the time they lived on Volta Place, but that impression had now been changed by the information discovered by his counsel with respect to the Catletts.

He concluded his testimony with the emphatic statement that he had entered a plea of not guilty to the indictment against him and was "in truth and in fact" not guilty.

In marked contrast to Stryker's "hammer and tongs" technique, Murphy went about the cross-examination of Hiss quietly but with an unmistakable air of confidence and determination.

Hiss was led by Murphy's questions to admit that he had seen and talked to Chambers on fifteen different occasions. He admitted they might have become sufficiently familiar to call each other by their first names. What had they talked about on these numerous occasions? Always, said Hiss, about the activities of the Nye Committee, or art or literature, the subleasing of the 28th Street apartment, or casual incidentals; never anything about State Department papers, Communists or communism.

Throughout his long cross-examination Murphy kept probing the weak spots in Hiss's story—the old 1929 Ford, the Woodstock typewriter, and the suspicions and rumors of Hiss's Communist connections before Chambers had made his charge. The cross-examination was deliberately disorderly and, therefore, disconcerting—a series of questions which seemingly exhausted a particular subject, then a shift to an entirely different topic, and then, sometimes hours later, a return to the first subject from an entirely new approach.

About the old Ford, Chambers, said Hiss, had told him he had no means of getting about and Hiss had lent him the car once or twice while he occupied the 28th Street apartment. In the fall of 1935, with Hiss's permission, he used it continuously for about two months. Chambers returned the old car and with it the keys. Meanwhile Hiss had bought a new car. Then, several months later—May or June 1936—Chambers called on Hiss and reminded him of a previous promise he had made to give Chambers the old car when he got a new one. Hiss then turned over the Ford to him, together with the keys and a District of Columbia certificate of title. This, according to Hiss, was the last time he saw Chambers before the confrontation in the Commodore Hotel in 1948.

With deadly persistence Murphy brought out the improbabilities in the story. Hiss was made to admit that he had given Chambers the car, despite the fact that Chambers had then defaulted in the payment of the rent of the apartment, that Chambers owed him a balance of twenty dollars for cash advances, and he had come to regard Chambers as an undesirable associate and a "dead beat." Although Chambers may have considered the gift of the Oriental rug a discharge of his obligations, Hiss said he had not regarded it as a "satisfactory equivalent" of what Chambers owed him.

Hiss denied ever having said to Chambers that he wanted to give the old car to some deserving organizer or that he ever assigned the title of it to a man named Rosen. Confronted with the assignment on the reverse side of the certificate of title to the Cherner Motor Company, dated July 23, 1936, purportedly signed "Alger Hiss" and acknowledged before one W. Marion Smith, a notary public, Hiss remembered that someone brought the assignment into his office in the Department of Justice and told him he had disposed of the car some time before but had not completed the formal assignment of it; that he thereupon signed the paper and acknowledged his signature before the notary.

All of this, as Murphy then proceeded to show, was widely at variance with Hiss's sworn testimony before the House Un-American Activities Committee.

Hiss's handling of the troublesome Woodstock typewriter was not much better. He remembered the old Woodstock. It was an office machine given to Mrs. Hiss by her father. He admitted after some hedging that he had testified before the grand jury he had a "visual recollection" of the typewriter at Volta Place and had told the FBI agents that Mrs. Hiss had disposed of the typewriter to the Salvation Army or some junk dealer in 1938. Now, however, he testified, he was positive, in view of the Catletts' testimony, that the typewriter had been given to the Catletts in December of 1937 when the Hisses moved from P Street to Volta Place. Confronted with more of his testimony before the grand jury, Hiss was compelled to admit that he had made no mention there of the gift of the typewriter to the Catletts and, when asked the names of his former house servants, had not mentioned "Clytie" Catlett. He said he thought she was dead.

Hiss was questioned at length about his conversation with Secretary of State Byrnes in March 1946, concerning a rumor which had come to the secretary that Hiss had Communist affiliations. Hiss said he had been called into Byrnes's office and the secretary had told him that he had been informed two or three members of Congress were going to make speeches on the floor of the House to the effect that there were a number of Communists in the State Department and that they had named Hiss as one of them. That afternoon, said Hiss, he went to Ladd of the Federal Bureau of Investigation and told him of his conversation with Secretary Byrnes and said he wanted to submit himself to any interrogation the bureau might propose. He said that at that time he answered frankly and fully all questions put to him concerning his membership in various societies and his previous associations with Lee Pressman and others.

Hiss admitted that shortly before he was elected to the presidency of the Carnegie Foundation, he had had a talk with John Foster Dulles, one of the trustees, in which they discussed rumors which had reached Dulles that Hiss was a Communist. Hiss said he then told Dulles of his previous talk with Secretary Byrnes and his subsequent interview with representatives of the Federal Bureau of Investigation, and he had "checked with Secretary Byrnes specifically" as to whether the issue had been laid to rest. He was told it had been. On further cross-examination it appeared that the "specific checking" had not been with Secretary Byrnes personally but with Assistant Secretary Dean Acheson. Hiss also testified that he had two later talks with Dulles about the rumors or charges that he had been a Communist: the first, in March of 1947, after he had assumed the presidency of the Carnegie Foundation and had appeared before the grand jury, and the second, in the summer of 1948, after the congressional-committee hearing had started. He denied that on the latter occasion Dulles suggested to him that out of consideration for the endowment he should resign as president.

Under further cross-examination Hiss testified that the first time he heard the name Whittaker Chambers was in May 1947, when some FBI agents called at his office in the Carnegie Endowment Building and asked him what he knew about some forty or fifty persons whose names they mentioned, and the name Whittaker Chambers was in the list. It was next mentioned to him by a personal friend in March or April of 1948. He said he heard it a third time on August 2, 1948, when he was called on the telephone by a number of different newspapermen, who told him they understood from "someone close to the committee" that a man named Whittaker Chambers was going to appear before the committee the next day and say that he (Hiss) was a Communist. He added that before August 3, 1948, he made no attempt to find out who Whittaker Chambers was.

Hiss admitted knowing Noel Field[15] well enough to have entertained him at dinner at his house. He denied ever having discussed the subject of Field's services for the Communist party with a woman known as Hede Eisler, Hede Gumpertz or Hede Massing, or that he had ever known a woman under any of those names.

For the alleged purpose of impeaching Hiss's direct testimony, Murphy read practically the entire transcript of the House committee's proceedings in the confrontation of Hiss and Chambers in the Commodore Hotel.

Mrs. Hiss followed her husband on the stand. Her testimony paralleled his—sometimes literally. She had never known the Chamberses under any name but Crosley. She had never called them by their first names, and they had never called her by her first name. The Chamberses, she

---

15 Field was well known as a Communist at the time of the trial.

said, had spent two nights with them at the P Street house, while they awaited the delivery of their own furniture to the 28th Street apartment. She denied Mrs. Chambers' testimony as to the furniture in their various residences and its arrangement. She admitted that Mrs. Chambers had painted and given her a picture of her son "Timmie." She denied they had ever celebrated any anniversaries or holidays with the Chamberses or that she ever visited the Chamberses at any of their various addresses or tended the baby while Mrs. Chambers painted.

Mrs. Hiss said she had never taken a trip with either of the Chamberses to Peterboro, Smithtown or anywhere else. She testified, as her husband had done, that she had spent the entire time during the first half of August 1937 at Chestertown or at Baltimore where she was taking a summer course in college. She told of her withdrawal of $400 from the Washington bank. The Volta Place house, she said, was much larger than the 30th Street apartment and required considerable additional furniture. She told of the things she bought with the money—a new bed, a mattress, a bureau, a chair, a rug, lamps, candlesticks, curtains and a workbench for "Timmie." She denied most emphatically that she had ever made any typewritten copies of State Department papers or that she had ever handed any such documents—original or copies—to Chambers.

Murphy's cross-examination was quiet and gentle. He covered her history before her marriage to Hiss. When she lived on Central Park West, above 96th Street in New York, she had been a member of the Socialist party, hadn't she? She didn't think so. Confronted with the election register for 1932, which showed her registered as a Socialist, she admitted she voted that year for Norman Thomas. She denied knowledge that she was shown as a Socialist on the records of the Morningside branch of the Socialist party. She admitted typing the Bryn Mawr alumnae report and the letter to the University of Maryland. The typewriter, she said, was in bad order; the ribbon puckered and the keys did not always fall down. She now knew she had given the typewriter to the Catletts in 1937 because of what Mc-Lean had told her and the testimony of the "Catlett children."

Murphy developed numerous inconsistencies between her testimony on the trial and what she had sworn to before the grand jury six months before, particularly as to when first and on how many different occasions she had seen the Chamberses and with respect to the typewriter. Hadn't she told the grand jury she had seen the typewriter at Volta Place? Hadn't she told the grand jury she could recall no defects such as broken letters or keys jamming? Hadn't she told them she had no idea when she got rid of the old Woodstock? To all of these inquiries, she answered, "Yes"; but that was her recollection then, not now.

The last witness called by the defense was Dr. Carl A. L. Binger. He had sat in the courtroom taking notes throughout all of Chambers' testimony. Prosecutor Murphy, aware that Dr. Binger, a psychiatrist, was prepared to testify that Chambers' life history and erratic conduct indicated a mental condition which destroyed his credibility as a witness, insisted that the proposed testimony be stated for the record but out of the presence of the jury, as an "offer of proof." Under this procedure the Court could have ruled on the admissibility of the testimony before any questions were put to the doctor in the hearing of the jury. Although in a preliminary discussion the Court had expressed its doubts as to the admissibility of the evidence, it overruled the objection, rejected the proposed offer of proof and permitted the examination to proceed.

Dr. Binger was qualified as a physician who had been thirty-five years in practice and had latterly specialized in general psychiatry. He had read and studied Chambers' various writings and translations and had observed him on the witness stand. Stryker then proceeded for exactly forty-five minutes to propound a hypothesis reciting with well-placed emphasis every incident, discreditable or considered suggestive of abnormality, developed in his long cross-examination of Chambers—the insanity of his grandmother, the suicide of his brother, Chambers' expressed reaction to that suicide, his youthful habits and idiosyncracies, his having run away from home when he was sixteen and lived in New Orleans among drunkards and prostitutes, his early atheistic views, his career at Columbia, the stealing of books from the library, the writing of a blasphemous play which caused his expulsion, the lying to the dean to obtain reinstatement, his writing of an erotic poem, his translations of pornographic literature, his living with a woman not his wife whom he brought to his mother's home, his becoming a Communist, his expressed reasons for joining the party, his use of many aliases, his readiness to lie, cheat and steal for the party and his statement as to why he broke with it, his pretended fears for his safety, his perjury in his application and oath made to obtain employment with the WPA, his deliberate leaving of an old typewriter on a streetcar because it reminded him of his past, his hiding of the secret papers, his charges against Hiss, his admitted perjuries before the House Un-American Activities Committee and the grand jury, his recovery and production of the papers after his pretrial examination in the libel suit, his withholding of some of them and secreting them in the pumpkin, and his nervous breakdown while working for *Time* magazine.

The long hypothesis was followed by the question:

Now, Dr. Binger, assuming the facts as stated in the question to be true, and taking into account your observation of Chambers on the witness stand, and your knowledge of his writings and translations, have you, as a psychiatrist, an opinion, within the bounds of reasonable certainty, as to the mental condition of Whittaker Chambers?

Mr. Murphy was immediately on his feet, objecting to the question on the ground it was argumentative and that it did not correctly or completely represent the evidence and that it usurped the function of the jury. Judge Kaufman declared that on the basis of briefs previously submitted he had about decided to admit the testimony, but on second thought he had concluded to exclude it; that the question of the credibility of Chambers was "one of the crucial elements" in the case and "the record was sufficiently clear for the jury, using its experience in life," to appraise the testimony of all the witnesses.

Although the hypothetical question had not been answered, Stryker had every reason for gratification. He had drawn his picture of Chambers for the jury. Every venireman had a general idea of what Dr. Binger's answer would have been. He had not been cross-examined and his unuttered but apprehended answer had gone unchallenged. As an old trial lawyer Stryker was not too much concerned with the Court's direction to the jury to disregard the question. He knew from experience that this was like telling an unprotected man in a rainstorm he should not consider that the water falling on him was wet.

The Government's rebuttal case, while relatively brief, punctured a number of holes in the not-too-solid defense. Burnetta Fisher, daughter of "Clytie" Catlett and sister of the Catlett boys, took the stand to testify that she got the Woodstock typewriter when she was a high-school student and used it to type her homework. She did not have it fixed before she used it.

A daughter of Ira Lockey, the man from whom McLean had bought the typewriter, testified she also used the typewriter in her schoolwork, that she did not have it fixed, and that she used it until she moved to New York in 1948. While the keys sometimes stuck, she said, she was able to type on it—she would "just pull the keys back."

To rebut the testimony of Perry Catlett that after the Catletts got the typewriter he took it to a repair shop at the corner of K Street and Connecticut Avenue to have it re-

paired, the Government called a real-estate man who testified from his records that the Woodstock Typewriter Company rented space in the building at the corner of K Street
and Connecticut Avenue for two years succeeding September 15, 1938. (It was the Government's evidence that the
secret papers were typed in February and March of 1938.)
McLean, in an attempt to avoid the effect of this evidence,
suggested that the previous location of the Woodstock Company was also on K Street, just a block away. To meet this
the Government later in the trial produced another real-
estate man who testified that the previous occupancy of the
Woodstock Company commenced May 1, 1938; that the
lease had contained a ninety-day right-of-cancellation clause
which had been exercised, and the premises were vacated in
September of 1938.

The next witness, and an important one, was John Foster Dulles, chairman of the board of the Carnegie Endowment for International Peace. He testified that shortly
before Hiss assumed the presidency of the endowment on
January 1, 1947, he had questioned him about rumors that
he had Communist affiliations. Hiss told him, he said, that
he had voluntarily gone to the Federal Bureau of Investigation and submitted himself to its interrogation, and he
had thought those rumors had been laid to rest. Dulles continued that in March of 1938 he again heard reports that
Hiss had Communist affiliations; this time from a more
responsible source than on the first occasion. He again
questioned Hiss and Hiss told him that he had just appeared before the grand jury and had been asked about a
number of persons. Hiss said he had known some of them
and told the jury what he knew about them; others he had
known and had so told the jurors. The witness next talked
with Hiss on the subject of Hiss's Communist connections
on the eighteenth of August, 1948, while the House Un-
American Activities Committee's hearings were in progress.
At that time, said Dulles, he told Hiss the situation had

posed a rather serious and embarrassing problem for the trustees; that he had no doubt that Hiss was considering what his duty was as president of the foundation and it would be well for him to come to a conclusion that, regardless of whether the charges were true or false, his ability to discharge the duties of president had been somewhat impaired by the publicity which had been given to the testimony of Chambers and his denial of it. In response to that, said the witness, Hiss suggested that he (Hiss) was conscious of his duty and had given the matter considerable thought and had in mind a resignation at an early date, probably in September.

Under cross-examination by Stryker, the witness testified he wouldn't say Hiss had made a "definite, flat, binding promise to resign in September." Stryker seized the opportunity to show that the inquiries made regarding Hiss before his appointment to the presidency of the foundation and the laudatory character of his recommendations had all been presented to the trustees.

Murphy next advised the Court of his intentions to call three witnesses: Hede Massing, ex-wife of the notorious Gerhart Eisler, by whom he expected to corroborate Chambers' testimony that Hiss had been a member of the Washington Communist underground; an official of the Cherner Motor Company, of Washington, by whom he expected to prove that Hiss had transferred his 1929 Ford to that company, which had in turn signed it over to one William Rosen; and William Rosen, whom he expected would testify that he had received the car. On Stryker's objection all three witnesses were excluded from the stand on the ground that their suggested testimony was not proper rebuttal.

One of the last witnesses to take the stand was Courtland Jones, Washington FBI agent, who denied emphatically that he had ever offered Mike Catlett $200 for the recovery of the Hiss typewriter.

In surrebuttal the defense called four witnesses. A keeper of the medical records of the Delavan Hospital in Washington, where Mrs. Hiss said she had taken a sick relative in the summer of 1937, testified that the hospital records listed Mrs. Hiss's addresses as "care of Mrs. Wickes, Chestertown, Maryland." Miss Stafford, assistant registrar of the University of Maryland, who had previously appeared as a Government witness, testified Mrs. Hiss enrolled for a summer course in inorganic chemistry in June of 1937, and her grades were mailed to her at Chestertown, Maryland, on August 5, 1937. Norman Grieg, a camp counselor, testified Mrs. Hiss frequently visited her son Timothy at the Chestertown Camp during the summer of 1937, and he once saw Hiss when he visited the Hiss apartment in Chestertown. The last piece of evidence was the deposition of Mrs. Wickes, the Chestertown landlady, who deponed that the Hisses had been subtenants of one of her apartments during July and part of August in both 1936 and 1937.

This concluded the evidence.

Stryker began his argument to the jury on July 6, 1949, with the experienced criminal lawyer's stereotyped approach—the mantle thrown by a merciful rule around any defendant, that he is presumed innocent until proved guilty beyond a reasonable doubt. More concretely, the Government was required to prove beyond such a reasonable doubt that Hiss gave the secret documents to Chambers. Chambers was the only one in the long array of witnesses who had so testified; and if the jury didn't believe beyond a reasonable doubt that Chambers was telling the truth, it must acquit the defendant. Murphy himself had said it, declared Stryker, and said it better than he could: "If you don't believe Chambers, we have no case."

Stryker then proceeded to exhaust his extensive and picturesque vocabulary in a castigation of Chambers. His whole career, he charged, was "marked by trickery and deceit. . . . Roguery, deception and criminality have marked this man Chambers as if with a hot iron." Referring to Chambers' testimony that he withheld as long as he could

his knowledge of Hiss's espionage activities because he did
not want to injure him any more than was necessary, Stryker shouted in tones of mingled emotion and irony that
Chambers was "not only a traitor, a thief, a liar, a perjurer,
an enemy of his country, but a hypocrite!" Chambers
hadn't wanted to injure Hiss! Oh, no! All he did was to
testify under oath that "Hiss represented the concealed
enemy against which we are all fighting.

"Believe Chambers!" cried Stryker. "I would not believe him on a stack of Bibles if the FBI stacked them as
high as this building. He believes in nothing: not God, not
man, not in the sanctity of marriage or motherhood, not
even in himself."

Stryker tried to supply what the evidence clearly lacked
—a motive for Chambers' charges against Hiss. "This man
was ambitious," said Stryker. "In a Presidential compaign
he thought he could deliver a fast sideswipe at Alger Hiss—
Dumbarton Oaks—Yalta—Communism! Great stuff for a
political campaign to take the public's mind off the Eightieth Congress. . . . Chambers," he declared in another connection, "concocted this story to get out of the $75,000 libel
suit which Hiss has filed against him."

Chambers was not the only target of Stryker's wrathful
invective. The Federal Bureau of Investigation came in for
a full share. It had gone to every possible length to bolster
Chambers and discredit Hiss. It had oppressed the Catlett
boys; one of them it had tried to bribe with an offer to pay
$200 for the Woodstock typewriter. The House Un-Amer-
ican Activities Committee received special attention. Stryker likened it to the French Revolutionary Tribunal,
where the mere identification of a suspect, and the inevitable mob yell of "guilty," hustled the victim into the tum-
brel and started him on his way to the guillotine. "For
eleven months," shouted Stryker, "Alger Hiss has suffered
under the travail of that committee's work."

Leaving the offensive for the defensive, Stryker argued
that Wadleigh—"that miserable, abject specimen of human-

ity"—could have obtained the four handwritten memoranda by taking them off Hiss's desk or out of his wastebasket.

As to the typewritten copies of the State Department documents, the evidence showed the Woodstock typewriter had been given away by the Hisses before the papers could have been typed on it. "Clytie" Catlett, who had testified about the typewriter, was "a lovely Christian character . . . whose testimony was at least as credible as that of a man who had spent twelve years of his life trying to tear down his country." "Pat" and "Mike" Catlett were "undoubtedly very ignorant colored boys, but honest."

Stryker played up the character witnesses. No one but a paragon of virtue and loyalty could have summoned such a distinguished array of witnesses to his defense. Hiss, in contrast to Chambers, had led a "pure, wholesome, sound, clean, decent, fine life."

In his peroration, Stryker apologized for his zeal and his shortcomings, but he begged the jury to charge them to him, not to hold them against Hiss. "This is not a case," he thundered, "but an outrage—the long culmination of the job that was done by the House Un-American Activities Committee—an Un-American Committee, the way they handled the job." Lowering his voice and in his sweetest tones he said, "Ladies and gentlemen, the case will be in your hands. I beg you, I pray you, to search your consciences, and I have no fear, 'Yea, though I have walked through the valley of the shadow of death.' " And turning to the pale, drawn face of his client, he ended, "Alger Hiss, this long nightmare is drawing to a close. Rest well. Your case, your life, your liberty are in good hands."

It was a splendid effort. No one could justly accuse Lloyd Paul Stryker of not having given Hiss a full defense and an advocate's "full measure of devotion."

Murphy's summation was a deliberate, calm, assured review and analysis of the evidence, largely free from discreditable characterizations or strong invective, but punc-

tuated throughout with sarcasm and ridicule. Step by step
he went over the Government's case. There were, he said,
"three solid witnesses" to the essential facts: the typewriter,
the original State documents and the documents Chambers had in his possession. There was no contradiction of
the fact that Chambers had indubitable copies of the original secret, confidential State documents, all of them dated
in the first three months of 1938. The proof was positive
that all but one of them had been written on the Hisses'
Woodstock typewriter. From those undisputed and indisputable facts, the jury could draw but one conclusion:
that "that smart, intelligent, American-born man gave them
to Chambers."

It was true, conceded Murphy, that in a trial in a Federal
court for perjury the law required proof by two witnesses
or by one witness and corroborating circumstances. Here,
he declared, they had the direct testimony of Chambers
that he got the documents from Hiss and that the copies he
produced had been typed by Mrs. Hiss on the Woodstock
typewriter. That was the testimony of one witness. The
copies themselves (replicas of original State papers) and the
telltale typewriter were the corroborating circumstances.
He disposed of Hiss's denial by repeating an illustration he
had used in his opening statement: The small boy might
deny that he had raided his mother's pantry and helped
himself from the jam pot, but the denial availed little if
the boy's face was covered with jam. "The typewriter and
the copies are the jam on Hiss's face," he said.

But the documents and the typewriter were not the only
corroborating circumstances, said Murphy. There was the
testimony of Chambers and his wife as to their intimate
knowledge of the Hisses, of their homes—those on 30th
Street and Volta Place, as well as those on P Street and 28th
Street—and their furnishings, and of their habits and hobbies. Referring to Mrs. Chambers' detailed description of
the Volta Street home, Murphy put it bluntly to the jury:
"She was either there or she is psychic. Consider that, when

you decide who was lying." What about the $400 which
Chambers says Hiss gave him in November of 1937 with
which to buy a new car? Well, the uncontradicted evidence
showed Mrs. Hiss withdrew $400 from their joint bank ac-
count on November 19, 1937, and that Mrs. Chambers
bought a new car with something over $400 in cash on No-
vember 23, 1937. "Just how psychic do you have to get?"
asked Murphy.

The government prosecutor reviewed Hiss's confused
and implausible version concerning the old 1929 Ford and
the Oriental rug. He ridiculed Hiss's "absurd performance" to make certain of his identification of Chambers
when they confronted each other at the House committee's
session in the Commodore Hotel.

As to the attempt of the defense to show that the Hisses
had disposed of the Woodstock before January 1, 1938, all
of the facts, declared Murphy, proved the contrary. Hiss
before the belated discovery of the machine by the Catletts
had had a "visual recollection" of the typewriter at the
Volta Place house. Mrs. Hiss had been quite sure that after
they moved to the Volta Place house she had given the machine to the Salvation Army or some Georgetown junk
dealer. The Hisses hadn't mentioned the Catletts in their
testimony before the grand jury. They had thought "Clytie" Catlett was dead. Then the defense lawyers turned up
the three Catletts and the Hisses developed a new recollection. And the testimony of the Catletts, said Murphy, had
been completely discredited.

The prosecutor gave the jury his idea of the real facts
concerning the Catletts and the disposition of the typewriter. The Hisses knew the Woodstock had been used to
copy the secret State documents. When Chambers told Hiss
he had broken with the Communist party, Hiss realized the
danger to him of that typewriter—the "immutable witness"
against him. How best to get rid of it? Not by a regular
open sale, because then there would be a record of it. So
they gave it to the Catletts, hoping it would just disappear—

"end up in the ash can." Hiss had not mentioned the Catletts to the FBI because he hoped the government would
never trace the Catletts. But the FBI did trace the Catletts.
And what happened? The Catletts ran to Donald Hiss and
told him the FBI men had been asking about the typewriter. Why Donald Hiss? Probably because Alger had
told them to go to Donald and tell him if the government
men got hold of them. And when did the Catletts get the
typewriter? Not in 1937, but in 1938. What did Perry Catlett remember about it? He took it to a Woodstock repair
shop on the northwest corner of Connecticut Avenue and
K Street, but not in 1938—probably in 1939.

The evidence of the real-estate men, said Murphy, called
by the Government showed that the Woodstock shop had
not come to the Connecticut Avenue and K Street address
until September of 1938, and if the defense wanted to con-
tend that Perry really meant that he took it to the former
address of the shop a block away, that wouldn't help them
any because the shop hadn't come to that address until
May of 1938. Furthermore, the Catletts testified they took
the typewriter to their own house on P Street and the evidence showed conclusively that the Catletts did not move
into that house until January 17, 1938. That, summarized
Murphy, pretty well disposed of the Catletts and their testimony.

The most dramatic part of Murphy's summation was his
treatment of the defense's character witnesses. Stryker, he
said, had called some fifteen or more such witnesses—two
justices of the Supreme Court of the United States among
them. Maybe the jury would want to think for itself
"whether two judges of the United States Supreme Court
could with propriety come into this courtroom. . . . Just
how important," said the prosecutor, "is a person's reputation? . . . I dare say Judas Iscariot had a fairly good reputation. . . . He was next to God, one of the Twelve, and what
did he do? Brutus, Caesar's friend, I dare say he had a good
reputation. He got so close to his boss that he stabbed him.

And Major General Benedict Arnold? He came from a fine
family—what happened? . . . He sold out West Point. He
wasn't caught, but if he had been, couldn't he have called
George Washington as a reputation witness? . . . And take
the devil, Lucifer himself was one of the fallen angels. He
traveled in the sight of God. Now he had a reputation, I
dare say, and what happened to him?

"All window dressing," cried Murphy. "Those"—he
pointed to the typewriter and the Government's exhibits—
"those are the facts." Murphy concluded his argument
with a flower of speech which, if it failed to match the ex-
alted and picturesque figures of Stryker, had its own peculiar fragrance: "Someone has said that roses that fester stink
worse than weeds, and I say that a brilliant man like this
man who betrays his trust stinks, and under that smiling
face his heart is black and cancerous. He is a traitor."

The arguments were concluded on the seventh of July,
and on the afternoon of that day Judge Kaufman delivered
his oral charge to the jury.

When it is considered that the trial had lasted twenty-
seven days and that upward of seventy-five witnesses had
testified and piled up a record of more than four thousand
pages, the Court's instructions were surprisingly brief.

The Court instructed that the Government had established that Hiss had given the testimony alleged in the
indictment and that the statements made by him were
material to an investigation into espionage then being conducted by the grand jury. The Court explained that the
essential charge of the indictment was that Hiss had testified falsely when he swore that he had not turned over secret and confidential State papers to Chambers. The issue
for the jury to determine was, therefore, a narrow one:
Did Hiss deliver secret and confidential papers to Chambers in February and March of 1938? If he hadn't, he could
not be found guilty. If he had, the jury might find him
guilty.

The Court further instructed that the law in a charge

of perjury required proof by two witnesses or one witness
and corroborating circumstances. The only witness who
had testified that Hiss gave secret and confidential papers
to Chambers was Chambers himself. Therefore, Chambers'
testimony was to be considered seriously. Murphy had
been correct in his opening statement that if the jury did
not believe Chambers, the Government had no case. Chambers, the Court declared, was an interested witness, first,
because he had made a charge against Hiss and would naturally want to sustain it and, second, because of the pendency
of the civil damage suit against him. In determining Chambers' credibility, the jury should consider that it had been
proved that Chambers had previously made false and inconsistent statements, that he had failed earlier to disclose the
existence of the papers and denied that he had such papers,
that he had been a member of the Communist party, and it
should take into account all of the evidence concerning his
life and actions. If, after such considerations, it did not believe Chambers beyond a reasonable doubt, its verdict must
be not guilty. If, on the other hand, it did believe Chambers, it must further find that his testimony was corroborated by proof of supporting circumstances. Such proof, said
the Court, was what is called "circumstantial evidence,"
and such evidence must not only be consistent with the
guilt of the defendant, it must be inconsistent with any
reasonable hypothesis of innocence. It was for the jury to
say whether Chambers' testimony had been so corroborated.

As to the defendant Hiss, the Court charged that the jury
should consider "his life, education and standing in the
community," his later conduct when he learned of Chambers' charge against him, his challenge to Chambers to repeat his charge in circumstances where there would be no
protecting privilege against an action of libel, and the institution of such an action by Hiss when Chambers made
his charge publicly. It should consider, too, Hiss's explanation of the Government's exhibits and the typewriting.

The defendant had called character witnesses—"prominent persons"—who had testified to his previous good reputation for integrity, loyalty and veracity. Such evidence was competent to be considered in connection with all the other evidence in the case.

If, said the Court, the jury believed Hiss as against Chambers, its verdict should be not guilty. If, on the other hand, it believed Chambers and that his testimony as to the documents had been corroborated, its verdict might be guilty. In order to arrive at a verdict, all twelve of the jurors must come to an agreement; in other words, the verdict had to be unanimous.

Certainly the charge was, as the charge in every criminal case should be, eminently fair to the defendant. Neither side objected to it.

At 4:20 P.M. the jurors retired. Seven different times during the ensuing nineteen hours, they communicated with the Court. Once it was to ask for a copy of the indictment, the bill of particulars and the exhibits; twice it was to have portions of the judge's charge reread to them; and on four occasions it was to advise the Court that they could not agree.

It later appeared that from the outset of their deliberations they stood deadlocked—eight for conviction, four for acquittal. At nine o'clock on the evening of the eighth, it was apparent that a unanimous verdict was out of the question. With no objection from either the prosecution or the defense, the Court discharged the jury.

THE SECOND TRIAL

The second trial was begun on November 17, 1949. There were important changes in the old line-up. Judge Kaufman had been supplanted by Judge Henry W. Goddard. District Attorney McGohey had been succeeded by Irving H. Saypol. Lloyd Paul Stryker, for some unexplained reason, had been dropped. Claude B. Cross appeared with McLean as counsel for Hiss. Robert von Mehren had taken the place of Harold Shapero as an assistant attorney for the defense. Murphy and Donegan were again on hand to shoulder the burden for the prosecution.

Seventy-four-year-old Judge Goddard was the senior Federal judge of the district. He had served for over twenty-three years, and he enjoyed the esteem and confidence of the bar and the public. Cross was a highly regarded, scholarly lawyer, known and respected for his industry and thoroughness in the preparation of his cases. He had not, however, had any considerable experience in the trial of criminal cases. He was as unlike Stryker as it was possible for a man to be. His trial method was the mild, composed and persuasion-inducing type rather than the forceful, bellicose and persuasion-compelling type of Stryker.

A jury was obtained even more rapidly than on the first trial. As finally passed it held four men and eight women. Seven of the women were housewives; one was gainfully employed. Of the four men, one was an office man, one an optician, one a plant manager and one a retired manufacturer.

From the outset it was apparent that Judge Goddard's disposition was to discourage technical objections and afford each side the widest permissible latitude within which to get all relevant facts before the jury.

Murphy's opening statement took a line quite different from that which he had followed in the first trial. Instead of emphasizing the testimony of Chambers with the declaration, "If you don't believe Chambers, we have no case," he stressed as of primary importance the "immutable" evidence of the documents and that they were in Hiss's handwriting or had been copied on Hiss's typewriter. He faced frankly the many weaknesses of Chambers as a witness. All of these, he said, were immaterial if the jury believed Hiss gave the secret documents to Chambers.

Chambers, Murphy declared, had had an unguided and unfortunate boyhood. He had become a Communist, a secret agent. He had cheated, lied and stolen for the party. Because of his sincere belief in communism as a philosophy of government, he had thought at the time he was doing what was right. The day came when he was disillusioned. He broke with the party. He repented of his errors. He attempted to redeem himself and succeeded. Then suddenly he was summoned before a committee of the Congress of the United States and put upon his oath. He testified before that committee because he felt it was his conscientious duty to do so. He had not produced the documents which had so hopelessly entangled Hiss until he had been forced to do so by Hiss's libel action. Chambers' testimony, concluded Murphy, would be corroborated not only by the documents but by a wealth of supporting detail and the testimony of other credible witnesses.

Cross's opening followed closely the pattern which had been set by Stryker—Hiss's magnificent record and reputation and Chambers' utter worthlessness as an accusing witness. He imported some new discreditable details from Chambers' past and promised the jury the evidence would show that Chambers got the secret documents from someone other than Hiss.

The evidence for the Government followed pretty closely the lines set in the first trial. There were, however, several new witnesses and important additional facts developed in the examination of some of the previous witnesses.

Chambers was much more assured in facing Cross than he had been when confronted with Stryker. There were several additions to his former testimony. In 1937, he said, he had bought a farm in Maryland (not far from the one he presently owned) which he and Hiss had located a year or two earlier. Hiss had liked it so well that he made a down payment on it, but he had later changed his mind and withdrawn it. Chambers had then bought the farm. This was confirmed by the later testimony of the real-estate broker who produced the correspondence he had had with Hiss in the transaction.

Chambers also told of having once met Hiss in a restaurant and of Hiss's having introduced him there to a woman named Plum Fountain. The peculiarity of the name stuck in his memory. He recalled another automobile trip he had taken with Hiss, this one to Erwinna, Pennsylvania, in 1935. He could not recall what the occasion for the trip was. He was permitted over defense objection to tell what Hiss had said to him in disposing of his old 1929 Ford—that he wanted to pass it along to some deserving organizer who lacked means for needed transportation, and that the Cherner Motor Company was used as a conduit for that purpose.

Cross's cross-examination of Chambers, judged by the record, was quite as effective as Stryker's had been. He brought out all of Chambers' previous delinquencies and added others. He compelled Chambers to admit again the many contradictions and inconsistencies between his direct examination and the testimony he had given before the House Un-American Activities Committee and the New York grand jury.

The examination of Mrs. Chambers covered the same ground as in the first trial. While she appeared much more at ease than on the former occasion, Cross had little difficulty in developing many inconsistencies between her present testimony and her answers on the previous trial and in the Baltimore pretrial hearings of the civil suit. These concerned mostly dates when she said she had seen Mr. and Mrs. Hiss.

As on the first trial, copies of the secret documents which Chambers said he had received from Alger Hiss were compared with the originals and received in evidence. The one document which had previously been withheld was now offered. It was part of a cable from Paris, dated January 25, 1938, from United States Ambassador Bullitt to the State Department—a highly confidential communication regarding French, German-Russian relations and the attitude of England toward Mussolini and Italy.

McLean's cross-examination of the witness Anderson, a State Department official, with respect to the secret documents was even more extensive and effective than his previous cross-examination of this witness had been. He went into a detailed examination of each paper and made the witness admit from the markings on a number of them it could not be told with certainty that they had ever gone through Sayre's office.

The cross-examination of Wadleigh was likewise much more thorough than on the first trial. Cross's cross-examination, however, failed to establish, as he had promised in his opening statement, that Chambers had got the secret documents from Wadleigh or someone other than Hiss. The stubborn fact that all but one of them had been written on the Hiss typewriter stood in the way.

As additional witnesses the Government called a vice-president of the Cherner Motor Company, who identified a bill of sale, dated July 23, 1936, by which Hiss transferred his 1929 Ford to that company. On the same day it was reassigned to a William Rosen.

William Rosen was called to the stand. He denied knowing either Hiss or J. Peters. He declined to answer any further questions on the ground his answers might incriminate him.

Hede Massing, former Viennese actress and ex-wife of Gerhart Eisler, took the stand. She testified she had been a Communist and had known Hiss as one. Specifically, she recalled a conversation she had had with Hiss in the summer or fall of 1935 regarding the services of Noel Field, another Communist.

The woman who had rented the Volta Place house to the

Hisses corroborated Mrs. Chambers' description of the draperies and wallpaper there.

Cross did not succeed by his cross-examination in weakening substantially the testimony of any of these witnesses.

The Government put in evidence a memorandum made by Adolf Berle, Presidential adviser in charge of State Department security, after his interview with Chambers in 1939. It was captioned "Underground Espionage Agent" and listed as members of the Soviet underground, among others, Alger Hiss, Donald Hiss and Priscilla Hiss.

Practically all of the witnesses who had testified for the defense in the first trial appeared in the second. The line-up of the character witnesses was changed somewhat. Justices Frankfurter and Reed did not appear. Dr. Jessup, who had given his deposition on the former trial, appeared in person. Some additional witnesses were called. Francis B. Sayre, former Assistant Secretary of State, described Hiss as "a man of utter integrity and reliability, who had never in any way tried to influence American policy." Murphy, on cross-examination, however, got him to admit that he did not recall that Hiss had ever made for him any memoranda of the type of the four memoranda that had been produced by Chambers; also, that Hiss had recommended Noel Field to him as a prospective assistant.

Murphy forced the admission from Dr. Hornbeck that in 1939 he and Ambassador Bullitt had discussed a rumor that Alger Hiss was a Communist. He also got this witness to admit that the four Government exhibits in Hiss's handwriting were not of the kind ordinarily prepared by Hiss in the course of his employment.

The testimony of Mr. and Mrs. Hiss was not substantially different from that they had given on the first trial. Hiss denied ever having gone with Chambers to see a Maryland farm which Chambers afterward bought. He admitted he had looked at the farm and had considered purchasing it. The fact that Chambers had later bought it was a mere coincidence. He also denied Chambers' new testimony that he had made a trip with him to Erwinna, Pennsylvania, or that he had ever introduced him to a woman named Plum Fountain. He, however, admitted knowing a woman of that name.

Hiss denied again that he had ever met Mrs. Massing or talked to her about Noel Field. In his cross-examination Murphy produced a letter which Hiss had written to Noel Field in May of 1948. It was addressed "Dear Noel." Hiss again admitted he had known Field and that the Hisses and Fields exchanged social visits. Murphy also brought out in his cross-examination of Hiss that Hiss's father and sister had committed suicide (important to offset the testimony of suicide and insanity in the Chambers family) and that Hiss had dodged the lie-detector test when it was suggested by members of the House Un-American Activities Committee.

Murphy's cross-examination of Mike Catlett pretty well destroyed his testimony. His statement that the Catletts got the typewriter when the Hisses moved from P Street to 30th Street (July 1, 1936) was clearly absurd. One of the typewritten exemplars (the inquiry to the University of Maryland) written by Mrs. Hiss was dated May 25, 1937. His testimony that his family moved into their house on P Street in 1936 was disproved by the rental agent's record that the Catletts actually moved there on January 17, 1938. Mrs. Hiss had testified that the Catlett boys took the typewriter away in their little express wagon. Mike Catlett had said Mrs. Hiss delivered it to the Catlett home from her automobile.

Donald Hiss took the stand to deny that he had ever had any Communist connections, that he had ever given his brother any State papers, or that he had ever seen or known of Chambers.

In further refutation of Chambers' testimony that he had driven to Peterboro, New Hampshire, with the Hisses sometime during the first half of August 1937, and in cor-

roboration of their claim that during that period they were
at Chestertown, Maryland, the records of a Chestertown
bank were introduced to show a deposit in a Hiss bank
account there on August 10, 1937.

The most startling variation in the two trials was the
admission in the second of the co-called expert psychiatric
testimony. After hearing argument Judge Goddard ruled
that while the admissibility of such testimony had not
theretofore been passed on by any Federal court, such testimony had been admitted by a number of state courts and
its use had been advocated by leading authorities on the
law of evidence, and he would admit it.

Dr. Binger was called to the stand. His direct questioning followed rather literally that of Stryker in the first trial.
The hypothetical question had been embellished with
some further details and its reading time extended to seventy minutes. Dr. Binger's answer was impressive. Chambers, he declared, was in his opinion "suffering from a condition known as a psychopathic personality, a disorder of
character, the outstanding features of which are amoral and
asocial behavior." By "amoral" he meant that it was behavior against established convention. By "asocial" he meant
that Chambers had no regard for the good of society or
individuals. He said he based his answer on what he found
in the hypothetical question and in Chambers' writings:
evidence of repetitive lying, stealing, withholding truth, in-
sensitivity, play-acting, bizarre behavior, vagabondage, pan-
handling, inability to form stable attachments, abnormal
emotionality, paranoid thinking and pathological associations. It could all be summed up as "a defect in the formation of conscience."

The doctor went on at some length to tie up particular
recitals in the hypothetical question or excerpts from
Chambers' writings to the stated symptoms and characteristics of the abnormal type of personality he had described.

Dr. Binger was a large, heavy-featured, deep-voiced man
who spoke slowly and punctuated his testimony with tell-

ing emphasis and well-timed gestures. If his direct examination had not convinced the jury of Chambers' unreliability as a witness, it was fair to assume it had, at least, raised a disturbing doubt. The situation demanded an effective cross-examination. Prosecutor Murphy rose to the occasion magnificently. He had, of course, known since the first trial that the defense would renew its effort to get this testimony before the jury and was fully prepared to meet it.

Murphy first attacked the doctor's qualifications and interest. He had graduated from medical school some thirty-five years before but had been certified as a psychiatrist for less than three years. His wife was acquainted with Mrs. Hiss—they had been associated in some educational work. He was donating his services.

The prosecutor then undertook to isolate the different symptoms which the doctor had aggregated as the basis of his opinion. You cannot pick out "specific parcels of information" like that and make each one the basis for a conclusion, said the psychiatrist; "you must consider the totality of the picture." He was asked to point out the particular facts assumed in the hypothetical question on which he based his conclusion that Chambers was a "panhandler." He fumbled and finally admitted that he could not do it. Similarly, about the conclusion of "vagabondage" his answer was unconvincing—the evidence that Chambers had wandered about the country for a year or two after he had run away from home and his later jaunt to Europe, both before he was twenty-three years old. Did the fact that he had been married and had lived with one woman for more than eighteen years evidence instability in his attachments? asked Murphy. No, admitted the doctor, that one fact would not.

The doctor had concluded among other things that Chambers was a "repetitive liar." How many lies, asked Murphy, had the doctor counted in the hypothetical recital? Possibly ten, the witness replied. That was over a period of thirty-three years, pursued Murphy. Yes, answered the witness, but he was not basing his opinion on any "statistical count of lies." "What's par?" concluded Murphy, amid the audible chuckles of the jury and the spectators.

The doctor professed to have read everything Chambers had written, but under the prosecutor's searching cross-examination it developed he had read nothing but what had been handed to him. He had not read any of the widely commended articles that had appeared during the last ten years in *Time* magazine. In Chambers' translation of Franz Werfel's *Class Reunion,* the doctor professed to find the inspiration for some of Chambers' conduct. The central character's name was "Adler," quite similar, said the doctor, to "Alger." In the Werfel story Adler had been unjustly accused by his friend Gregory. There was a suicide pact, the same as had been suggested between Chambers and his brother. These and other incidents impressed the doctor as "extraordinary analogies." Sarcastically, Murphy asked him if he found any such analogies in Chambers' translation of the innocuous children's book *Bambi.* Of course not, said the expert.

The prosecutor took up the doctor's inclusion as one of the bases for his opinion that Chambers was a "psychopathic personality" the assumption of his youthful untidiness and carelessness of dress. "Well," said Murphy, "Will Rogers and Bing Crosby were rather casual in their dress, weren't they? Were they psychopathic personalities?"

"Oh, they were quite different," said the doctor.

The witness had attached an importance to Chambers' having secreted the papers and microfilms in the pumpkin.

"Well," said Murphy, "how about the concealment of the Connecticut charter in the Hartford Oak? Were our colonial forefathers all psychopathic personalities?"

"That, too, was quite different," replied the harassed witness.

Dr. Binger, according to his direct testimony, had been particularly impressed by the fact that Chambers so frequently qualified his answers. How many times had Chambers qualified his answers? inquired Murphy. The doctor didn't know, exactly. "Well," said Murphy, "I will tell you: ten times in 700 pages of transcript." The doctor did not dispute the prosecutor's count. "Now," pursued Murphy, "do you know how many times Hiss qualified his answers?" The doctor didn't know. Again Murphy acted as statistician. "One hundred and fifty-eight times out of 550 pages," cried the cross-examiner.

Another of Chambers' abnormalities, according to psychiatrist Binger, was his constant gazing at the ceiling during his examination. Here Murphy made a "ten-strike." "Doctor," said Murphy, "I have made a count of the number of times you looked at the ceiling. During the first ten minutes you looked at the ceiling nineteen times; in the next fifteen minutes you looked up ten times; for the next fifteen minutes, ten times; for the next fifteen minutes, ten times; and for the last fifteen minutes ten times more. I counted a total of fifty-nine times you looked at the ceiling in fifty minutes. Now I was wondering whether that was any symptom of a psychopathic personality?" The doctor shifted uneasily in his chair, and, without much enthusiasm, managed to reply, "Not alone."

Murphy, in an effort to bring the professional jargon of the alleged expert to the level of the ordinary layman, asked the doctor for a simpler definition of the high-sounding phrase, "psychopathic personality." Would he explain for the benefit of uninformed laymen like himself and the jurors just what the term meant? As is so often the case with assured phrasemongers, the explanations simply begat the need for further explanations, with an end result of increased confusion. Murphy finally summed it up, evidently much to the doctor's relief, for he acquiesced in it by suggesting it was a sort of a "wastebasket classification" in which you could conveniently dump a lot of unrelated and otherwise unclassifiable symptoms.

To support the testimony of Dr. Binger, the defense

called Dr. Henry Murray, former director of the Harvard Psychological Clinic, who qualified as having made a specialty of analyzing psychopathic personalities by studying their writings. He testified, although he had never seen Chambers before he entered the courtroom, that he was competent to express an opinion as to Chambers' dominant characteristics and traits of mind solely from a study of his writings. He declared unhesitatingly that the writings showed Chambers to be a psychopathic personality; that they contained "a higher proportion of images of disintegration and destruction, filth and dirt, decay and decomposition and death than any writings" he had ever examined. He answered the long hypothetical question and corroborated Dr. Binger that Chambers was a psychopathic personality and that the outstanding characteristics of such an individual were instability, disregard of social relationships, intrigue, deceit, fantastic falsehoods and false accusations.

Dr. Murray, who styled himself a psychologist rather than a psychiatrist, possessed a more solid background of knowledge and experience than Dr. Binger and proved on cross-examination to be a more resourceful witness. Emboldened with his success with Dr. Binger, Murphy took the Harvard psychologist over much the same ground. The results were not wholly disappointing. If Dr. Murray's answers were sharper than Dr. Binger's, as most of them were, they did not much advantage the defense, for they served not only to remind the jurors of Dr. Binger's inadequacy but also emphasized Murphy's suggestion that doctors, by whatever name they were called, frequently disagreed and were often wrong.

Murphy's bull's-eye came as the result of a week-end adjournment. Dr. Murray was still under cross-examination when court recessed on a Friday evening, to reconvene the following Monday. In the interim the ever-alert FBI unearthed a new witness, a former writer on *Time* magazine, who informed them that during the preceding November Dr. Murray had got in touch with him and inquired as to Chambers' history and habits; moreover, that the doctor had got into quite an altercation with the newsman when the latter had resented the doctor's referring to Chambers as a "pathological liar."

On Monday, when Dr. Murray resumed the stand, he was led to repeat, under Murphy's deceptive gentleness, his previous statement that he knew nothing of Chambers personally and had based his opinion solely on an examination he had made of his writings and the recitals in the hypothetical question; and that he had not formulated that opinion until Christmas. His talk with the *Time* representative was then "sprung" on him. When he left the stand it was quite obvious to disinterested observers that the attempt of the defense to induce the jurors to substitute professional psychiatric opinion for their own observation and judgment had not been conspicuously successful.

The so-called psychiatric testimony, on which the defense so heavily counted and which, it is apparent, caused the Government's lawyers no little concern, had proved a "dud." The jury, after Murphy's cross-examinations, was quite prepared to accept and act on his argument that, so far as its attempted application to Chambers was concerned, the "psychiatric stuff" was pure buncombe. This inclination was aided by the later specific instruction of the Court that this testimony, like all expert testimony, was purely advisory and the jury might reject the doctors' opinions entirely if it found either that "the hypothetical situation presented to it in the question was incomplete or incorrect" or "the reasons [given in support of the opinions] unsound or not convincing"; that "the jurors had seen and heard Mr. Chambers for several days while he was on the witness stand," and it was for them to say "how much weight, if any," they would give to the testimony of the experts.

The rebuttal of the Government was brief.

All the witnesses who had been permitted to testify in rebuttal on the previous trial were recalled and repeated their earlier testimony.

Since the first trial, the Federal Bureau of Investigation had located Edith Murray, a Negro woman who had worked as a maid for the Chamberses at two of their residences in Baltimore. She remembered having seen Mrs. Hiss at the Chamberses' homes on four different occasions and that once she stayed overnight. She had seen Mr. Hiss on one occasion. She readily identified both of them in the courtroom.

An ex-secretary of the Social Democratic Federation, who had been an organizer for the Socialist party in 1932, produced a membership card of Priscilla Hiss, dated March 23, 1932.

From the Aleutian Islands the Government had brought an Army sergeant named Roulhac, who testified that he signed as a surety the agreement by which the Catletts were enabled to rent their house on P Street in January of 1938. He said he remembered seeing an old typewriter in the hallway, but not until about three months after the Catletts moved in.

To demonstrate that the old Woodstock typewriter was even now not in such bad condition, Murphy produced a typist from the Federal Bureau of Investigation who, in the presence of the jury, struck off a copy of one of the Government's exhibits. It was a good performance. None of the keys stuck or jammed.

Cross spoke for just four minutes less than five hours. Throughout his long summation his manner was quiet and his tone conversational. One of the attendant reporters described his argument as a "folksy sort of talk" to good neighbors.

There was, Cross declared, but a single issue: Who was

to be believed, Hiss or Chambers? Meticulously and somewhat tiresomely, he went over Chambers' entire testimony.
He contrasted his "Godless upbringing" with the Christian
rearing of Hiss. He compared their early careers. He
pointed out the many contradictions, inconsistencies and
improbabilities in Chambers' story—the repeated occasions
when he had glibly and shamelessly confessed perjury and
the withholding of facts. You could not rationalize his actions. The psychiatrists supplied the only answer: Chambers was a psychopathic personality, indifferent alike to his
obligations to society or individuals, given to the making of
baseless charges and utterly incapable of telling the truth.
Hiss, on the other hand, had a spotless record. Nineteen
witnesses, some of them the most distinguished people in
America, had vouched for him; his reputation for integrity,
veracity and loyalty was of the highest.

Cross attempted an explanation for every item of damaging testimony. As to the typewriter, he argued that Chambers got it through a confederate after the Hisses had given
it to the Catletts. "Anyone clever enough to secure secret
documents through a confederate could easily have traced
it to the servants' children and could have obtained possession of it and made copies of the documents." He explained the contradictions between Dulles and Hiss on the
ground that Dulles was a "very busy man" and could not
be expected to keep clearly in mind the details of long-past
conversations with Hiss. Edith Murray's testimony had
been influenced by the "wicked" Chambers. Hede Massing was not to be believed because she had given three
different dates as the time of her marriage to Gerhart Eisler.

With a bad case, Cross did the best he could. There
were simply too many items in the Government's case
which could not be explained away.

United States Attorney Murphy faced the jury with supreme confidence. He had made a much stronger case on

this than on the first trial. This second trial had extended over nine weeks. The jury was tired and anxious to get down to the business of deciding the case. Murphy sensed the situation and concluded his argument in less than half the time that had been taken by Cross.

Answering the defense counsel's contention that Hiss had shown himself as a more credible witness than Chambers, Murphy replied that the jury had seen both men. "Hiss," declared the prosecutor, "was continually smiling, equivocating and fencing." Chambers, on the other hand, "for seven days on the witness stand displayed dignity and decorum. He was sincere, unhesitating and never evasive."

What sinister motive had been shown for Chambers' act? asked Murphy. Except that he had been summoned before the congressional committee and felt it his duty to lay bare his past and expose the Communist spy rings which were threatening the security of the United States, why should he throw away a $30,000-a-year job as the senior editor of *Time* magazine to accuse Hiss falsely? He scornfully dismissed the "psychiatric and psychological testimony." It had been thoroughly discredited—shown to be absolutely worthless. It represented mere opinions based on the assumption of a vague assortment of selected, unrelated and insignificant facts. Neither of the so-called experts had ever examined Chambers; indeed, one of them had never seen him before he testified.

Murphy repeated the effective argument he had made on the first trial as to the probative value of character witnesses.

The prosecutor's definite flair for the effective use of sarcasm found a fair target when he came to answer Cross's explanation of how the documents came to be copied on the Hiss typewriter. "What probably happened," chuckled Murphy, "is that somebody, not Chambers—he's too smart—one of his conspirators . . . went up to the Volta Place house and asked innocent Clytie Catlett: 'I'm the re-

pair man. Where's the machine?' I can just see it now.
It's terrific. You can have this guy coming with a Woodstock hat on—'Woodstock Repair'—saying, 'I am the repair-
man to fix the typewriter.' Then Clytie says, 'Well, which
one do you want? The Remington, the Royal, the L. C.
Smith?' . . . 'No, we want the Woodstock.' 'Oh, that's over
in my boy's house, over at P Street.' And then the next
scene: It is in the middle of one of these dances. [It had
been brought out that there were frequent revels at the
Catlett P Street home.] And you see Chambers sneaking
in at night, mingling with the dancers, and then typing,
typing the stuff, holding the State Department document in
one hand." Turning to the defense counsel, he concluded,
"Oh, Mr. Cross, you've got to do better than that."

The prosecutor made a telling point of Chambers' testimony, which Hiss denied, that Hiss had introduced him to
a woman named Plum Fountain. There was such a person,
declared Murphy; she appeared as a witness and testified
"Plum Fountain" was one of the names she was known by.
How could Chambers, how could anyone, he inquired,
"think up a name like that?"

Speaking seriously, Murphy referred time and again to
the "immutable witnesses"—the four memoranda in the
handwriting of Alger Hiss, the forty-six copies of secret
State papers and the microfilms. The real offense of Hiss,
declared the prosecutor—the stealing of restricted and confidential papers of the Department of State—was serious
indeed. The "siphoning" of the State documents had given
Soviet agents secret coded information, intended exclusive-
ly for State Department officials, which permitted Russia
to break the highly secret American diplomatic codes.

Murphy's closing appeal to the jurors was brief and stirring—a call to do their duty fearlessly, considering naught
but the law and the evidence; if they did that, there was but
one verdict they could return—guilty.

Judge Goddard's charge covered substantially the

ground which had been traversed by Judge Kaufman in the
first trial. While balanced and scrupulously fair, it lacked
the "defense cast" apparent in the earlier instructions.

Balancing the "respective interests" of the parties, he
charged:

> The defendant Hiss has a great interest in this case. Mr.
> Chambers also has a deep interest in the result. It was Mr.
> Hiss's denial of Mr. Chambers' testimony before the grand
> jury which led to the defendant's indictment for perjury, so
> that naturally they would both wish to have their state-
> ments sustained. Mr. Hiss has commenced a suit against
> Mr. Chambers for libel, and the result here may affect that
> suit. Their wives also have an interest in the outcome.

He instructed the jury generally as to the probative value
of expert testimony and made a particular reference, as previously indicated, to the testimony of Binger and Murray.

.   In the final paragraph of his charge, Judge Goddard, having in mind the previous disagreement, sought by a plain
statement of jurors' duties to prevent a similar result in this
second trial. He said:

> The jury is composed of twelve citizens and your verdict
> must represent the decision of each individual juror. The
> object of the jury system is to secure a unanimous verdict
> through an exchange of views, reasons, and arguments
> among the several jurors. And, as you confer in the jury
> room, opinions may be exchanged or changed. Although
> the verdict should represent the considered judgment of
> each juror, a juror should not refuse to listen to the argu-
> ments of other jurors equally intelligent and equally ear-
> nest in the effort to mete out justice.

His final word was addressed to their ultimate duty as
jurors:

> Now, ladies and gentlemen, if you find that the evidence
> respecting the defendant is as consistent with innocence as

with guilt, the defendant should be acquitted. If you find
that the law has not been violated, you should not hesitate
for any reason to render a verdict of acquittal. But, on the
other hand, if you find that the law has been violated as
charged, you should not hesitate because of sympathy or
for any other reason to render a verdict of guilty, as a clear
warning to all that a crime such as charged may not be committed with impunity. The people of this country are entitled to be assured of this. I submit the case to you with
confidence that you will faithfully endeavor to render a
verdict.

At 3:10 P.M. on Friday, January 20, 1950, the jurors retired. It was almost twenty-four hours before they announced they had reached an agreement.

The forewoman of the jury announced the verdict:
Guilty on the first count and guilty on the second count.

The following Wednesday morning Judge Goddard
heard and overruled the defendant's motion for a new
trial. Hiss was asked if he had anything to say before the
Court passed sentence upon him. Hiss, after thanking the
Court for the opportunity of again denying the charge
made against him, added the remarkable statement: "I only
want to add that in the future the full facts of how Whittaker Chambers was able to carry out forgery by typewriter
will be disclosed."

The Court then pronounced its sentence: five years' imprisonment in the penitentiary on each of the two counts,
the terms to run concurrently.

AFTERMATH

Hiss promptly appealed his case to the Federal Court of
Appeals for the Second Circuit. On December 7, 1950, that
Court (Justices Chase, Augustus Hand and Swan) handed
down its unanimous opinion, affirming the judgment of
the district court.[16]

---

16 185 F. (2d) 822.

After restating the law that to convict of perjury there must be the testimony of two witnesses or one witness corroborated by facts or circumstances, the Court said:

Chambers testified in great detail concerning his relations with Hiss in Washington. . . . Indeed, it is perfectly plain that his testimony, believed as it evidently was by the jury, is of such breadth and scope that if it was adequately substantiated by other evidence, as the law requires, there was enough to support the verdict.

After commenting that the jury might well have believed that Hiss "had been less than frank in his belated recognition of Mr. Chambers as the man he had known as Crosley," the Court concluded:

The jury had ample evidence other than the testimony of Chambers on which to find, as it evidently did, that the documents of which Mr. Chambers produced copies were all available to Mr. Hiss at the State Department, and that finding, coupled with the fact that they were copied on a typewriter which the jury could well believe was used for that purpose when in the possession of Mr. Hiss in his home, supplied the circumstances which strongly corroborated the testimony of Mr. Chambers. Indeed, such known circumstances tend to fill out a normal pattern of probability when so interpreted, while in attempting to reconcile them with appellant's denial of association with the delivery of State Department documents or their copies to Mr. Chambers one approaches the realm of sheer speculation.

The alleged procedural errors were shortly disposed of as insufficient support for the claim that Hiss had not had a fair and impartial trial.

The carefully considered, vigorously worded, unanimous opinion of the Court of Appeals made practically certain the failure of Hiss's final effort to escape the consequences of the jury's verdict. On March 12, 1951, the Supreme Court of the United States denied his petition for further review. Ten days later he surrendered to the United States marshal and commenced the serving of his five-year sentence. As the doors of the Federal penitentiary at Lewisburg, Pennsylvania, closed behind him, he was still protesting his innocence and confidence in his ultimate vindication.